SUPER 8 HANDBOOK

by
George D. Glenn & Charles B. Scholz
University of Northern Iowa, Cedar Falls

Howard W. Sams & Co., Inc.
4300 WEST 62ND ST. INDIANAPOLIS, INDIANA 46268 USA

PREFACE

Much has happened in the field of Super 8 film making since we wrote the First Edition of this book in 1973. The advancements in cameras, lenses, film stocks, and sound equipment have been only slightly short of fantastic. However, the basic principles of film making have not changed despite the growth in Super 8 technology.

So, our purpose in this Second Edition is to reemphasize the basics of motion-picture production using the medium of Super 8. We will review the new technology and tell you what we have found out about the new gadgets and gimmicks. But our primary purpose is to give you as much information as we can to help you to make better movies in any gauge.

CHARLES B. SCHOLZ
GEORGE D. GLENN

Preface to the First Edition

A few years ago in his book *My Autobiography*, the great Charlie Chaplin made the following statements about film books:

> Although many worthwhile books have been written on the subject, the trouble is that most of them impose the cinematic taste of the author. Such a book should be nothing more than a technical primer which teaches one to know the tools of his trade. Beyond that, the imaginative student should use his own art sense about dramatic effects. If the amateur is creative, he needs only the barest technical essentials. To an artist, complete freedom to do the unorthodox is usually most exciting. . . .[1]

In preparing this book, we have attempted to keep Charlie Chaplin's precepts firmly in mind. This is intended to be more of a "how-to" book than a study of film theory—a technical primer, rather than a treatise on aesthetics. We have written this book for you, the person who desires to produce interesting, high-quality movies in the Super 8 medium. We chose to limit ourselves to Super 8, because we believe it is an excellent, low-cost starting point for the beginner, an expressive medium for the serious amateur, and a fertile field for the professional.

The Super 8 field has grown enormously since its introduction in 1965; it seems that new advances in cameras, film stocks, and laboratory services are reported every day. The latest information available has been incorporated into this text; but, we realize that we have not solved every problem, thought of every shortcut, or even reported every advancement in the field. If you know of anything that has been missed, forward it to us, and we will attempt to inform our students and readers.

---

[1]Charles Chaplin: *My Autobiography*. London: Bodley Head Ltd., 1964.

Acknowledgments

Special thanks are due to Bob Lippert for his original photography, Nancy Hinshaw for her photography and printing, and Dan Grevas for his great cover shots.

Thanks to The Chinon Corporation and Thomas J. Coyne III, Eastman Kodak, especially Richard G. Anderson and John Johnson, Super 8 Sound and Robert Doyle; all of these for their advice and help.

Thanks to Robert Meyer and the Bell and Howell/Mamiya Company, Smith-Victor Corporation and Mr. G.C. Anderson, Eumig (U.S.A.) Inc., and Kenneth J. Marissael, and Robert H. Reibel and Hudson Photographic Industries, Inc. for their generosity.

And thanks to the Minolta Company and Basil Vorolieff, Jean Anwyll and the folks at Polaroid, Art Kramer, Sales Manager of Lowell-Light, Yashica, Inc. USA Main Office, Don Myrus for Bolex and EPOI, Canon USA, Inc. and William Wuest, George Corbett of Berkey Marketing Companies for Cosina, and ELMO and the Elmo Mfg. Corp., and Stan Brown and AIC PHOTO INC. for Bauer.

Dedication

To Nancy for reading along and to Sandy for her encouragement, and to Shelly Johnson, Jane Bock, and Jackie Tinker for their typing and proofreading.

Contents

Introduction to Super 8

In the 1890s, George Eastman, the inventor of the Kodak Camera, used the slogan, "You push the button, we'll do the rest." Today, Super 8 movie making is nearly that simple. It is necessary only to load your camera with a cartridge of Super 8 film, aim the camera, and press the trigger. The electric-eye metering system maintains near-perfect exposure of every frame and the electric motor drive provides smooth running speeds throughout the run of your 50- or 200-foot film cartridge. If you have autofocus, you will not even have to touch the lens; the camera will keep the action in focus for you no matter where you aim.

If you already own a Super 8 camera, you do not need to be sold on the advantages of its easy operation. But, perhaps you would like to do more with it than just take pictures of your family and friends. Perhaps you would like to make real movies. That is what this book is all about. It will tell you how to plan and how to produce movies of your own. It will tell you what tools to use and how best to use them. And, it will give you helpful hints on how to solve all kinds of film-making problems.

Now is a good time for you to begin making movies with your Super 8 camera. To paraphrase George Eastman, "You load the camera, we'll do the rest."

SECTION I

Planning

CHAPTER 1

Vocabulary

Every profession or hobby seems to have its own special language. This list of strange sounding words and phrases is not consciously designed to confuse the beginner, but is intended to aid communication among the knowledgeable. Film making, too, has its own language. So that we will be able to communicate through the rest of this book, we'll briefly discuss the essential language of film making.

THE FILM

First of all, let's look at the primary ingredient—the film itself. Any motion-picture film can be broken down into several component parts. The smallest of these is the single *frame*, which is only one of the thousands of individual still photographic pictures that make up the completed film. The movie you see is the projection, in very rapid sequence, of many frames of film, with each picture slightly different than the last. This gives the illusion that the pictures themselves are moving.

Since the individual frames flicker by at a rate of 18 or 24 per second, the viewer is unaware of seeing any individual frame(s). For this reason, the frame may not seem important. However, it is important to the film maker because, when he/she is editing the film, a given frame will be the exact point on which the picture should be changed to the next *shot*.

A shot is really the basic unit of the film. It can be defined as any single strip of movie film which represents an uninterrupted run of the camera. The camera is started, several frames or feet of film are exposed, and the camera is stopped. One shot has been made. When the camera is restarted, a second shot is made, and so on. A shot can be as short as a single frame or as long as the cartridge of film in the camera.

After the shot, the next largest subdivision is the *scene*. A scene is a sequence of shots which are related in some way—by location, by action, by the characters involved, or by time. A scene may consist of one or two shots, or it may be assembled from hundreds of shots. The complete film, then, is a series of scenes which consist of sequences of shots which are made up of hundreds or thousands of frames. These bits, the scenes and shots, are arranged in order and joined together by a process called *editing*.

EDITING

Editing really has two meanings. It refers to the process we just described, that of arranging or ordering the shots into scenes and then putting the scenes in some sequence to make the film. But, the other part of editing, that of physically cutting apart and joining together pieces of film, is called *cutting*.

Cutting is so named because it describes the physical action of cutting the film apart and putting it back together again. From this process, we get our simplest form of the editing arrangement, *the cut*. The cut is only one of many possible transitional devices that are available to the film maker, but it is the one which the amateur (and even the professional) film maker will use the most often, if only because it is the easiest and least expensive way to edit. The cut is as abrupt as its name suggests—one shot ends and another begins. The pieces of film are physically cut and joined together with the last frame of the first shot attached to the first frame of the second shot. Entire films have been made, successfully, using only the cut.

After the simple cut, the most common transition is the *fade*, shown in Fig. 1-1. It is used as either a *fade-in* (Fig. 1-1A) or a *fade-out* (Fig. 1-1B). The fade-in begins with the film completely black. Gradually the image appears, becoming more and more visible as the shot progresses. The fade-out is the reverse; at the end of a shot, the image gradually becomes darker until it has become black. Traditionally, fades have been used to begin and end a scene or a film, and they often indicate a passage of time in a less abrupt manner than does the cut. A fade-in or -out can be as short as a few frames or it can last several seconds. "Slow fade to black" is an old way of ending a film and it is a very common way to break a television show.

The *dissolve*, illustrated in Fig. 1-2, is a more complicated transition, one that requires either a sophisticated Super 8 camera or some laboratory work on the film after it is edited. A dissolve is a deliberate double exposure of a fade-out over a fade-in. This produces a transition which consists of the last part of a shot gradually being superceded by the first part of the next shot. Dissolves traditionally have been used as transitions from reality to unreality, to indicate a compression of time, to show a move from reality to memory, etc.

Like a dissolve in its "soft" effect, we also have the *focus shift*. This is shown by Figs. 1-3 and 1-4. If attention must be shifted between two objects in different planes in a shot, use the focus shift. The film maker can end a shot by throwing the image completely out of focus and then beginning the next shot out of focus (see man in Fig. 1-3) and gradually sharpening the image (Fig. 1-4). This is a transition which is easily done by anyone with a focusable reflex camera.

FILM CONTENT

However, editing and making the transitions between shots is only a part of the film. Each shot has its own content. We generally express this in terms of the *field of view* that we see in the shot and the *point of view* from which we see it. We also describe shots in terms of the camera movement that creates them.

The field of view (Fig. 1-5) in the shot is described in terms of its appearance on the screen and how close the subject appears to us. You can see that a *close-up* or C.U. (Fig. 1-5A) has a very small field of view with a relatively large image size. Similarly, the *long shot,* or L.S. (Fig. 1-5C), is a large field with relatively small image size. The *medium shot,* or M.S. (Fig. 1-5B), has a normal field of view with normal image sizes. Notice that we speak of these fields of view as if we were moving closer or farther away from them. That is the effect that these different shots will give on the screen. Actually, what we are seeing in a C.U. is a smaller part of a "normal" field of view. A field of view, then, is that picture that is contained within the limits of a frame (or the viewfinder of the camera).

The field of view can be seen from either an objective or a subjective *point of view,* or P.O.V. When the P.O.V. is *objective,* we are in the position of invisible observers, looking on from a sort of God-like vantage point. Most films are shot using the objective P.O.V. A *subjective* P.O.V., however, can be used. This implies that the camera is a character, and we are seeing exactly what that character would see.

CAMERA MOVEMENT

There are two kinds of camera movement that are used to describe shots, those in which the camera *moves* and those in which the camera is *moved.* The camera moves in a *pan, tilt,* or *zoom* shot. The camera is moved when using the *dolly, truck,* or *crane* shot.

The panorama, or pan shot (Fig. 1-6), is one of the simplest and most basic of those shots in which the camera moves. In a pan shot,

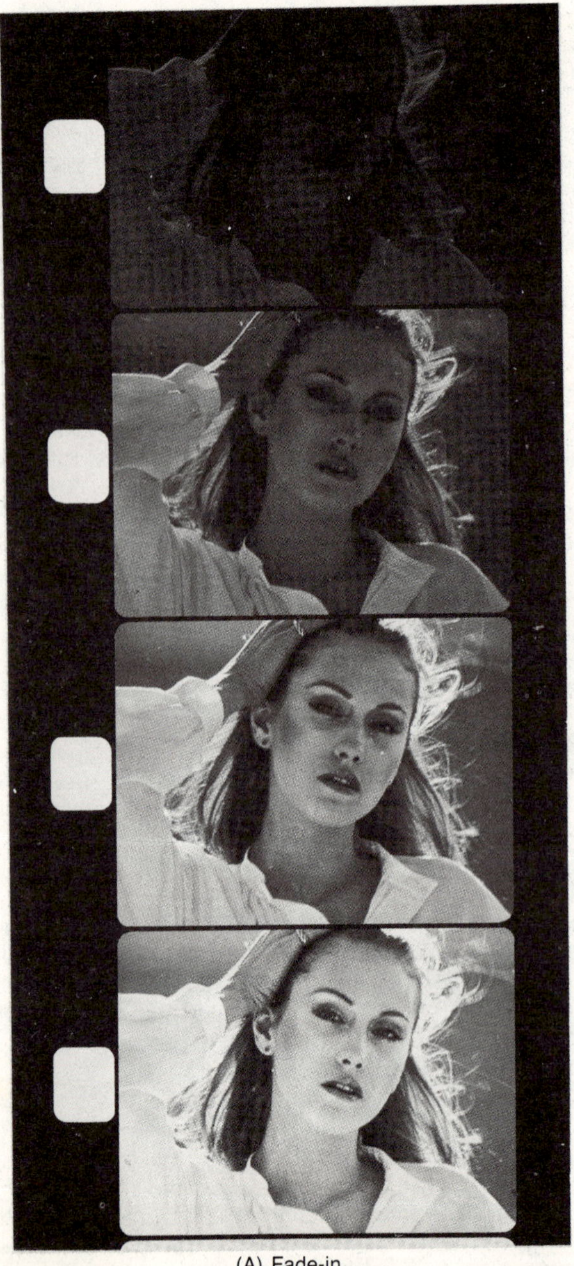

(A) Fade-in.

Fig. 1-1. The fade transistion is accomplished by

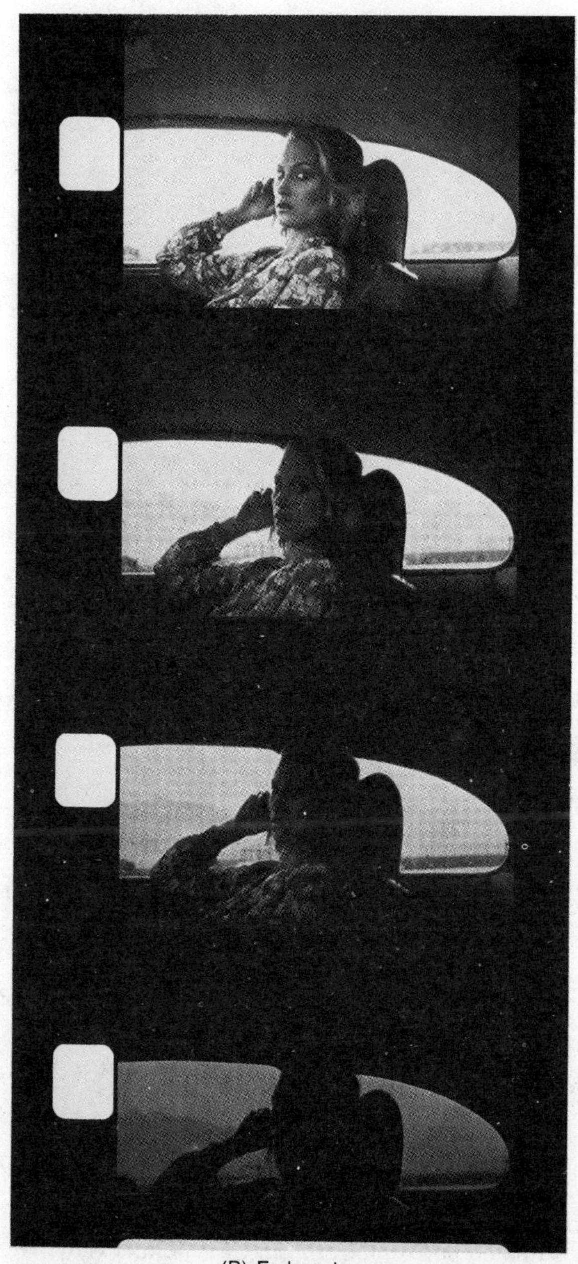

(B) Fade-out.

stopping down the aperture or closing the shutter.

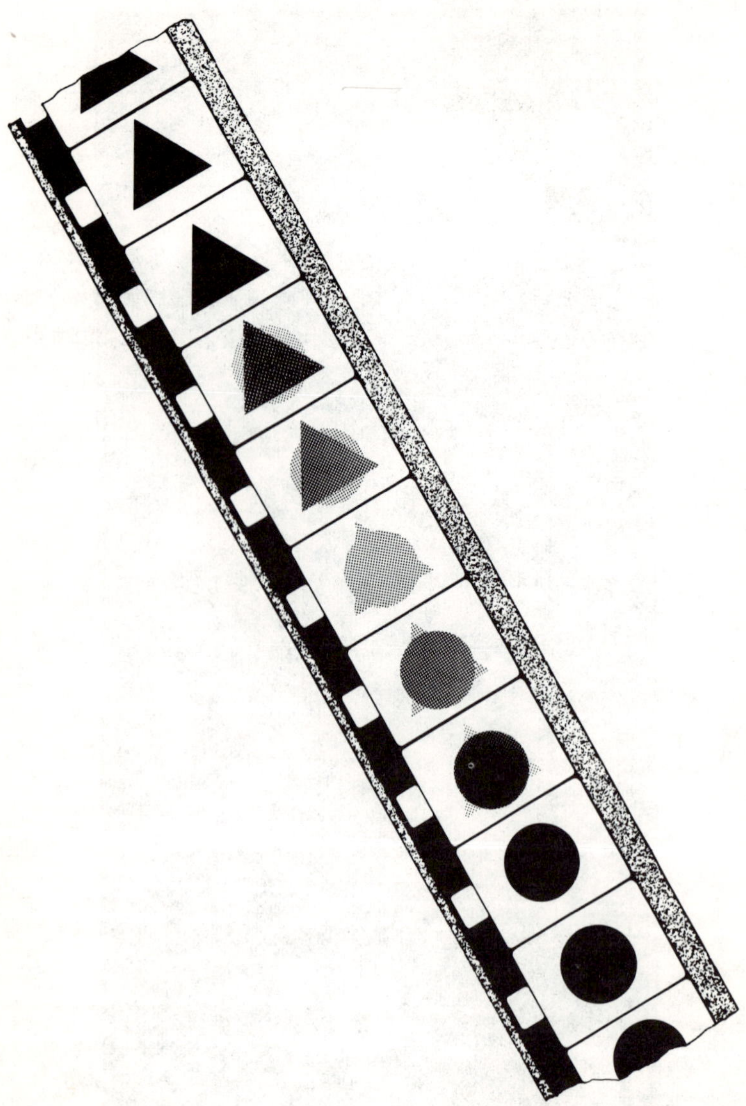

Fig. 1-2. With a dissolve, one image slowly turns into another.

the camera pivots on a stationary point (usually a tripod), and the camera is rotated horizontally through the field of view. The tilt shot is a vertical pan. However, instead of being pivoted from side to side, the camera is pivoted up and down.

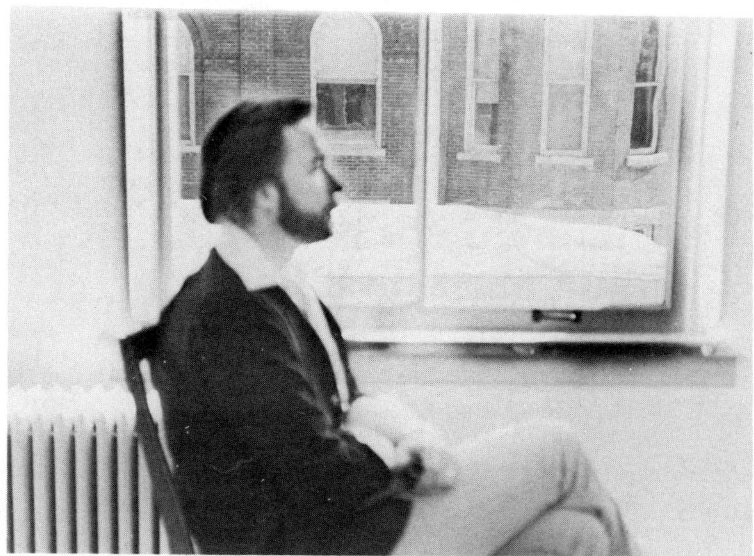

Fig. 1-3. Man is out of focus, building in background is clear and sharp.

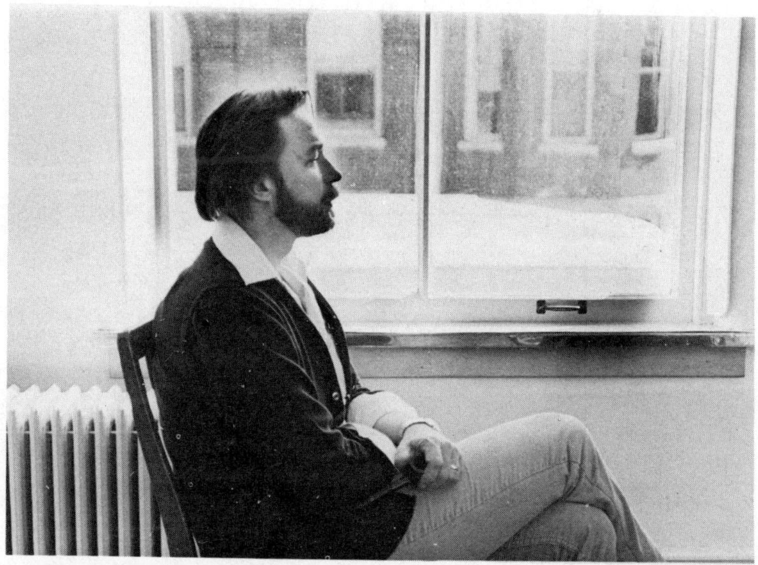

**Fig. 1-4. Man is clear and sharp while building in background
is fuzzy and indistinct.**

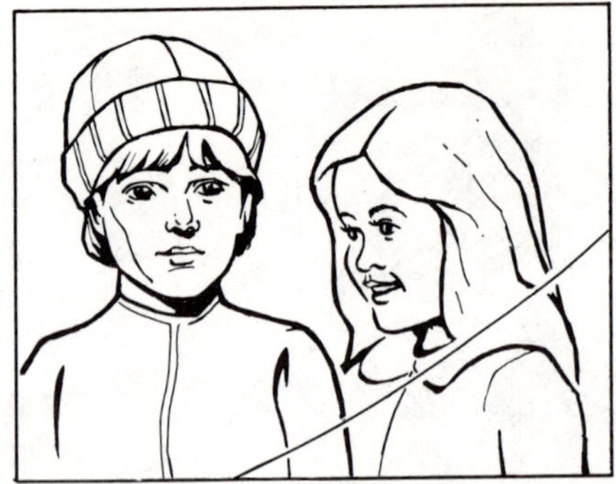

(A) A close-up shot.

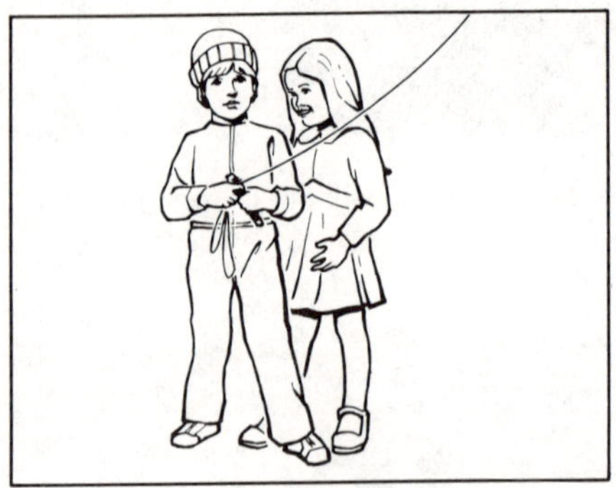

(B) A medium shot.

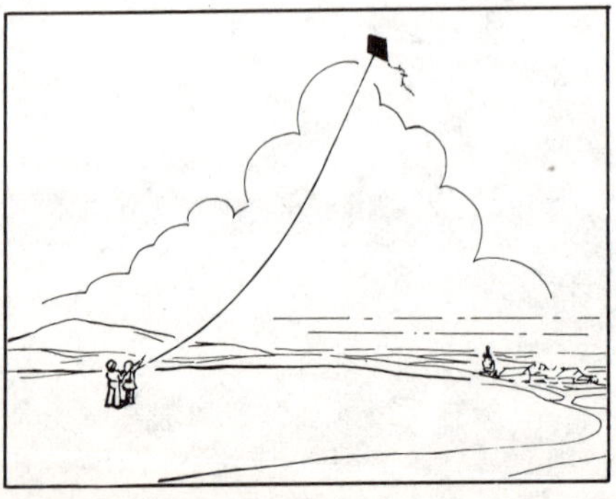

(C) A long shot.

Fig. 1-5. Movies are made up of shots that are taken at various distances.

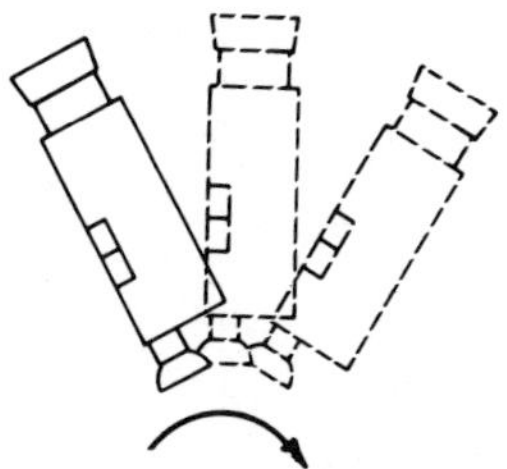

Fig. 1-6. Panorama or "pan" shot.

The zoom shot (Fig. 1-7) involves a movement within the camera itself rather than a movement by the camera. By turning the zoom ring and changing the *focal length* of that lens, the field of view can be altered from a long shot to a close-up (or the reverse), without moving the camera closer (or farther away) from the subject. The subject appears to move closer and get larger as we zoom in. Actually, we are looking at just a very small portion of the normal field of view from this distance. (See Chapters 3 and 7 for a further discussion of focal lengths.)

There are camera shots where the camera really moves, however, that can also be used to alter the field of view. One of these is the *dolly* shot (Fig. 1-8). Here the camera remains locked in place on the tripod while both camera and tripod are moved toward (dolly-in) or away from (dolly-out) the subject. This shot gets its name from the little cart that is used to move the camera in or out. The *trucking* shot (Fig. 1-9) is similar to the dolly shot in that both camera and tripod move but, in this case, they are moved parallel to the subject or along with a moving subject. In the *crane* shot, both the camera and tripod are moved up or down as well as in or out. This shot gets its name from the device used to raise and lower the camera and camera operator when making such a shot.

CAMERA AND FILM SPEEDS

There is a final item of vocabulary that we should look at before we begin planning our films, and that is the concept of *speed*. We can affect the content of shots (and the meaning of our film) by the speed at which things happen in the shots. If something unfolds in *slow motion*, we have more time to examine and analyze its impact than if it happens at *normal speed* or if it happens in *fast action*. All these speeds are related to the *running speed* of the camera and the running speed of the projector. Normal running speeds for Super 8 are 18 and 24 frames per second, or fps. If the film is shot and projected at the same running speed, the action will appear to happen at normal speed. If the film is shot at one running speed and projected at a slower running speed, the result will be slow motion. The reverse is

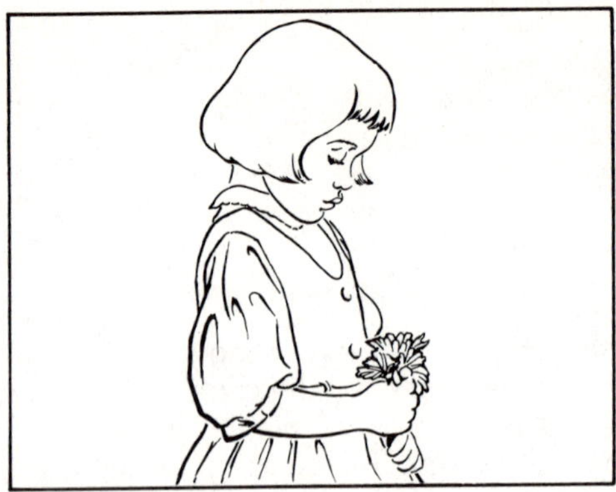

ZOOM-IN TO

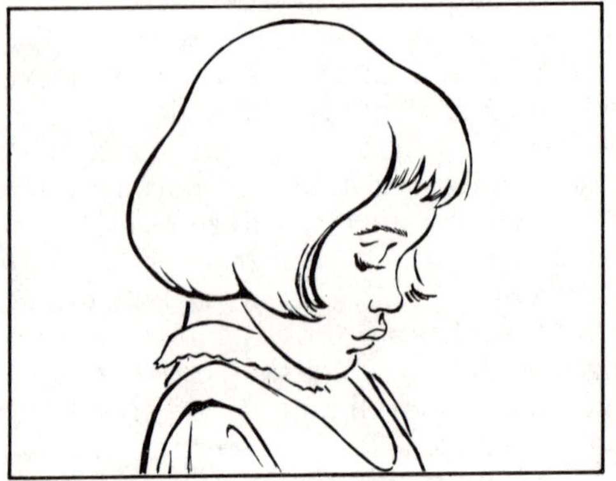

Fig. 1-7. The subject appears to move closer and get larger
as the camera zooms in.

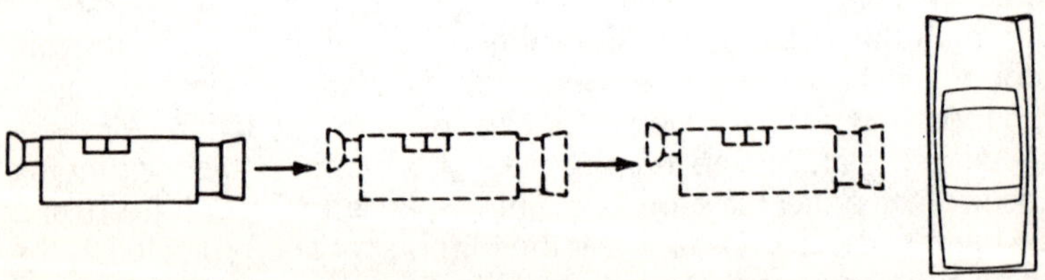

Fig. 1-8. A dolly shot.

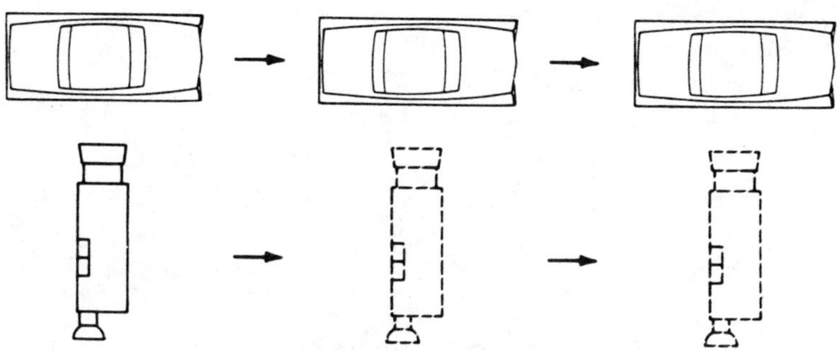

Fig. 1-9. A trucking shot.

also true. If the film is shot at one speed and projected at a faster speed, the motion will appear to be faster than normal. There are three other definitions of the term speed that we will use in our discussions. They are *shutter speed, film speed,* and *lens speed.*

Shutter speed is the length of time that the shutter of the camera is open in order to expose an individual frame. It is expressed in fractions of a second and can be determined by finding one-half the reciprocal of the running speed. For example, if the running speed was 18 frames per second, then $\frac{1}{2} \times \frac{1}{18} = \frac{1}{36}$. A setting of $\frac{1}{36}$ of a second would be the shutter speed. It is necessary to know shutter speed when using light meters.

The sensitivity of the film, itself, to light is called the film speed. Film speed is measured in ASA numbers which refer to an agreed upon rating system of film sensitivity. Films that are less sensitive to light, those that require longer exposures or greater amounts of light for good exposure, are called "slow" films and have lower ASA numbers. Kodachrome II, with an ASA rating of 40, is a good example of this type. Films which are more sensitive to light are called "faster" films and have higher ASA numbers.

Finally, there is lens speed—the potential or maximum light gathering capacity of the camera's lens. This is always expressed in f/stops with the smaller numbers (like f/1.2 and f/1.4) being "faster" or capable of admitting more light, than larger numbers like f/8 or f/11. The f/number the lens is rated at refers to the largest aperture that the lens can be opened to; the smaller the number, the larger the lens opening, and the larger the number, the smaller the opening.

This concludes the discussion on the basic vocabulary of a film maker. As we get into the actual process of planning and producing movies, these terms, and others, will be discussed in more detail. However, you know enough of the basic language to follow our explanations. How to apply these concepts will be our next concern.

CHAPTER 2

The Script

Two important steps should be taken before any film is run through the camera. These are *scripting* and *production planning*. Professional film makers often take as much time in scripting and planning a film as they take in shooting and editing it. They are aware that time spent in preparation results in time saved on the set. While amateur film makers cannot be expected to use Hollywood-style production methods (and really should not bother trying to use them, either), they should expect to script and plan their films as carefully as if they were risking a Hollywood-size budget. (Note that we are exercising our poetic license in the use of the word "scripting." This means everything necessary to have a working plan—from the original idea to the written script with its revisions to the dialogue and the placement of the actors.)

FILM CONCEPT

In this chapter, we will concentrate on the writing of the script. The first challenge is in determining the kind of film you want to make. This usually does not take much time. Most film projects start with somebody saying, "Wouldn't it be fun to make a film about. . .?" But what is really important here is your *film concept*. Concept is defined as "a mental image of an action or thing." It is the idea that you want to express in your film, the impression you want the audience to receive from the images that you show them and the sounds that they hear.

While you do not have to write the concept out, you do have to think it through. Your concept should include the message of the film, how it is to be expressed to the audience, and who that audience might be. A primary weakness of many amateur films is the lack of a definite concept. If the film maker is not clear as to what he or she wants to say, or how best to say it, or to whom the message is aimed, then it is usually difficult to find the proper images or arrangement of images. It is necessary for the film maker to formulate a clear and concise statement of concept. At this point, a question that must be asked is, "Is my concept a suitable one for film production?"

There are many instances when a motion picture is the best medium for expressing and illustrating a concept. But there are times when some other medium might be more suitable. For example, a well arranged slide and tape show on your recent tour of Mexico might be the most effective way for your audience to see and appreciate that country in the way that you did. Also, a short story or a novel might be a better form of expression than a dramatic film, if you want to reveal the inner thoughts and motivations of a character. The point is that you should make a film only when you are convinced that practically or artistically, this is the best way to treat your concept.

FILM STYLES

Now that you have decided on film as the medium, what kind of film should you make? We have categorized movies into five general types:

1. *Home movies* are the "snapshot" movies of everyday activities. Usually not staged, they are similar to a visual diary and often have little continuity.
2. *Documentary films* document or illustrate some aspect of real life, sometimes from a personal point of view, sometimes from an objective viewpoint, as in a news story. Although documentaries sometimes utilize reconstructed events in their making, they are usually not fictionalized. They examine and document an existing condition, situation, or problem.
3. *Instructional films* are related to documentaries, but concentrate on how to do something, how it works, or what it is.
4. *Dramatic films* are serious or comic treatments of fictional stories.
5. *Art films* are often considered to be a film for film's sake—often made up of pure or abstract images that are related thematically or visually.

These divisions are never as clear-cut and arbitrary as we have stated, but division into these types can serve as guidelines for further discussion.

Now that you have a clear concept and know what type of film you want to make, you should have a working knowledge of *filmic conventions* before you start to write your script.

FILMIC CONVENTIONS

In every type of communication media, there are certain ways of introducing information, certain modes of expression, and certain forms for presenting specific kinds of information. These ways, modes, and forms are called *conventions*. Conventions are the agreed-upon rules about communication that give it structure and order. We observe conventions in simple forms when we answer the telephone or write a note. We observe more complex ones when we make speeches, write novels, or tell jokes.

Motion pictures have a series of conventions about continuity, point of view, time, place, action, characterization, light, and sound. There are certain forms that are followed in scripting, planning, shooting, and editing movies that observe these conventions. You will probably recognize each of these conventions as they are discussed, since you have seen most of them on the movie screen or read about them in scripts.

Continuity

It is the sequence or arrangement of the scenes and shots in the film that determines the "meaning" of the film. This is also how the story is created. This idea, of the form shaping the content, seems to be at odds with an important literary convention which states that it is the story that is important, not how it is told. In fact, this is not really the case, for several types of literature, including the classic detective story, always follow a specific form. In a film, however, continuity is of primary importance. It determines how the story is to be expressed and it makes sense of the story line.

Point of View

Movie audiences always assume that they are the camera or that the camera is operating in their behalf. They are never surprised that they can see the most violent part of the battle and not be hurt, or that they can be present at the most intimate moments in a person's life and not be noticed. In addition, film audiences are willing to accept almost any camera angle or field of view that the camera can show them. They do not seem to mind when the camera switches from an objective to a subjective point of view, or when the camera plays the opposite side of a conversation. Again, this tends to violate a literary convention wherein the author usually chooses one "voice" or point of view, and stays with it throughout the story. The film convention of "point of view" allows us to see and hear whatever we choose.

Time

There is no fixed relationship between real time and screen time. Movies can compress time (days, weeks, and months) into a few minutes on the screen, just as other kinds of stories can. Or, movies can stretch time out, to heighten the tension or increase the suspense. Movies, again like other forms of literature, can take things out of chronological time and present them to us in different arrangements. The *flashback* and *flash forward* are good examples of this.

Place

Many story-telling forms demand that you establish the locale before you get into the story. A film does this by showing a place. Places in movies exist—they do not have to be explained. Since we are capable of filming in almost any place, there seem to be no limits as to where movies can take place. And, editing allows us to move from place to place as fast as we can change shots.

Action

The actions of persons in the movies and the action of the plot do not seem to need any justification to the audience. Unlike other forms of drama, movies do not seem to need to establish motivation[1] for the actions of their characters. Just as the movie exists, so the action happens.

Characterization

Acting performances in a film are more dependent upon the way the actor is shown than on the actor's own performance. Characterization need only be internally consistent within the film for it to be effective. This might be one of the reasons for the many one-dimensional portrayals by screen actors that we now see in films.

Light

We observe a number of nonrealistic conventions about lights and lighting in the movies. For example, how does it happen that the place where the lead actress chooses to sit is always beautifully lit? Or, where does the light come from that allows us to see outdoors at night? Since none of these lighting situations bother the audience, they should not bother us. Although most professional camera people make an effort to light realistically, there is still no reason to avoid observing this convention just for the sake of realism. As most photographers realize, good lighting (and the resultant good exposure) are much more important to the film than devotion to realistic light sources.

---

[1]Although a perceived motivation on the part of the characters involved will help make the actions of the character more believable, and will help to raise a film above the level of mere entertainment.

Sound

We do not object to nonrealistic sound in a film either. The conventions about sound in films include a nonrealistic background sound (especially music), the lack of real sound (like street noise), sound effects in silent movies, and an exaggeration of real sounds. Again, as with lighting, it has become customary to make the soundtrack sound like the background noises should sound in that location. But there is nothing wrong with using the existing sound conventions to enhance the effect of sound in your film.

We accept and use filmic conventions because they give us a basis for understanding the transmission of information in film form. If we did not have them, we would find it difficult to understand and to make films.

STAGES OF A SCRIPT

There are several scripting stages you should go through before writing the final script. You can expand the idea of a written statement of concept into a *treatment*. This is a brief written description of the supporting visual images. It is not a story in the literary sense, but rather a summary of the action, with some thought given to expressing the specific images suggested by the concept. The treatment should also include some indication of what the viewer will hear as well as see in the film.

For the short movie, a simple treatment will be sufficient. Write out the main ideas and images in a few sentences. This serves to focus your thinking about the concept and provides a basis for the next stage of scripting the film. When planning more complicated films, the treatment will undoubtedly become more extended. We find, however, that three paragraphs, or about one typewritten page, is as long as any treatment needs to be. Keep in mind that the treatment is not the *scenario* or *shooting script*, so details like dialogue and camera angles need not be included.

After completing the treatment, the next step is to write the *scenario* or *screenplay*. Where the treatment is an outline of the action, the scenario fills in all the details. The scenario states, in specific terms, what is going to occur in the film. The scenario includes such items as a precise description of the action, all the dialogue, a description of sound effects needed, descriptions of the locations, and the *general* point of view of the camera: i.e., close-ups, reverse angles, pans, etc. In addition, it should provide the general continuity by indicating where cuts, fades, dissolves, etc., will occur.

There are several types of scenarios that can be used depending on the kind of film contemplated. The most common type is the one used for fiction films, called the *screenplay*. This kind of scenario indicates not only all the visual images, but, also, the all-important dialogue. The *narrative scenario* is used for a *voice-over* or *narration film* such as travelogues, teaching films, documentaries, etc. Other scenarios might employ no dialogue or narrative at all, such as would be the case in a film that relies entirely on visual images to tell its story or make its statement. Documentary films may have a partial scenario to begin with and the narrative or commentary is written as the film is edited.

One method of scripting that has been used to good effect, either alone or in conjunction with a written scenario, is the *storyboard* (see Fig. 2-1). This consists of a series of still pictures, drawings, or sketches of the scene as visualized by the film maker. This technique is commonly used for animated films, but many professionals use it for every kind of film. The Disney organization popularized the storyboard scenario, and is still a firm supporter of the technique.

When drawing storyboards, make one picture for each shot in the film. Write the field of view and camera movement instructions under each picture. If a zoom shot is indicated, use two pictures, one to indicate the start of the zoom shot and the other to indicate the end. Pan and tilt shots should be illustrated in a similar manner. Do not worry about your artwork on these sketches. It is more important to have accurate camera angles and figure sizes.

The written scenario not only indicates the kinds of visual effects that your film will require, but it is also the place to indicate in detail how information will be supplied through sound and through written titles. Let's briefly explore both these aspects of a complete scenario.

Sound

Sound is becoming as increasingly important in amateur films as it has been for years in the professional film. Ever since 1927, when Al Jolson sang in *The Jazz Singer,* sound has been inseparable from the picture in the professional film. Today, sound is taken so much for granted that we feel a real lack whenever a silent film is watched. However, with the increased availability of sound-film systems for the amateur film maker, you may run the risk of over-emphasizing sound at the expense of effective visual images. Careful planning for the sound that will go into a scenario makes this possibility less likely.

The question of what kind of sound and how much sound to include cannot be answered in absolute terms. The best answer, albeit an ambiguous one, is that sound should be subordinated to the picture while at the same time being an integrated artistic element. Unless the need for sound arises organically from the film (like dialogue), and unless it functions either practically or symbolically, it

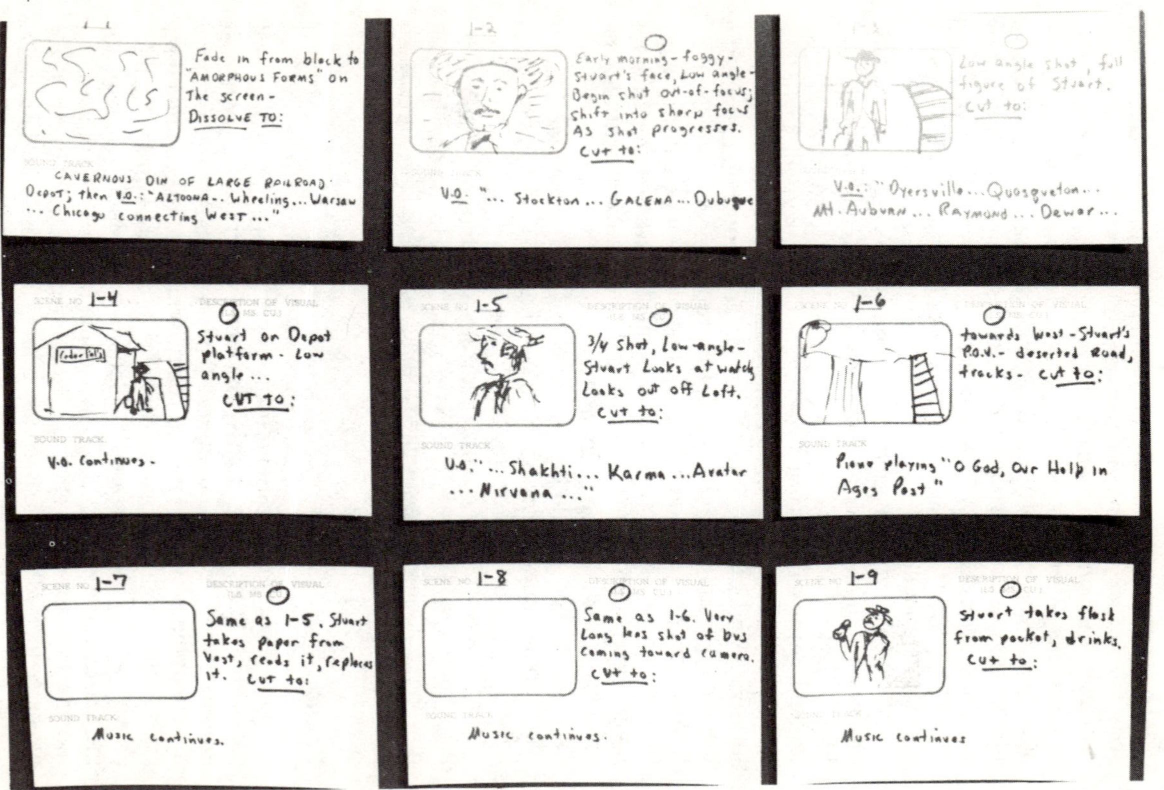

Fig. 2-1. A storyboard.

is probably best to use no sound at all. The sound should *mean* something—it must support and strengthen the visual images. Sound should never be thrown into the film in the hopes that the audience will be so dazzled by a Super 8 "talkie" that it fails to notice a poor story line or bad camera work. A good rule of thumb is to plan your film first in terms of the visual elements and, then, determine where and how sound can enhance those effects.

Titles

Titles, like sound, should be planned in advance of exposing any film. The most common use of titles today is informational. Titles are the most efficient and effective way to tell your audience what the name of your film is, who made it, and who is in it. Further, titles may be used in silent films to show necessary dialogue or to impart information that otherwise could only be known through sound. Titles are often used even in sound films to set locale, time, or to provide exposition for the action to follow. The kind of title you will use depends entirely on the requirements of your film and the information you must impart.

Once you have planned your titles, your next step is to decide where in your film they should be placed. Often the bulk of the informational titles are shown at the beginning of the film, but often, too, they are saved until the end. A recent trend has been to delay displaying the titles until the film is fairly under way. The decision may depend on the nature of the film. If it is a silent film, a more immediate reliance is placed on the titles than if sound were used. A silent film will probably require *more* titles than a sound film.

A SAMPLE SCENARIO

Although the scenario is more detailed than the treatment, it still does not supply the specifics needed to actually shoot the film. It may include the location, action, and point of view, but it does not specify the exact camera angle, field of view, focal length, and lighting. These specifications are stated more exactly in the *shooting script,* the final stage in the planning process.

The shooting script is an accurate technical description of the movie superimposed on the information supplied by the scenario. The shooting script is the equivalent of a contractor's blueprint. In the shooting script, each shot is described with the camera angle from which it is to be filmed, the field of view that is to be encompassed, and, possibly, the length of the lens that is needed, as well as the shooting location, and the direction of the light.

When transforming the scenario into a shooting script, the film maker should attempt to visualize exactly what he wants to occur in front of the camera (as well as what he wishes to suggest is happening off camera). Then, he can block out the action in terms of camera positions. Simple sketches are necessary at this point, even if the storyboard scenario has not been used, to show the relative positions of the actors and the action.

To illustrate all we have said about scripting so far, we offer the following example:

The Bandits

CONCEPT: "The Bandits" is a segment of a larger-scope dramatic film, episodic in nature, that uses the same characters caught in nightmare situations, in which one of the characters inevitably destroys the other. There will be four or five episodes altogether. This is a fiction film for adult audiences.

TREATMENT: In this segment, which we can subtitle "The Bandits," our two characters find themselves as Western outlaws hiding the loot from their most recent holdup. One outlaw is digging a hole at the base of a large cliff while the other watches and directs his activities. A map of the location of the cache is in evidence. The money box is placed in the hole and the hole is filled in. As the two men start to return to their horses, the leader orders the henchman to retrieve the forgotten map. As the first bandit picks up the map, the leader shoots and kills him, recovers the map, and rides off, his secret safe.

At this point, you could probably make a short film based on this idea. And you are free to do that if you want to. But it would not necessarily look like the film we have made. Why? Because the concept and the treatment by themselves do not contain enough detailed information about how we visualized each of the shots. Nor, for that matter, do they give you a shot breakdown. Obviously, to complete this film, we need a scenario and a shooting script. (We have written this as a sound film but it could be done just as well as a silent film. Perhaps you might need a title or two to compensate for the lack of dialogue but we think everything else would work.)

The outline shown in Fig. 2-2 is our scenario. Why did we choose to use these specific shots and arrange them in this order? We did it to tell the audience certain things about the story and about the two men in it. Let's examine how we did that.

Our first shot, the long shot showing the entire location, is called the *establishing shot*, since it establishes the locale for the scene. But,

<pre>
                    THE BANDITS   SCENARIO

Shot
Number   Description
____

  1   Long Shot of portion of secluded ravine. Under an over-hanging
           boulder, a man is digging a hole. He is dressed like a cowboy. A
           small iron-bound chest lies near him. Another man, holding a rifle
           or shotgun, stand guard a little ways off. He is dressed in western
           style also, but of a finer cut than the first man. He smokes a cigar.
           It is late afternoon. Cut to:

  2   M.S.   The two men, second moves closer to first. Cut to:

  3   M.C.U. of the Boss. He glances from side to side, flicks ash from his
           cigar, looks down at Henchman. "How much more you have to dig?"
           Cut to:

  4   M.C.U.   Henchman digging. He pauses, wipes sweat from face with a
           grimy handkerchief. "I almost got it." Takes a drink of water, resumes
           digging.

  5   C.U.   Boss watching with narrowed eyes. He looks at sky. "We ought to
           be out of here before sundown." Cut to:

  6   C.U.   Henchman digging, "Yeah." Cut to:

  7   M.C.U.   Boss sets gun down, takes pencil and paper from pocket, starts
           to draw map. Dissolve to:

  8   E.C.U.   Boss' point of view. Finishing map. Cut to:

  9   M.S.   Henchman finishes digging, throws spade down. Boss folds map,
           sets it on rock. The two men put strongbox in hole. Boss, "Cover it up
           good." Dissolve to:

 10   M.C.U.   Zoom to M.L.S.   Pan to follow action. Henchman finishes
           tramping down earth; they pick up tools and walk toward horses. Cut to:

 11   M.C.U.   Boss feels his pockets, looks back toward hole, turns to
           Henchman. "Where's the map?" Cut to:

 12   C.U.   Treasure map on rock. Cut to:

 13   M.C.U.   Boss gestures Henchman back to map. Cut to:

 14   M.L.S.   From Boss' point of view. Henchman picks up map, turns to go
           back.

 15   M.C.U.   Boss draws revolver, carefully aims, and fires. Cut to:

 16   M.C.U.   Henchman lies dead near rock, hand still clutching map.

 17   M.S.   Boss walks over to body, picks up map, drags body behind rock.
           Cut to:

 18   L.S.   Boss returns to horse, mounts, and rides slowly off with other
           horse trailing behind. Fade Out.
</pre>

Fig. 2-2. Example of a scenario.

what are the men doing in those rocks? We are too far away to tell that they are bandits. They might be picnickers or even archeologists. We need to know more about them so we move in closer for our next shot, which is a medium shot. This shot includes only a small portion of the surrounding country. Most of the frame is filled with the two robbers. Now we can see more clearly that one of the men stands guard while his companion digs a hole for the loot under the rocks.

We want still more information so we shoot some close-ups. These shots concentrate on one or the other of the two men. We can see, for example, that the digging robber is dirty and perspiring, and has dug to a depth of three or four feet. The other man, obviously the leader, is relaxed. He, alternately, scans the horizon for signs of intruders while continuing to watch his companion dig. Now we introduce an extreme close-up of the leader's face showing the cruelty in his eyes above the thin cigar clamped in his teeth. We then begin a series of shots, both medium and close-ups—showing the men finishing the digging, marking the map, placing the strong box in the hole, filling it in, and walking toward their horses. The dissolve is used between several of these shots to compress the time it would take to portray these actions in real life.

Now we want to set the scene for the killing. We insert an M.C.U. of the leader showing him searching for something in his pockets. He asks his henchman for the map. Here we change to a cut-away shot from the leader's point of view—a closeup of the map left behind on the rock. We cut back to the leader ordering the henchman to retrieve the map. As he obeys, we cut to a closer shot of the boss drawing, cocking, and firing his .45. We cut to a closeup of the henchman's sightless eyes to see the results of the gun being fired. Then, in a few quick shots, we have the boss hide the body, get the map, and ride off secure in the knowledge that only he knows where the treasure is buried. Note that we did not use much dialogue at all in the script. Just enough to give us a few pieces of information about the action and the characters.

While there is nothing particularly original in this little scenario, it serves to introduce the possible ways of combining shots to give certain types of information to the audience. Each type of shot has its inherent emotional and informational values, which are determined, in part, by the shots that precede it and follow it and, in part, by the duration of the individual shots themselves. (Remember that every shot in a film must be considered in relation with other shots. None exist independently of any other.)

In the early days of film making, all the operations were done by relatively few people. Many cameramen wrote and directed their own shows. In many ways, we have come full circle, since the person who operates the camera in most Super 8 productions is again the writer-director. And, as that person, you will soon realize that there is more to movie making than just following a scenario or aiming and shooting the camera. The director must envision the action, block it out, rehearse the actors, and direct the shot. The director must also know how to maintain visual and story continuity within the shots and throughout the picture. In other words, the director must have a thorough grasp of the filmic process. This is why you, the director, should do this final task in the scripting process—writing the shooting script.

THE SHOOTING SCRIPT

The shooting script is the blueprint of the film. It is the place where we detail such information as camera angle, field of view, camera location, and actor placement. This script is what we will take on location.

The shooting script is divided into two parts. On one sheet of paper, we write a description of the camera information, the action, and the sound. On another piece of paper, we sketch a ground plan of the location of the shot (or scene). Then, we fill in the information for each shot. The two pages are put in a loose-leaf binder or notebook, facing each other. When we get on location, it is a simple matter to turn to the correct shot, look at the sketch, place the camera, block and rehearse the actors, and take the shot. A sample shooting script is shown in Figs. 2-3 and 2-4, illustrating the first two shots of "The Bandits."

Note that the information contained in the written part of the shooting script (Fig. 2-3) is similar to that in the scenario. The major difference is that the shooting script is more detailed. The camera information, for example, tells us that the first shot is to be a slow pan, from a high angle, of the entire location. This is somewhat of a change from the scenario in which "long shot" was the only camera instruction indicated. The shooting script makes the instructions more specific and the subsequent filming more precise. Note also that the wide-angle lens is specified. Obviously, this is an attempt to get the largest field of view without moving the camera too far back.

The instructions in the action section are virtually the same as those in the scenario, but the sound section is detailed and specific. The scenario said nothing about sound in the first shot. The shooting script tells us that we should record the horses, the wind, and the sounds of the henchman working. We could have figured out most of these things from the scenario if we stopped to think about it once we got on location. However, the reason we write them down here is so that we will not have to stop in the middle of our setup to think of what we want to do next.

```
                        SHOOTING SCRIPT

                          SCENARIO

     TITLE:  THE BANDITS        DIRECTOR:  GLENN        PAGE   1
```

SCENE	Master Shot Description
1	CAMERA: Slow pan high angle L.S. of secluded ravine, late afternoon, air is dusty. Use wide-angle lens.
	ACTION: Under an over-hanging boulder, a man is digging a hole. A small iron-bound chest lies near him. Second man stands guard on fallen tree over ravine. He holds a shotgun and smokes a cigar.
SHOTS	SOUND: Wind in background, grunts and digging sounds from first man, horses whinny and stamp their feet off screen.
1	Special Editing
	None
SCENE	Insert Shot Description
1	CAMERA: Medium shot eye level of first and second man.
	ACTION: Second man moves closer to first to inspect hole.
SHOTS	SOUND: Subdued wind, digging and spurs of second man as he walks over.
2	Special Editing

Fig. 2-3. Example of a shooting script form.

The other important part of the shooting script is the blocking sketch (Fig. 2-4). The simple drawing shown here is a plan view of the location on which we filmed "The Bandits." We have drawn in the camera, the actors (Boss and Henchman), and the major features of the terrain (the rock, the canyon, and the hole). Movement by the camera, or on the part of the actors, is shown by arrows, and their positions are indicated at the beginning and the end of their movement. The direction of the major source of light is also indicated. In this case, it's the sun. If this were an interior shot, we would have shown where existing lights were and where we would place supplementary lighting. The sketches are kept as simple as possible since they are merely instructions to ourselves. Blocking the film out this way enables one to plan the action before going on location.

We have designated the first camera position in this shooting script as the *Master Position*. This idea comes from a concept in film making called the *Master Shot*. This concept can be stated by mentioning that in every scene, there is one camera position that can be used to film the majority (or all) of the action in a continuous run. After the camera positions are blocked out in the shooting script, one position is determined to be the Master Position. This is usually a medium long shot with a good view of all the action in the scene. During production, this shot is taken first with the entire scene being run, from start to finish. Then, the camera is switched to those other

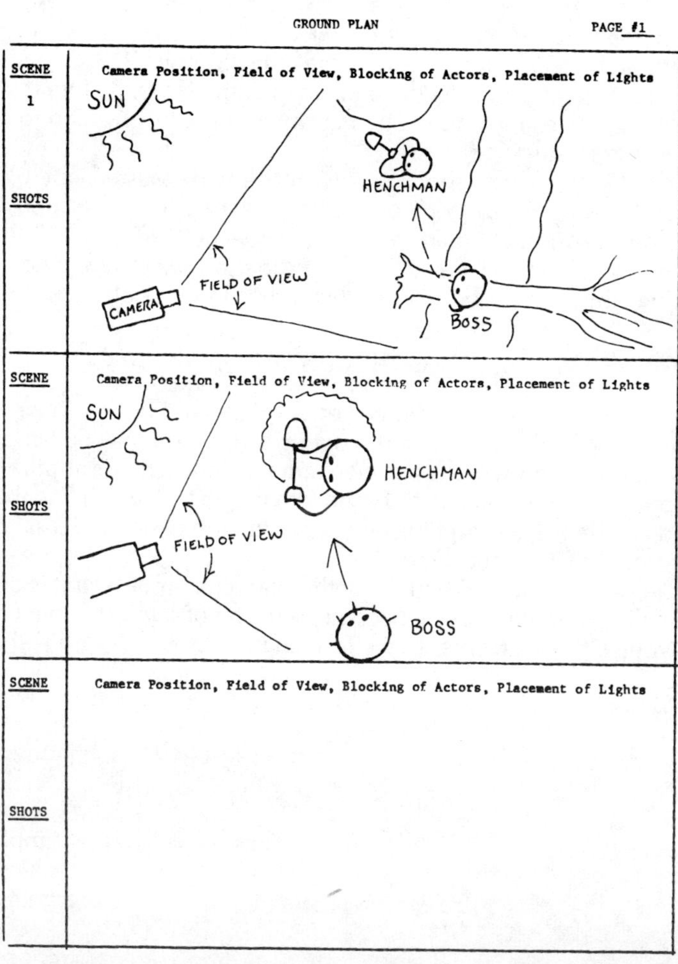

Fig. 2-4. Example of a blocking sketch for a shooting script.

camera positions that are necessary in order to shoot the other bits of action. The result is one shot that includes all the major action and dialogue, and a series of insert shots (or short takes) that contain the close-ups, the details, etc., that make up the remainder of the scene.

There are several advantages to shooting a master shot—advantages for the actors, the production crew, and the editor. The running through of the action and dialogue in one long shot gives the actors a chance to do a better job of creating their roles in the film. It simplifies the production crew's job, too, as they will only have to set up the whole scene one time. There are two advantages to the editor that accrue from this concept. There is always one complete shot with all the action in it. When editing, the editor can return to this shot if the inserts lack continuity or fail to convey the message. And the master shot has the whole action/dialogue in the time it took to film it (real time). This gives the editor a good starting point from which to edit the scene for timing.

To determine which shot you will choose as the Master Shot, block the scene in shooting script form, then pick the camera position that best covers the action from a wide-angle field of view. With a complicated scene, it may be necessary to shoot two Master Shots. In editing, they would be intercut like other insert shots.

CONCLUSION

It may seem like a lot of unnecessary work and bother to write a scenario or work up a detailed shooting script. You may be tempted to shoot first and write it up afterwards (or not write it at all). But scripting is an essential part of good film making. You will find that a solid and thorough script makes your entire job easier and it saves a great deal of film and time.

The same things apply to the entire planning process. If it is done carefully, your film making becomes a matter of saying to your crew (or yourself), "Here's what we're going to do next."

SECTION II

Preparation

CHAPTER 3

The Camera

Anyone who plans on becoming a film maker should also become familiar with the tools of the film maker. They should understand fully the camera, the lighting equipment, the different types of films, and the other accessories that are available for his or her use.

The camera is the basic tool of the film maker. And, since a worker is only as good as his knowledge of his tools, the film maker must understand how the camera works before he or she can plan or produce a film. However, the automatic nature of Super 8 cameras means that many of their functions can take place without the constant supervision of the film maker. Nevertheless, you need to know how the systems of the camera work in order to use them to best advantage in your film production (see Fig. 3-1).

The basic function of any movie camera is to expose a perforated strip of film with a certain number of pictures (or frames) in a specific length of time. (The normal running speed for Super 8 cameras is 18 frames per second.) The movie camera takes each picture by pulling the film downward into the film gate and opening the shutter for a fraction of a second, so that the light coming through the aperture can expose one frame of film. Then the shutter is closed, and the exposed film is wound onto a film spool by the takeup mechanism. From this simple description, we can see that there are three basic systems necessary to the operation of every movie camera—the *lens* system, which gathers and focuses the light; the *exposure* system, which takes the picture; and the *transport* system, which brings the film to and takes the film from the exposure system. In practice, there is another system that all movie cameras have (the *monitoring* system) that tells the camera operator what each of the other systems is doing and how well each is doing it.

Although the functions of all movie cameras are generally the same, there are some major design differences between Super 8 cameras and those of other gauges. Most Super 8 cameras use a

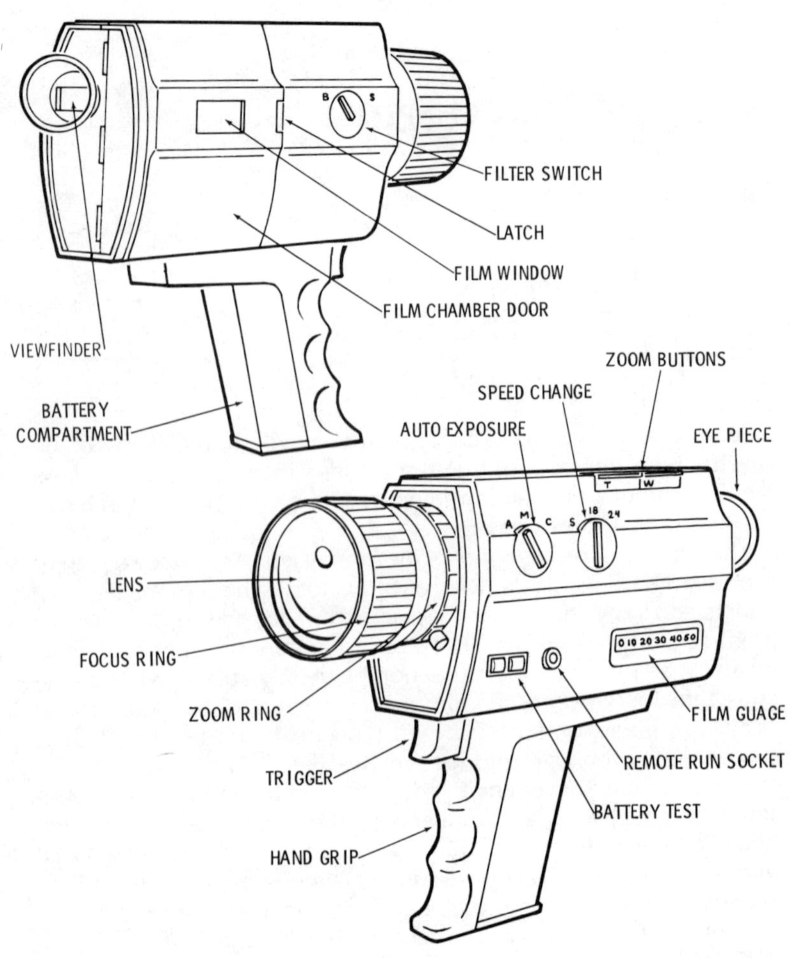

Fig. 3-1. Two views of a typical Super 8 camera.

permanently mounted *zoom lens*, while other types of movie cameras have detachable lenses, often of a fixed focal length. Super 8 exposure systems, from the beginning, have been more automatic in nature, allowing the camera operator to concentrate more on taking the picture than on worrying about getting the correct exposure. Most other movie cameras have exposure systems that must be set manually and which do not compensate automatically for changes in lighting. The transport system in Super 8 cameras uses a film cartridge that snaps into place. In most other movie cameras, the film must be threaded from the feed reel through the film gate to the takeup reel. Finally, Super 8 cameras have always had more complete monitoring systems than other cameras, due primarily to the automatic nature of the other operating systems in the Super 8 camera. Only recently have professional cameras in other gauges (like 16 mm) gone to the kinds of monitoring devices that most Super 8 cameras have had for years.

There are three common types of Super 8 cameras—the reflex-viewing zoom lens camera, the nonreflex zoom lens camera with coupled rangefinder, and the fixed focal length lens camera with viewfinder. However, contemporary Super 8 cameras come in all sizes, shapes, and price ranges (see Fig. 3-2). The most widely used type is the reflex-viewing zoom lens camera. This is the kind of camera that allows you to see what the camera sees because you actually look through the lens as you are filming. Since it is the most popular type, we will use it as our primary example while explaining the systems of the camera.

THE LENS SYSTEM

The *lens system* consists of the lens barrel (which contains the focusing ring, the zoom ring, and the elements of the lens itself), the lens cap and lens shade (which are attached to the front of the lens barrel), the beam splitter and the viewfinder (both located in the body of the camera). Fig. 3-3 shows a typical lens barrel. Note that the focusing ring, the zoom ring, and the reference marks are located on the lens barrel. The purpose of the lens system is to gather the light reflected from the subject, bring it into sharp focus at the film plane, allow the film maker to choose a certain size picture or field of view, and, at the same time, let the film maker see the image that is being photographed.

The Lens

The lens portion of the lens system is a collection of optically correct, highly polished, glass or synthetic elements that are arranged to gather the light that is reflected from the subject into the camera and focus it on the film plane. (By focus, we mean the way the lens causes the light rays to converge at the film plane; we do not mean image sharpness.) The lens elements are coated with metallic salts in order to allow more light to pass through them than would be possible if they were just plain glass. This is especially important in zoom lenses where there are often ten or more elements in the lens. The elements are packaged in groups, which are arranged to give the various focal lengths needed, with the least amount of movement of the camera or lens.

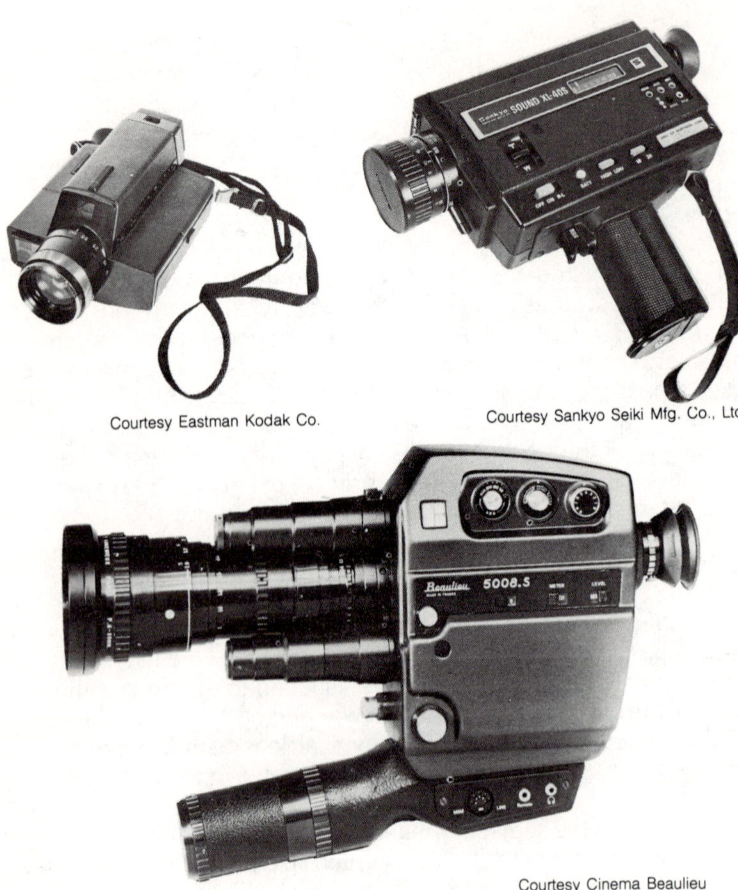

Courtesy Eastman Kodak Co.   Courtesy Sankyo Seiki Mfg. Co., Ltd.

Courtesy Cinema Beaulieu

Fig. 3-2. Three common types of Super 8 cameras.

The Focus Ring

Image sharpness, more commonly called *focus*, is controlled by the front ring on the lens barrel. This ring is usually calibrated in both feet and meters. In a reflex camera, the eye sees the same image that the film records (Fig. 3-4). Thus, focus is achieved by sighting through the viewfinder and then turning the focus ring until the image is sharp. There are three kinds of focusing systems that are commonly used on Super 8 cameras and each type looks different in the viewfinder. They are:

Split Image—Split-image focusing appears to be a small circle in the center of the lens, split into two halves. By moving the focus ring, the top and bottom halves move either farther apart

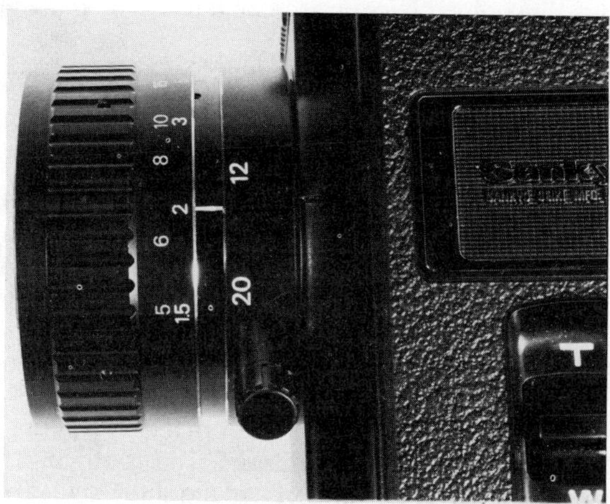

Fig. 3-3. A typical lens barrel.

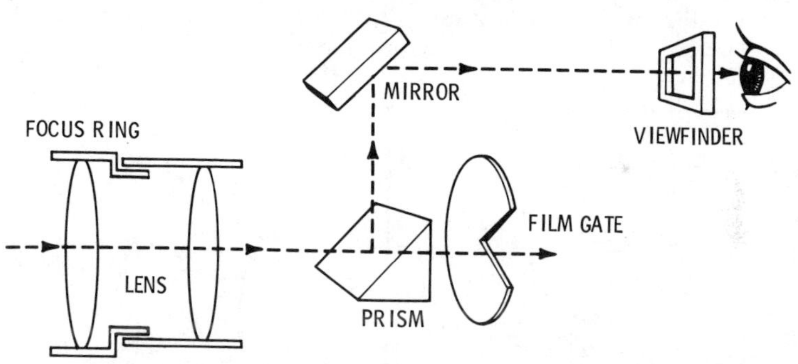

Fig. 3-4. Diagram of a lens system.

or closer together. The subject is in focus when the top and bottom halves are aligned (Fig. 3-5A).

Ground Glass—Ground-glass focusing (Fig. 3-5B) works on the principle that when the subject is in focus, the image in the viewfinder will appear to be in sharpest view. Moving the focus ring causes the subject to change from a blurred image to a sharper "in focus" image.

Microprism—The microprism system uses the center of the lens, like the split-image system and the blurred-to-sharp principle of the ground-glass system (Fig. 3-5C). The focusing field is a small circle in the center of the lens that is filled with tiny prisms. When the focus ring is turned, the subject in the prismatic area appears to be either sharper or more blurred until the point of focus is reached. Then the microprism becomes almost clear.

The Zoom Ring

The zoom effect is controlled by the second or inside ring on the lens barrel and by buttons on the top or side of the camera body. The zoom ring is calibrated in millimeters (abbreviated mm) which represent the focal length of the lens at that particular zoom setting. Focal length is the distance between the optical center of the lens and the film plane (see Fig. 3-6). The zoom ring varies the focal length of the lens by moving the lens elements in relation to each other to vary the point at which the rays of light will converge. A zoom lens is a lens with variable focal length.

It is common practice to refer to the zoom lens of a Super 8 camera by its zoom ratio, such as a 5-to-1 Zoom. The zoom ratio expresses the relationship between the longest and the shortest focal lengths in the zoom lens range. Unfortunately, this zoom ratio does not tell us what the upper and lower limits of the zoom range really are. A 5-to-1 zoom ratio might refer to a lens that zooms from 8-mm to 40-mm focal length, or it could refer to a lens that has a range from 9.5 mm to

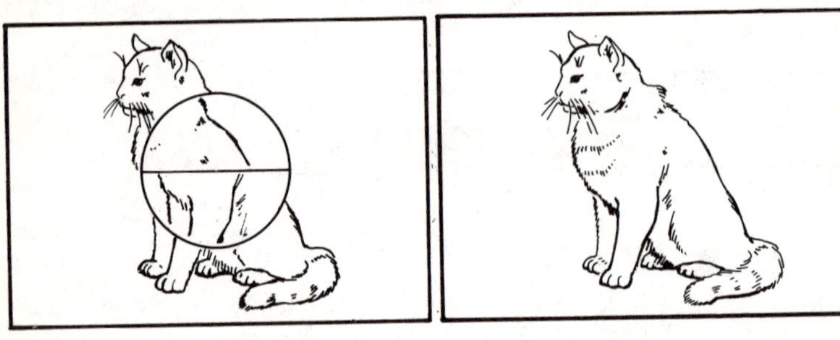

(A) Split-image focusing.   (B) Ground-glass focusing.

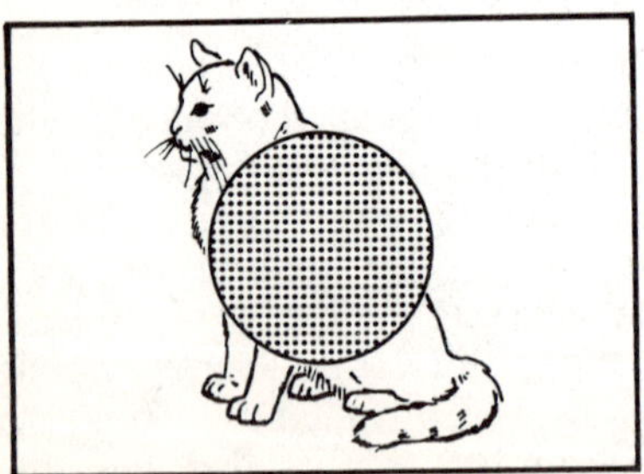

(C) Microprism focusing.

Fig. 3-5. Each type of focusing system looks different in the viewfinder.

47.5 mm. These are two different lenses that cover somewhat different fields of view, but they happen to have the same zoom ratio. It would be more correct to refer to zoom lenses by their focal length range, like an 8–40-mm zoom lens. This is commonly done in still photography where zoom lenses are now becoming quite popular.

By varying the focal length of the lens, the zoom ring controls the field of view that the camera "sees" (Fig. 3-7). The "normal" field of view for Super 8 cameras is about 12.5 mm (Fig. 3-8). Any focal length shorter than that (a lower number) is considered to be a larger than normal field of view and is called a "wide angle" view. In the wide-angle field of view, more area is seen but the objects in that area appear to be smaller, or farther away (Fig. 3-9). Conversely, any focal length longer than 12.5 mm (a higher number) is considered to be a "telephoto" field of view. In a telephoto shot (Fig. 3-10), the area of view is smaller than normal and the objects appear to be larger (or closer) than normal.

In most modern Super 8 cameras, there is another field of view setting to complement the wide-angle and telephoto settings. This field of view is called *macro focus*. Macro focusing means the camera has the ability to focus sharply on objects that are closer to the lens than the limit of the normal focus setting, which is usually about one meter. This special focus condition is accomplished by moving some elements of the zoom lens in relation to other elements, much like the manner in which a change in focal length is accomplished. The difference here is that one must switch to the macro setting on the camera in order to activate the macro-focus mode. Camera manuals give specific directions for doing this. What macro focus does,

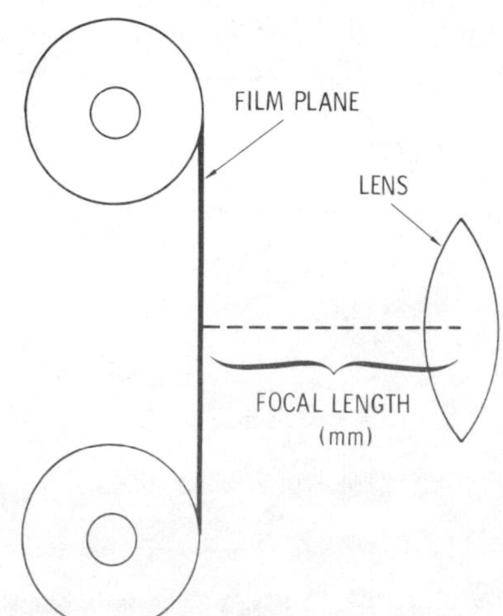

Fig. 3-6. Focal length.

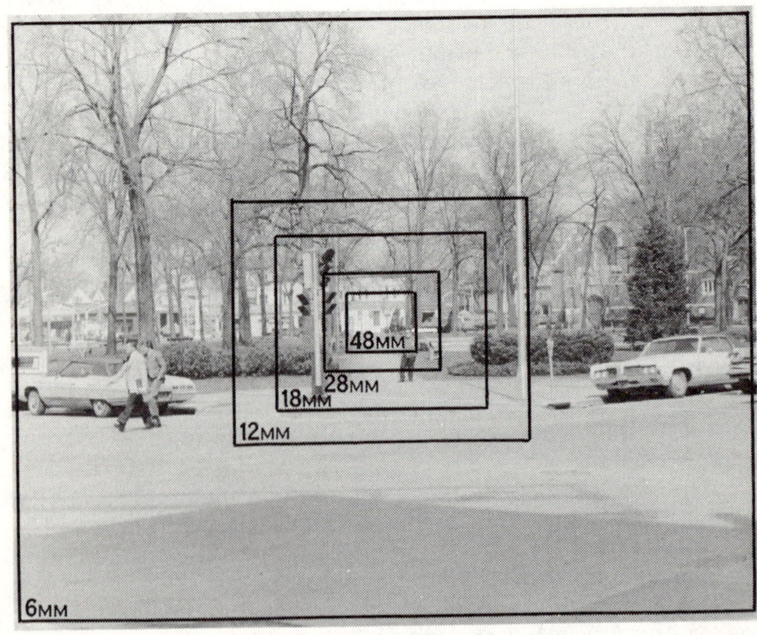

Fig. 3-7. Field of vision covered by different focal lengths—wide angle (6 mm), normal (12 mm), and telephoto (18 mm, 28 mm, and 48 mm).

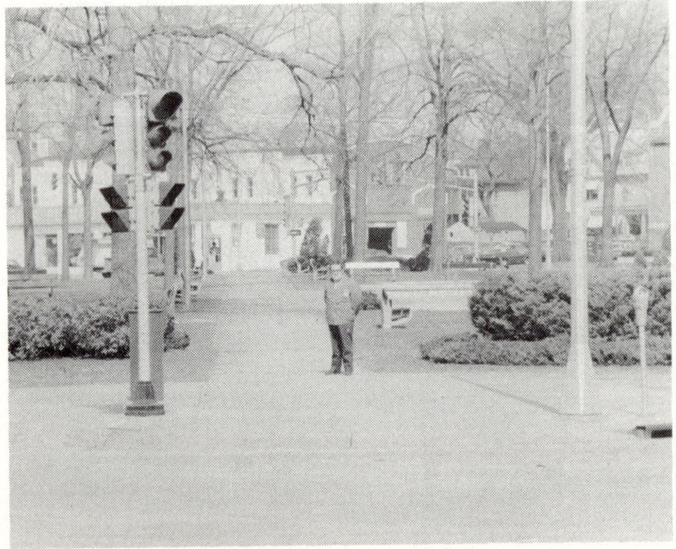

Fig. 3-8. Lens is set at 12.5 mm (normal).

however, is allow you to see a much smaller field of view than you could even with full telephoto because you can get much closer to the object. An extremely small object, like a postage stamp, can fill the screen with its image.

The Viewfinder

All these fields of view can be seen by the camera operator through the viewfinder in the reflex camera. On nonreflex zoom cameras, the viewfinder is usually coupled with the zoom ring so that the size of the field of view will change in the same proportions as the zoom lens "sees" it. Actually, the field of view you see in the viewfinder is slightly smaller than the field of view the camera is seeing. This reduction is caused by the problems of transmitting the image, as seen by the lens, through a series of mirrors, in the viewing system, to the viewfinder. The viewfinder is usually equipped with a *diopter* adjustment (Fig. 3-11). This device enables the camera operator to adjust the viewfinder to bring the reflex image into correct focus for the operator's vision.

The other parts of the lens system, such as the lens cap, the lens shade, and the eyepiece, are primarily protective devices. The lens cap, usually made of plastic or rubber, fits on the end of the lens barrel to protect the surface of the lens from dirt and scratches. The lens shade, or lens hood, attaches to the lens barrel by means of screw threads in the focus ring. Its purpose is to prevent direct

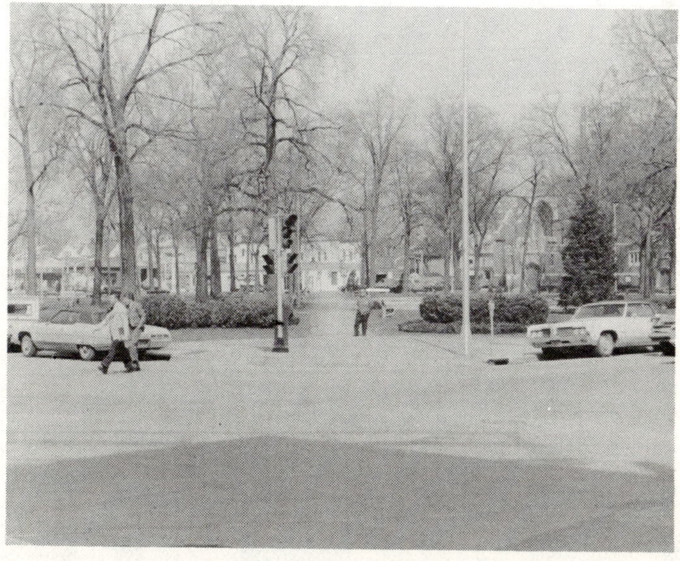

Fig. 3-9. Lens is set at 6 mm (wide angle).

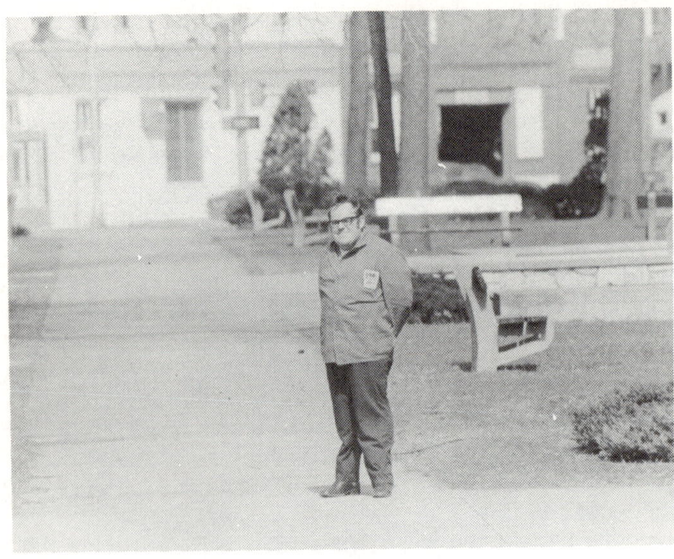

Fig. 3-10. Lens is set at 28 mm (telephoto).

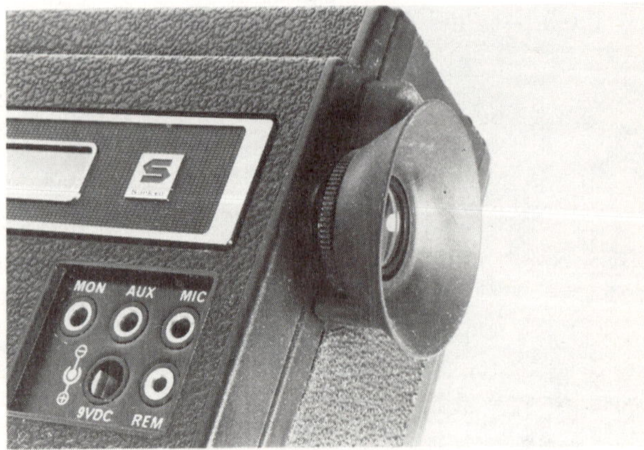

Fig. 3-11. The viewfinder with a rubber eyecup and a
diopter adjustment ring.

sunlight from striking the surface of the lens and causing glare in the
picture. The eyepiece, sometimes called the eyecup, is attached to
the viewfinder. It has two functions; it protects the viewfinder from
getting scratched, and it shrouds the viewfinder when you are using it
so that unnecessary light does not interfere with focusing or viewing.

THE EXPOSURE SYSTEM

The *exposure system* located directly behind the lens system, and usually integrated with it, consists of the aperture and metering system, the shutter, and the filter (Fig. 3-12). This system controls the exposure of the individual frames of film by regulating the amount of light that each frame receives. The lens, rated in f/numbers as to its maximum opening, "gathers" the light and focuses it on the film plane. The metering system "reads" the incoming light and decides how much to open the aperture (measured in f/stops) to give a correct exposure. The filter corrects the color balance of the film and has nothing directly to do with exposure.

The Aperture

The aperture is the opening at the back of the lens which is designed to respond to the reactions of the light meter that are caused by the amount of light coming in the lens. The aperture (see Fig. 3-12) is opened up or stopped down by a series of overlapping blades

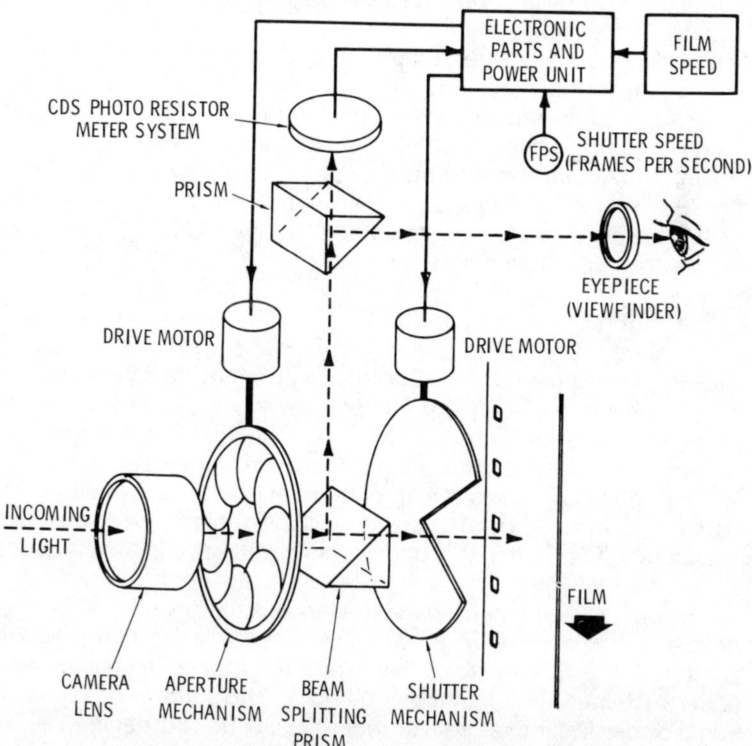

Fig. 3-12. An exploded view of the exposure system.

arranged in a circle and called an iris. In operation, the iris in the aperture resembles the iris in your eye, hence the name. Some Super 8 cameras use a series of forked blades to control the passage of light through the aperture but the effect is still the same as the more commonly used iris.

The Metering System

The metering system consists of a light-sensitive cell that moves a mechanical linkage to open or close the aperture in response to the amount of light coming through the lens. This cell is powered by the electrical system in the camera or, in some cases, by a separate battery. In considering how much to open up or stop down the aperture, the metering system takes into account the type of film being used in the camera (its ASA rating), the running speed of the camera (frames per second), and whether or not the filter is in place. In most Super 8 cameras, the metering system actually reads the light coming through the lens. This type of metering is called *through-the-lens* (or TTL) *metering,* and it is the most accurate automatic metering system.

On many Super 8 cameras, the automatic functioning of the meter (and aperture) may be overridden by a manual adjustment or some other form of over/under exposure control. This manual control works directly on the linkage of the aperture allowing the camera operator to directly control the size of the opening (in f/stops) and, consequently, control exposure. Both manual and automatic control of the metering system are monitored by the light-meter display, which reads in f/stops.

The Shutter

The shutter is the third part of the exposure system. It is located directly behind the aperture and right in front of the film gate (just ahead of the film plane). The shutter is a disc with a piece (a certain number of degrees wide) cut out of it. This disc is driven by the camera motor in synchronization with the film transport system. The shutter opens for a fixed length of time relative to the speed of the camera ($\frac{1}{36}$ of a second at 18 fps, the normal running speed of Super 8 cameras). The shutter only opens when the frame is in the film gate. It is closed when the frame is being changed (see Chart 3-1).

Low light or XL cameras have shutters that are open for 220–230 degrees of their travel. This, coupled with the larger than normal aperture in the XL cameras, allows them to give adequate exposure under extremely low lighting conditions. The shutters of conventional Super 8 cameras remain open for about 180 degrees.

There are some cameras that have variable shutter openings. These cameras can be used to make fades and dissolves by manipulation of

Chart 3-1. Camera Speed vs. Shutter Speed

For conventional Super 8 cameras with 180° shutters, the shutter speed (in fractions of a second) is calculated by multiplying the "reciprocal" of the running speed by ½.

Running Speed (fps)	Shutter Speed
8	1/16
12	1/24
18	1/36
24	1/48
36	1/72
54	1/108

For XL Super 8 cameras with 220°–230° shutters, the shutter speed (in fractions of a second) is calculated by multiplying the "reciprocal" of the running speed by ⅔.

Running Speed (fps)	Shutter Speed
8	1/12
12	1/18
18	1/27
24	1/36
36	1/54
54	1/81

the shutter opening and backwinding the film. Another advantage of the variable shutter is that one can use shutter control to effect a greater depth of field without changing the camera running speed, the focus setting, or the focal length of the lens. A further advantage is that the variable shutter will allow you to shoot in light that is too bright (normally) for the smallest aperture of the camera. When the camera is stopped down to its smaller aperture, by closing the shutter somewhat, you can further reduce the amount of light on the film and not worry about overexposing it.

The Filter

All Super 8 cameras are equipped with a built-in filter which allows you to use one type of film for both indoor and outdoor filming. The majority of film made for Super 8 is called Type-A film. This means it is "color balanced" for use under tungsten light (or incandescent light). In order for the colors to appear correct when the film is exposed under sunlight, the film must be filtered with an orange/yellow filter. If this were not done, the color of your film when exposed in sunlight would appear to be very blue. Conversely, the filter must be taken out when shooting in artificial light or the colors will appear to be more orange than normal. The filter is controlled in two ways—by a filter notch located on the film cartridge which signals a corresponding pin in the film chamber, and by a manual override switch on the outside of the camera. This manual override may be a filter switch (see Fig. 3-1), or it might be the mounting socket for a movie light. Some cameras are equipped with both. In any case, this filter switch (or movie light socket) allows the film maker to leave the filter in (normal position in most cameras), or take it out as needed, to get the correct color balance under various kinds of lighting.

THE TRANSPORT SYSTEM

The *transport system* is the heart of the movie camera. It is the one system that distinguishes the movie camera from the still camera. Although the still camera can be said to have a transport system, the system of the movie camera is much more complex and sophisticated. The transport system (Fig. 3-13) consists of the trigger, the speed change switch, the film chamber, the film gate, the pressure pad, the claw, and the takeup and remote run mechanisms. With the exception of the pressure pad which is located inside the

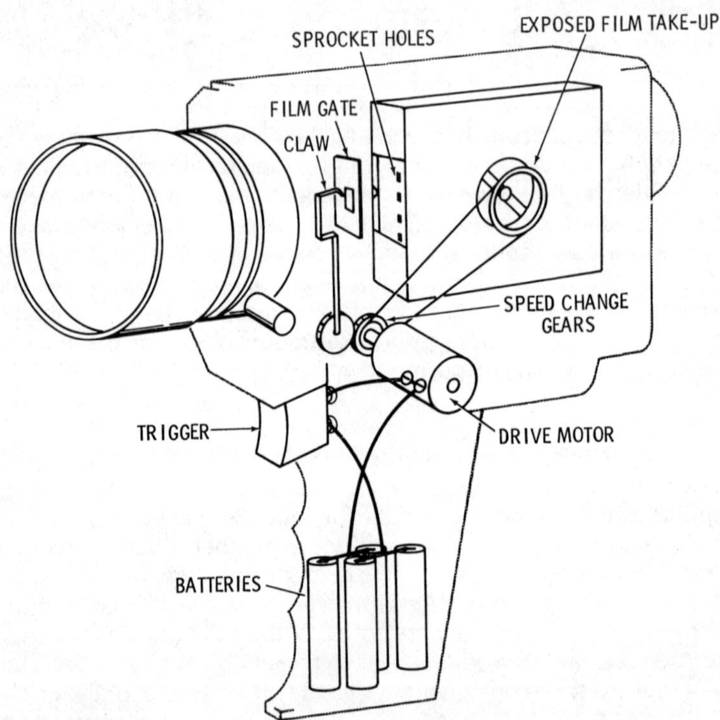

Fig. 3-13. The transport system, the heart of the movie camera.

film cartridge, all these devices are contained within the body of the camera. The purpose of the transport system is to bring the film to the exposure system, hold it still and flat while the frame is being exposed, and then take up the exposed film. The transport system does this consistently at the selected camera running speed.

The Trigger

The first part of the transport system is the trigger or shutter release. This switch, usually located at the front of the camera body, starts and stops the transport system by turning on or shutting off the electric motors that drive the system. These motors are powered by a series of batteries located in either the body or the handle of the camera. Most triggers are equipped with some sort of locking device. This enables them to be *locked off* so an accidental squeeze of the trigger would not accidentally expose some film or *locked on* to allow continuous running of the camera without holding the trigger.

Most cameras, now, are also equipped with a second trigger-like device called a *remote run*. This remote run mechanism takes one of two forms. Either, it is a threaded socket for a flexible shaft (called a cable release) or it is an electrical socket (usually miniplug size) that takes an electric switch. In either case, the results are the same; pressing the cable release or turning on the switch causes the trigger to be released and the camera to run. The purpose of the remote run mechanism is to allow the camera operator to run the camera without having to press the trigger. This, in turn, frees the camera operator from having to stand by the camera for every shot and, also, gives him opportunities for controlling the camera remotely at long distances. Any camera with an electric remote run can be operated by radio control and several camera manufacturers are now offering such equipment.

Speed Change Switch

The speed change switch is usually located on the side of the camera body (see Fig. 3-1). It is marked with numbers that indicate the specific frames-per-second speeds at which the camera can be run. There is another mark like an S or like SF that is used to indicate the single-frame setting. The normal running speed of Super 8 cameras is 18 frames per second. However, most cameras are designed to run at 18 fps, or at a slow-motion speed (24 fps, 32 fps, 36 fps, or 54 fps) and single-frame speed. The speed change switch shifts the speed of the camera by changing gears or rubber drive wheels inside the camera body. This change in speed also affects the shutter, the claw, and the takeup mechanism as they are all linked together. The automatic metering system also takes each camera running speed into account and compensates for the increased or reduced shutter-opening time by stopping down or opening up the aperture.

The purpose of having multiple running speeds in the Super 8 camera is to give the film maker greater flexibility in covering a given filming situation. The slow-motion speeds can be used for all kinds of effects, including motion analysis and instant replay. The fast-motion speeds (often 9 fps or 12 fps) give a hurry-up quality to shots and can be used to simulate the jerky effects associated with the old-time movies. Single frame, of course, is valuable for titling, animation, pixilation, and a host of special effects.

The Film Chamber

The film chamber, which contains the other essential parts of the transport system, is located in the body of the camera. Access to this chamber is through the film chamber door or cover, located on the right-hand side of the camera body or at the back of the camera body. The chamber is fitted with springs to hold the cartridge firmly in place when it is loaded. (On those cameras with rear doors, the springs are in the door itself.) The alignment pin, the film gate, and the claw are located at the front of the film chamber while the takeup mechanism is on the left-hand side of it.

The purpose of the *alignment pin* is to hold the cartridge in correct alignment with the film gate when the cartridge is loaded. The *film gate* is a "space" gate whose primary function is to maintain film alignment side to side. A *pressure pad* in the film cartridge holds the film flat against the gate.

The *claw* located in the upper right-hand corner of the film gate performs two functions. It pulls the film down into the film gate, frame by frame, so that it may be exposed, and it holds the film steady in the gate, so the exposure is done accurately. The claw moves in synchronization with the shutter and the takeup mechanisms.

The *takeup mechanism*, a small sprocket wheel on the side of the film chamber, winds up the exposed film on another film spool located inside the film cartridge. On those cameras that offer double-exposure effects, this takeup mechanism is usually disengaged during the process so the exposed film is *not* wound up inside the cartridge. The film, which piles up inside the cartridge for about 90 frames, is then drawn back through the film gate with the shutter closed. Then, the takeup mechanism is reengaged, the film is reexposed by a second pass through the gate, and it is wound up on the inside of the film cartridge. The reason that the takeup mechanism is disengaged for this operation is that the film cartridge is designed to wind one way only. Once the takeup mechanism has wound the film on the other spool inside the cartridge, it cannot be unwound back again without damaging the cartridge. So, the only solution is to not take up the film if you want to re-expose it. If your camera has this feature, the operator's manual will give you explicit directions on how to use this effect.

THE MONITORING SYSTEM

Every Super 8 camera contains a series of monitoring devices to tell the camera operator what is happening to the film transport system, the exposure system, and the batteries that power the camera. While each Super 8 camera seems to accomplish these monitoring functions in a slightly different manner, there are five basic monitoring functions that every Super 8 camera does have: film window, aperture or metering system indicator, film run indicator with end-of-run warning, film gauge, and battery check.

The Film Window

The film window is on the right side of the camera, often in the door of the film chamber. It shows whether or not the camera is loaded and what type and speed of film it is loaded with. The film cartridge is marked with this information in two places on its right-hand side because the film windows on some cameras are higher than those on other cameras.

Light Meter Indicator

The light-metering system indicator is often a scale or circular dial, calibrated in f/stops, that is visible through the viewfinder (Fig. 3-14). It reads the opening of the camera aperture. When the camera is set on automatic metering (or automatic exposure), the meter reading will change as the camera adjusts automatically to changes in the light. When the camera is set on manual exposure, or when you are overriding the automatic system, the meter will read the aperture that you have set or locked in. On those cameras that have no scale or dial for meter reading, the exposure can be monitored by a red light that appears when the camera is underexposing or overexposing the film.

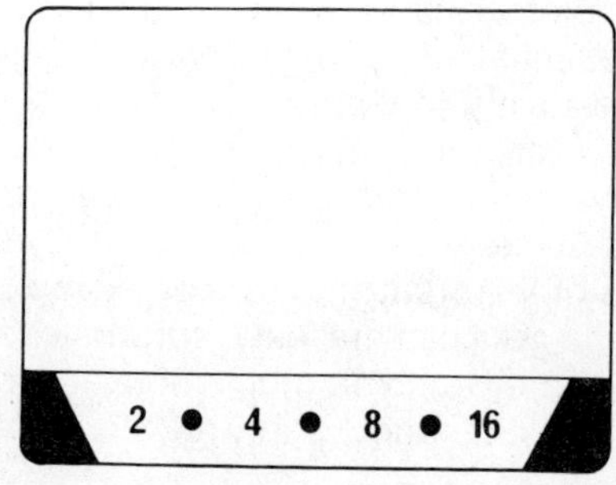

Fig. 3-14. Diagram of f/stops, as seen in the viewfinder.

Run Indicator

The film-run indicator is usually a blinking window or dot visible through the viewfinder. It tells you that the film *is running* through the camera. The film-run indicator is often paired with an end-of-run indicator, a flag, or warning light, which tells the operator that the film cartridge is running out of film. This end-of-run indicator is connected to the film gauge and resets automatically when the gauge resets.

Film-Footage Counter

The film gauge, or film-footage counter, is a dial or scale on the left side of the camera that indicates how much film has been *shot* (exposed) on the cartridge or how much film is *left* on the cartridge. The film gauge automatically resets to FULL (or START, or 1) when the cartridge is removed. The gauge measures the amount of film exposed by monitoring the takeup mechanism in the film chamber.

Battery Indicator

The battery check indicator, a small resistance meter, is located on the bottom or side of most Super 8 cameras. Its purpose is to tell the condition of the batteries that power the camera. Most meters use warning lights, but in reverse of the usual function. If the light goes on and stays on when you press the button, the batteries are all right for use. Weak batteries are denoted by a light that flashes when you press the metering button but it does not stay on. Dead batteries will not light up the metering light at all.

RECOMMENDATIONS

We began this chapter by saying that the camera is the basic tool of the film maker. Now that you understand how that tool works, you must choose the right tool for the job you intend to do. It would be foolish of us to recommend that you purchase an expensive (and complicated) Super 8 camera just to take pictures of your family. On the other hand, we would be remiss if we didn't tell you about the essential features that you can get and should expect even on relatively low-priced cameras.

Every Super 8 camera incorporates, in some manner or other, the systems that have just been described. It is how these systems are designed and the limitation of the component parts that they use that is of importance to us. For example, in the lens system, we suggest you get a camera that incorporates a macro-focus lens. This lens will enable you to do much more accurate close-up work, better titling, and better photography of very small objects. Macro lenses give you the flexibility of close-up lenses without the expense and bother of the attachment and storage of such lenses.

We think that the minimum zoom ratio that you should have in your camera lens is 4 to 1 (a focal length range of 8–32 mm, for example). Anything shorter than that ratio is like having no zoom lens at all. We further suggest that you avoid extremely long zoom lenses (those over 60-mm focal length), unless you are planning to do a lot of telephoto shots and feel you would need the range. Once the focal length of a Super 8 camera goes much beyond 40 mm, it is very difficult to hold by hand and still get a steady picture. In general, you are better off getting a camera that has a good wide-angle focal length (6.5 mm or 7 mm) rather than one that has an extremely long telephoto focal length.

We prefer zoom controls that can be operated manually by a lever attached to the zoom ring. We also like the feature, found on some cameras, of being able to run the power zoom without running the camera. We also recommend the split-image focusing system. We have found this type of focusing to be the most accurate, with all kinds of subjects, under all kinds of lighting conditions. In addition, the viewfinder of any zoom-lens reflex camera should be bright enough to see the subject under any lighting conditions in which the camera is capable of taking a picture. Viewfinders with eyecups are easier to use, especially if you wear glasses.

In the exposure system, the faster lenses of the new XL cameras, with their f/1.2 (or even f/1.1) aperture openings, have a distinct advantage over conventional-lens cameras with their f/1.7 openings. At the same time, most XL cameras incorporate a 220-degree shutter opening. This longer shutter opening also allows better exposures at low light. The XL cameras are a much more versatile group of cameras and we highly recommend them.

Regardless of which lens or focusing system you buy, be sure to get a camera with through-the-lens exposure metering. When the meter sees the same picture as the film does, it reads the amount of light needed for proper exposure more accurately. Some popular XL cameras do not have TTL metering since this kind of metering does take away some of the light that could be used for exposing the film. These cameras sacrifice accuracy of exposure in order to get a visible picture under very low lighting conditions. However, we think it is more important to have accurate control of exposure. For this same reason, we feel it is desirable to have some form of manual control or override of the automatic metering system. This will allow you to more accurately control the exposure of your film in those special lighting situations. Many cameras now incorporate manual-exposure control since it can also be used to produce special effects like fades and dissolves, right in the camera.

Also, be sure to get a camera that will take film with a 160 ASA speed. Even better would be a camera that is designed to use films that have ASA ratings up to 500, since such films are already on the market. Minimum specifications should be an ASA film speed of 25 to 160.

Since all Super 8 cameras come with a built-in type-A filter, we have only one recommendation here. Get a camera with a filter switch. This will give you easier control and more flexibility in a variety of lighting situations.

Almost all film transport systems are alike in Super 8 cameras. What is of concern is the access to the film gate, the filming speeds, and the remote run capability. The film gate should be easy to inspect and clean. For this reason, we prefer a camera with a side opening film chamber. End-opening doors may allow a more rigid camera body but they are a real disadvantage when it comes to camera maintenance.

Your camera should have at least two running speeds and a single-frame capability. We prefer running speeds of 18 and 24 fps since these are the standard speeds for Super 8 silent and Super 8 sound, respectively. However, a slow-motion speed (32, 36, or 54 fps) might be more suitable to your needs than the sound speed (24 fps). Or, a fast-motion speed (like 9 or 12 fps) could be just as desirable. Get the combination that you think you will have the most use for. And, by all means, get single-frame capability.

Most modern Super 8 cameras have electric shutter releases in their remote run controls instead of the old-fashioned cable release. We prefer the electric remote run control even though it requires that one purchase a more expensive switch rather than a simple cable release. The electric switch is more accurate, lasts longer, and has only one moving part. You should, of course, get a camera with remote run capability.

Any camera that you buy should include the five basic monitoring functions that we listed earlier. All cameras have film windows, but many cameras do not have f/stop scales or dials. Instead, they rely on over- or under-exposure warning lights. We feel that the meter reading should be available *in the viewfinder* and should read out in *f/stops*. This is especially important on cameras that have manual control of the aperture. If you cannot see what the f/stop reading is, you may accidentally leave it in the manual mode when you wanted automatic metering, or vice-versa. It is also important to know what your f/stop is so that you can accurately compute your depth of field.

Film-run indicators and end-of-film warning signals have been regular features on all but the cheapest cameras that we have seen or tested in the past few years. Both features are necessary in order to have good transport-system monitoring. We prefer a film gauge that measures the film in feet and meters. This allows the camera operator to keep more accurate track of how much has been shot on a given cartridge. Contemporary camera designs use film gauges that read from Full to Empty, Start to Finish, or 1 to 0. Until one becomes adept at interpreting these symbols and markings, it may be difficult to know exactly how much film is left on the cartridge. In addition to the film gauge, frame counters are absolutely necessary if you want to do any accurate animation or work extensively in single-frame filming.

We prefer the kind of battery meters that glow when the batteries are good, flash when the batteries are weak, and do not light up at all when the batteries are dead. The kinds of meters that show the relative strength of the battery are too easy to misinterpret.

Finally, when selecting a camera, remember that you are purchasing a tool for making films, not a collection of abstract specifications. Select a camera that "feels" good, one that is easy to operate, and one that is well put together. Assuming that you have already figured out the specifications you need, and chosen the camera model you want, here is a quick checklist for camera evaluation:

1. Are all the controls readily at hand?

   If it is necessary to change hands frequently while focusing, zooming, backlighting, or changing speeds, the camera will be juggled and the shot ruined. Select a camera that is easy to use or you will spend more time learning how it works than working with it.

2. Does the camera feel comfortable?

   Do not buy a camera that feels awkward. Make sure that the control knobs are easy to turn and are large enough, that the power zoom buttons work freely, and that the zoom and focus rings move easily. This last point is very important if you want to capture fast action. And, the hand grip should fit your hand comfortably.

3. Is the camera well balanced?

   If the handle is placed properly, the camera will be easy to hold for lengthy hand-held sessions as well as being correctly balanced when mounted on the tripod.

4. Is the camera well made?

   The film-chamber door should fit snugly, but open easily. All screws should be fastened solidly and the heads free from burrs. The zoom and focus rings should be easy to turn, yet there should be no excessive play in the lens barrel. If the hand grip folds or detaches, it should lock tightly when in position to allow a steady control of the camera.

5. Does everything work?

   Load the camera with batteries and try all the systems. If your dealer will allow you to, shoot a roll of film through the camera and get it processed before you buy the camera. If you cannot arrange this, then shoot a roll of film as soon as you buy the camera. Read the instruction book and put the camera through its paces. Get that roll of film processed as soon as possible to find out just how well everything is working.

6. Will the camera last?

      This is the hardest question to answer. Considering the complexity of modern Super 8 cameras, they have a remarkably good record of reliability. The students attending our Film Workshops have used some of our cameras for three years with no major repairs. These were lower-middle-priced reflex-zoom cameras with an average complement of features. All they have required was a little maintenance every semester. A good rule to remember regarding durability is that "the simpler the camera, the less there is to go wrong." For a corolary, "the more complex the camera, the more expensive it will have to be to assure reliability." For maximum reliability, we suggest you buy a proven design instead of the latest thing. That way, you'll probably avoid the "teething" problems that all new models go through. And, pick a good brand name.

The quality of film production depends much more on the vision of the film maker than on the complexity of the camera he or she uses. A person with good visual skills, a simple camera, and some skillful editing can produce an excellent film. Our final suggestion is get the *least* expensive Super 8 camera that will do the jobs you want it to do.

CARE AND CLEANING OF EQUIPMENT

Film production equipment will only perform up to its capability when it is clean and properly adjusted. Normal maintenance can and should be done by the film maker. However, your camera repair person is the one to handle the big repair jobs. There are three areas of the camera that need regular attention—the lens and viewfinder, the film chamber, and the batteries. These should be checked and attended to before each filming session.

Lens

A blower brush is essential to camera maintenance (Fig. 3-15). Blow all dust and grit from the lens before attempting to wipe it off. Any dust on the lens can scratch the lens when it is wiped off and that will cause permanent damage to the lens. After blowing the dust off, wipe the lens with a piece of lens cleaning tissue moistened with lens cleaner. Swab gently in a circular motion. Do not rub. Always put the

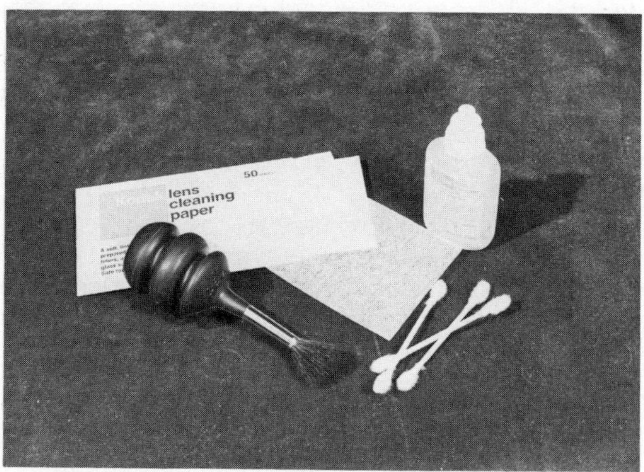

Fig. 3-15. Cleaning materials.

lens cleaner on the tissue, not on the lens itself. If you put it on the lens directly, it could get under the edges of the lens mounting and loosen the lens. Finally, take a dry lens tissue and wipe off the remainder of the fluid. If no lens tissue is available, you may use a soft cloth. But, *do not* use facial tissue or toilet paper as these contain abrasives that will scratch the lens. If no lens cleaning fluid is available, use a contact-lens cleaning solution.

Film Chamber

The film chamber can be cleaned with a cotton swab moistened with water or alcohol. Wipe away from the film gate so as not to leave any threads there. But, *do* wipe the gate itself to remove the accumulation of emulsion. On sound cameras, the recording head should be cleaned regularly with an audio head cleaner.

Batteries

Always take the batteries out when the camera is going to be stored. Swab the battery chamber with alcohol, and clean the tips of the contacts with an emery board or very fine sandpaper. Use only alkaline batteries in any camera or tape recorder as these have a longer life and are less likely to leak when they go bad.

Storage

If you have to store your camera for a long period of time (over a month), do the following:

1. After cleaning it thoroughly and removing all the batteries, put the camera in a plastic bag and seal the bag.

2. Store the camera in a dry place where the temperature will not exceed 90 °F for any length of time. (Try to avoid using the basement or the attic.)
3. When you take the camera out of storage, check all the systems for proper functioning before starting to use it again.

Adjustments

There are virtually no adjustments that you can make to repair your Super 8 camera. If something is not working right, take it to your camera dealer. His camera-repair personnel are much better prepared to diagnose and fix your camera's ailments than you are.

CHAPTER 4

Film, Lights, and Other Accessories

As we mentioned at the beginning of Chapter 3, anyone who plans on becoming a film maker should fully understand the film, lights, and other accessories that he will be working with. This chapter is designed to give you that understanding.

FILM

If the basic tool of the film maker is the camera, then it follows that the *film* is the basic material "worked" by this tool. In this section, we will discuss what film is supposed to do, how it accomplishes this through the composition of the film stock itself and through processing, and what kinds of film stocks are available to the Super 8 film maker. We will also give you some questions to ask yourself when choosing a film stock, and we will offer some tips on buying, storing, using, and processing film.

The purpose of film is to record the image that is gathered by the lens system and regulated by the exposure system. It does this by allowing the light that strikes the light-sensitive portion of the film to convert parts of this light-sensitive surface to a *latent image*. During processing, this latent image is developed, first to a visible negative image and, then, to a positive image—the one we see in projection. All Super 8 movie-film stocks are 8-mm wide strips of cellulose acetate or polyester (the base of the film), coated with a relatively thin layer of gelatin (the emulsion), and backed by a very thin coating of dyed material (the antihalation backing). This is illustrated by the drawing given in Fig. 4-1. The light that strikes the emulsion leaves a latent image that is transformed, during processing, into a visible picture.

The *base* is the thickest and strongest portion of the film. It is the means by which the emulsion is transported during exposure, processing, editing, and projection. The base is punctured on one

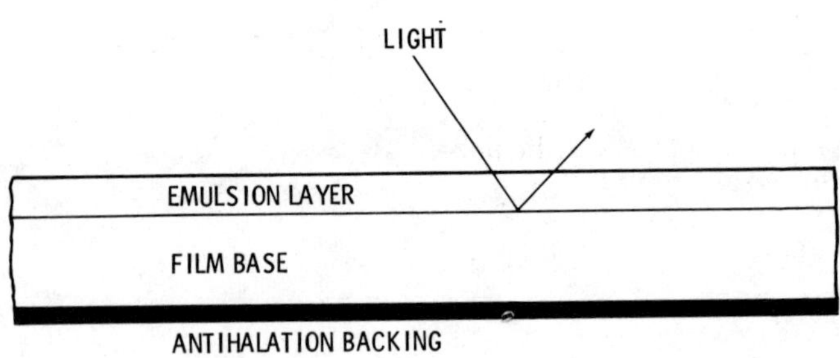

Fig. 4-1. Diagram of a piece of raw film stock.

edge with tiny holes called perforations. The purpose of these perforations is to keep the film in alignment during exposure, editing, and projection. The distance between these perforations is slightly larger than the height of one frame as exposed by the camera. (The remainder of the space is taken up by the frame line.) Most Super 8 cameras, however, do not take their pictures between the perforations but rather expose the frame with the perforation approximately in the center of that side of the frame.

The *emulsion layer* of a Super 8 film is a relatively thin coating of gelatin on top of the base. This gelatin contains light-sensitive silver-halide crystals in suspension and is the portion of the film in which the exposure takes place. The emulsion is that portion of the film that faces the lens at the film gate. Upon exposure to light, the silver-halide crystals in the emulsion change to metallic silver producing an invisible image called a *latent image*. When the film is processed, the unexposed silver-halide crystals are removed, the metallic silver is fixed, and the image is permanently recorded as a negative.

All Super 8 camera stocks are *reversal* films, which means that they are positive transparencies (like slides) created directly from the originally exposed film. This, in turn, means that they must go through *two* development stages. In the first stage, the film is developed as a negative, in the manner we just described. Then, the silver of that negative image is bleached out, the film is re-exposed to a controlled light (or it is *fogged* by a chemical solution), and it is developed again to fix the remaining metallic silver as the positive image.

The process just described applies to black and white film stocks. In the emulsion of color film stock, however, there are layers of color dyes which must undergo a separate development process. Color reversal films use the subtractive color system. Instead of using a mix of the primary colors, (red, blue, and green) to create the desired hue on the screen, the film employs the secondary colors (yellow, magenta, and cyan) in combinations to create the proper hue. In the emulsion of color reversal film, there are three layers of color dyes through which the light must pass. Each layer absorbs a certain color in the primary scale (from the light that is reflected off the object being filmed). During the second stage of processing, these dye layers are converted to positive dye images. This color-development step is done after the original negative development of the film and it removes all traces of the original negative.

The *antihalation* backing is a thin coating of dyed material on the back of the film base. Its purpose is to prevent light from passing through the base during exposure and being reflected back into the emulsion. Such reflections would cause glare around bright objects or cause double images of those objects to appear on the film. This backing is usually removed before the film is developed, often as the first step in processing.

The sensitivity of the film emulsion to light is called the *exposure index* of the film. The exposure index rating is expressed in ASA numbers. The lower the ASA number, the less sensitive the film is to light, or the slower the speed of the film. The higher the ASA number, the more sensitive the film is to light, and the film is considered to have a faster speed. What this means is that in a given lighting situation, a slower speed film will require a longer shutter opening or a larger f/stop (lower number) to get a good exposure than would be required by a faster film. However, the slower film will allow a greater margin of error in its exposure because it has a greater *latitude* than the fast film. Latitude, when referring to film stock, means a tolerance for over or under exposure. Slower films are generally more tolerant of (or less sensitive to) incorrect exposure. Consequently, they are considered to have more latitude.

The Cartridge

Up to this point, what has been written about Super 8 film stock, except for the information on the perforations and frame size, could just as easily have been applied to almost any gauge of color reversal film. What distinguishes Super 8 film from other film stocks is the way that it is packaged. All Super 8 film, for use in ordinary cameras, comes in plastic cartridges which contain a feed reel, a takeup reel, camera-coding information, and the pressure pad. As you look at the cartridge from the front, the feed core is on the left with the film coming down past the pressure pad. The takeup core, driven by the takeup mechanism on the left-hand side of the cartridge, is enclosed within the right-hand side of the cartridge.

There are four coding notches on the front edge of the cartridge (opposite the film side). The top notch tells the camera what the exposure index of the film stock is. The second notch positions the cartridge in correct alignment with the film gate. The third notch tells the processing machine what type of film is in the cartridge, and the bottom notch takes the Type-A filter in or out depending on the type of film in the cartridge. These notches are illustrated in the drawing of Fig. 4-2. Since only a small portion of the film is visible through the front opening of the cartridge, it can be loaded and unloaded in daylight without fear of exposing the entire roll. When the roll is run out, the word EXPOSED appears at the end of the film and is visible through this opening. When the film is processed, it is removed through this opening and put into the processing machine.

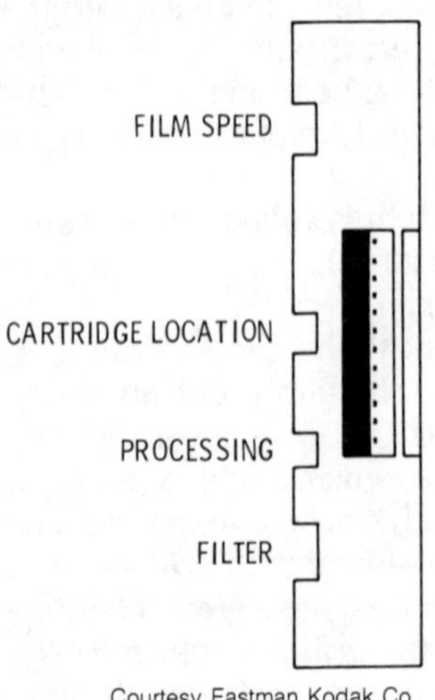

Fig. 4-2. Coding notches on the front edge of the Super 8 film cartridge.

Courtesy Eastman Kodak Co.

Kinds of Film Stocks

Although they all come in the same type of cartridge, there are a great variety of film stocks available in Super 8 format. Film stocks are generally classified by color, type, and exposure index (or speed). When we refer to Ektachrome 160, for example, we are talking about a color reversal film stock with a Type-A color balance and an exposure index of ASA 160, under the proper lighting conditions. Type-A film means color film in which the emulsion has been color balanced for incandescent light. In order to use this film in sunlight and still get correct color renderings, a color-correcting filter must be employed. The use of this filter drops the exposure index to ASA 100, since it keeps some of the light coming through the lens from reaching the film. The film stock listed in Chart 4-1 shows both the daylight and tungsten exposure indices for color-film stocks.

With the array of film stocks available in Super 8 format, it may be difficult for you to choose the one you need. We usually ask ourselves the following questions before picking a film stock.

Chart 4-1. Super 8 Movie Film Stocks

Black and White Film			
Film Name	**ASA Film Speed**		**Notes**
	Daylight	**Tungsten**	
Superior Bulk Film			
EK 4-X Pan	400	320	
EK Plus-X Pan	40	50	
EK Tri-X Pan	200	160	
Color Film			
Eastman Kodak Company			
Ektachrome 160	100	160	50-foot sound and silent.
Ektachrome 7242	80	125	200-foot sound.
Kodachrome 40	25	40	50-foot sound and silent, 200-foot sound.
Type G Ektachrome 160	160	160	
3M Company			
3M Super 8	25	40	
3M Super 8	100	160	

1. Do we want color or black and white?

    Color films can be more "realistic" looking than those made in black and white. However, black and white films have a more somber look that is better suited to some subjects. Productions that are trying for an "old-time" flavor can use black and white film to great advantage. Color film is cheaper to buy and process; it is also more readily available than black and white film.

2. What kind of lighting will we be using? Are we shooting indoors or outdoors?

    If we are shooting outdoors in sunlight, a slower speed film, like EKT 40 or K 40, would be fine. However, if most of the shooting would be indoors, EKT 160, a faster film, would give us a greater f/stop range and would be a better choice. If the indoor lighting is the fluorescent type, then EKT G will be our best choice. The same rules apply for the speed of the film stock when you are shooting in black and white. Use a slower speed film outdoors and a faster speed film indoors.

3. Are we going to make prints of this film or will we only project the original?

    If you are going to make prints of your original film, your original film should have a relatively low contrast and it should not have saturated colors. Printing will always increase the contrast and color saturation as well as exaggerating the grain. That means, as far as color films are concerned, EKT 40 or EF 7242 are better film stocks from which to make prints. However, if you only intend to project your original, then K40 or EKT 160 are perfectly acceptable. In black and white films, Plus-X is a good choice for originals that are to be printed. Tri-X and 4-X are both very acceptable camera originals to use for projection.

4. What film stock is the cheapest, most readily available, and the cheapest to process?

All color film stocks are cheaper and most are more readily available than black and white film stocks. Color processing is also cheaper, as a rule, than black and white processing. The most popular film stocks (Kodachrome 40, EKT 160 and EKT G) are always sold at the lowest market prices, are the most readily available, and (usually) are the cheapest to process. Although many manufacturers still make black and white film stocks in Super 8, very few of them process black and white film. The lack of popularity of the black and white film stocks, both for amateur use and in Super 8 format, has caused their prices to remain high both for film stock and for processing.

Tips On Film

The following lists give a few tips on buying, storing, using, and processing your Super 8 film.

1. Buying.
   (A) Always buy fresh film. Check the expiration date on the box before you pay for it. If the date is already past, do not buy it. If the expiration date is close, be sure you are going to use it before the date is past.
   (B) Buy from a volume dealer. Avoid the supermarket and quick-shop stores that sell only one roll of Super 8 film per month. Their film is not fresh.
   (C) Try to find out where your supplier stores his film. If he puts it on a high shelf in an overheated closet, buy from someone else. Film should be stored in a cool place, preferably in a refrigerator or cooler.
   (D) Buy name brands. We cannot say that we have never had problems with name-brand products, but we have never had any trouble getting our problems taken care of promptly and with great courtesy. Off-brand products may give you off-brand performance.
2. Storing.
   (A) Store all film in a cool place. We usually keep our film in

the refrigerator if we are not going to use it right away. If we buy a case of film for use in the indefinite future, we will put it in the freezer. Then, we take it out a day before we need to use it and let it thaw out completely.

(B) Leave the film in its protective foil wrapper until you have to put it in the camera. This will keep dust, dirt, and moisture from getting on the film, especially on the emulsion.

3. Using.

(A) Unless you have good storage facilities, use the film you buy as soon as possible.

(B) Read the instructions that come with each film cartridge and follow them carefully. They may save you a great deal of time and trouble in shooting and processing your movie film.

(C) Since the film cartridge actually has the film wound round itself on the feed core, occasionally the film will stick to itself. This will cause the film to jerk or chatter when it is being transported. Before loading the camera, rap the cartridge sharply once or twice against your palm. This will loosen any film that might be stuck together and might cause trouble during filming.

(D) Do not turn the film in the cartridge by hand. You might damage something. Do not touch the film.

(E) When you have finished shooting a cartridge, run the film all the way to the end (the *exposed* mark). This makes it easier for the processor to get your film out of the cartridge and into the processor.

4. Processing.

(A) Process your exposed film promptly. Do not let it sit around in your camera, on your dresser, or in your car. This can ruin your exposed film.

(B) If you are using processing mailers, take the film to the post office, and drop it off *inside* the post office. Do not let your carefully photographed film sit for hours in some hot letter box waiting to be picked up.

(C) Use a reliable processor. The company who manufactured your film is often your best bet. Cheaper processors are cheaper because they spend less money on the processing of your film. Often they will work their processing chemicals too long, which means that your film will not be as bright or as sharp as it could be. In addition, some of the cheaper processors skip the final lacquering solution which aids projection. Buy the best processing you can afford. Your film deserves it.

THE TRIPOD

The tripod is the most basic camera mount. Tripods come in a variety of sizes and types for different kinds of cameras and uses (Fig. 4-3). But every tripod contains the same parts. The tripod rests on three legs, hence its name. These legs are usually adjustable, in two or three sections, to vary the height of the tripod. At the bottom of the tripod legs are the feet, usually made of rubber, and sometimes containing small metal points called ground spikes. These ground spikes are used to anchor the legs in soft or rough ground. The legs are fastened together near the top of the tripod by the yoke. In addition to holding the legs together, this yoke acts as the guide for the center post which slides up and down through the center of the yoke. The tripod head is located on top of the center post and fastened to it by a

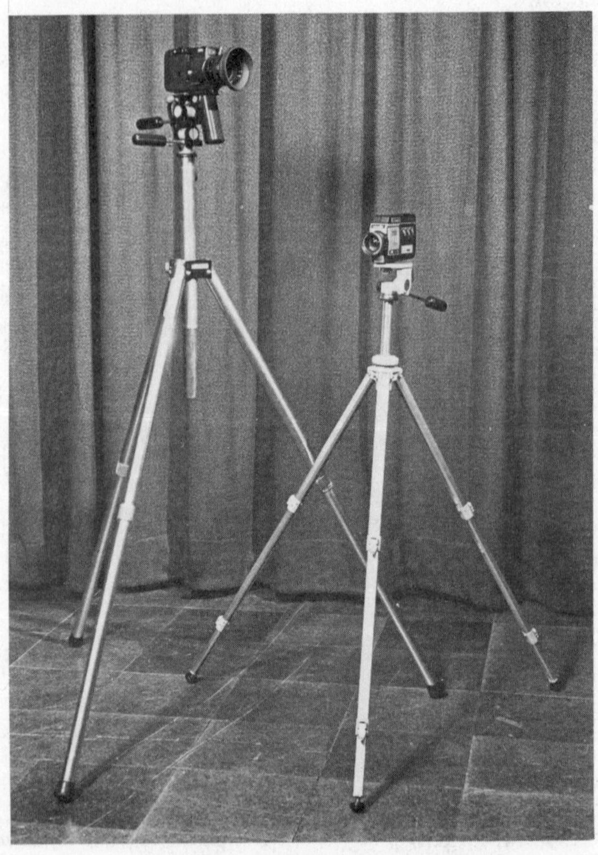

Fig. 4-3. Heavy-duty and light-weight tripods.

ball joint or swivel arrangement. The tripod head (Fig. 4-4) is usually equipped with two controls, one for panning and tilting the head and the other for leveling the head from side to side. In the center of the head is a small screw called the camera screw. It is used to fasten the camera to the tripod head. The tripod performs three functions for the film maker. It acts as a platform of varying heights for the camera, it is a stable base from which to shoot, and it is a fixed point upon which to pivot the camera in pans and tilts.

What we need then is a lightweight sturdy tripod, with adjustable legs, an extendable center post, and a combination pan/tilt head that moves freely. We need a lightweight tripod because much of the work in film making consists of moving, setting up, and taking down equipment. If we were only working in a studio, we could get by with heavy tripods but film making on location demands portability. However, the tripod should not be so light that the slightest movement will cause it to shake. The tripod should also be sturdy enough to support the weight of the camera without flexing or bending and it should be stable enough to stand still while the camera is being panned or tilted.

Adjustable legs on the tripod are important for two reasons; they

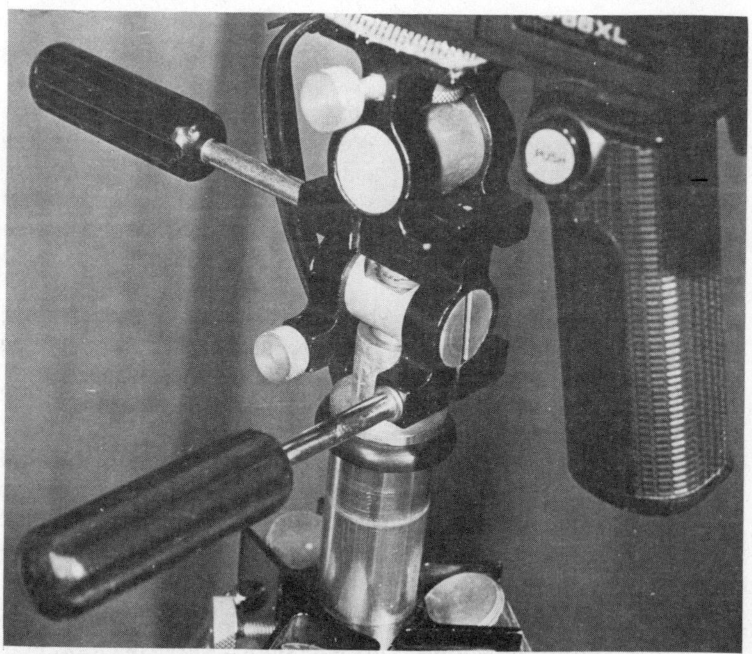

Fig. 4-4. A smooth-action friction-type pan/tilt tripod head.

allow a variety of camera heights with the same tripod, and they make storage and portability easier. Tripod legs can be either the tubular or channel kind with either collet locks or snap locks. They should be in at least two sections (three is better) for flexibility in setting the correct height.

An extendable center post, with or without a crank, is another important feature. It allows further adjustments of camera height without changing the length of the legs (and perhaps altering the steady base you have already established). If the tripod is equipped with a center-post crank, it is easier to do those "elevator" shots that are so popular on tv variety shows.

A combination pan/tilt head is a must. Some of the most graceful shots in film making are made with these simple movements. The preferred system is to have separate controls for the pan and tilt functions. In this way, the camera operator will be able to pan without tilting, and vice-versa. There should also be some means of controlling the rate of pan or tilt in the tripod head. The better tripods have small friction locks that can be adjusted to allow either quick movements of the head, or slower smoother movements. These are very valuable for making smooth pans and tilts.

The following is a quick checklist to use when choosing a tripod:

1. Pick a tripod that is sturdy and of lightweight construction. Make sure it will support your camera through all its movements.
2. Choose sturdy legs with positive locking devices. The legs should extend and retract easily, but should lock in place solidly at any extension.
3. Pick an adjustable center post with at least 15 inches of vertical travel. A geared center post is handy but not absolutely necessary. The center-post lock should be positive, yet easy to release.
4. Get a pan, tilt, and leveling mechanism on the tripod head. All controls should be easy and convenient to operate. Separate control handles for the pan and tilt operations are desirable.
5. Choose adjustable feet with ground spikes for that last bit of leveling and security.
6. A tripod should have a minimum height of 65 inches, at full extension. This will allow the camera height to be adjusted comfortably for most people. Persons who are over 6 feet tall will want a 72-inch total height.

Other Support Equipment

There are other camera supports which function like a tripod but are designed for more specialized applications. The *monopod* and the *C-clamp mount*, like the tripod, can have pan-tilt heads but their bases are different. The monopod (see Fig. 4-5) is very handy in situations where setting up a tripod would take too long or take up too much room. The monopod is very easy to carry around but it must be stabilized when set up. The C-clamp mount (and related specialty camera mounts like the suction-cup mount) is useful when you need a stable camera platform but have no room for a larger, more conventional mount (Fig. 4-6). These mounts also work well when shooting film from an automobile. The *chest pod* and the *shoulder-mounted gunstock mount* are two camera supports that are used to get steadier handheld shots. These camera mounts, which attach to the camera with the usual camera screw, can be worn or carried quite easily. They provide a much more stable camera platform than the regular holding of a camera by hand would do.

In addition to camera supports, there are also three common tripod supports that you should be familiar with. They are the *triangle*, the *spider*, and the *dolly*. The triangle is, as the name implies, a triangle of wood or metal that is set underneath a tripod to steady or level it. The triangle can be fastened to the floor with wood screws or nails, or it can be fastened to the ground with ground spikes. Its main function is to provide a level base for setting up the tripod.

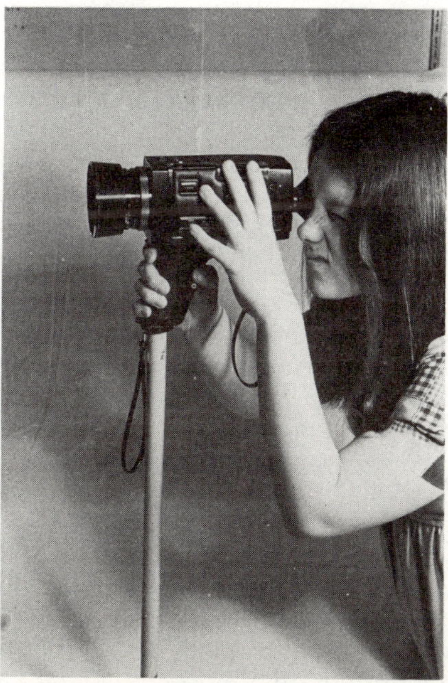

Fig. 4-5. A monopod camera mount.

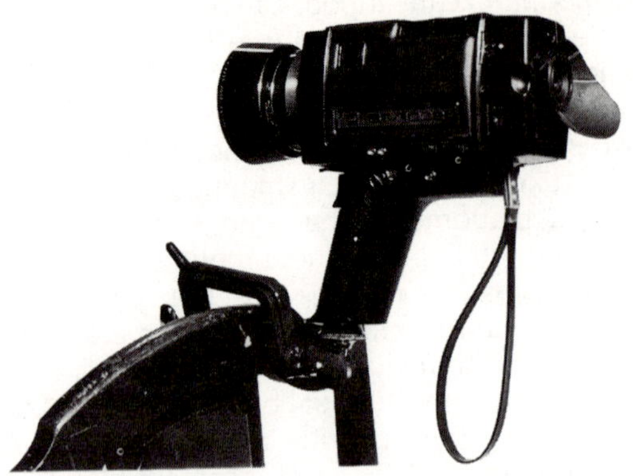

Fig. 4-6. A C-clamp camera mount.

The spider (Fig. 4-7) is another form of this idea. It consists of three metal tubes all joined at one end by a center support. At the opposite ends of the tubes are sockets for the tripod legs. These tubes are adjustable in their length so that a fixed-leg tripod may set at any height and still retain its stability. Spiders can also be fastened to the floor or ground.

The dolly is the most familiar tripod support. Many professional film makers use the dolly almost as the sole camera support since their dollies are heavy enough to provide a stable base for any camera shot. But, in Super 8 film making, the dolly is usually a lightweight triangular-shaped piece of wood or metal with small casters on it.

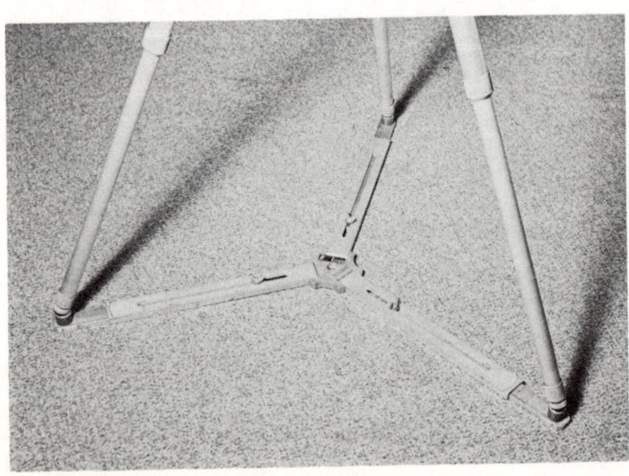

Fig. 4-7. A "spider" is used to anchor tripods on smooth surfaces.

The camera is fastened to a tripod mounted on top of the dolly in special tripod sockets or in small holes near the wheels. The tripod is anchored to the dolly by locking pins or spring clamps (see Fig. 4-8). Actually, any moveable object, with a provision to mount a tripod, can be used as a dolly. We have successfully used automobiles, skateboards, shopping carts, coaster wagons, and automotive creepers. Since the main object of using a dolly is to make the camera move more flexibly, anything that will accomplish this purpose can be used. The important thing is that the tripod and camera be mounted securely on your dolly.

Care and Maintenance of Equipment

There is little maintenance needed on most tripods. This is true, also, of light stands. As long as they are kept clean and straight, all they will normally need is a little lubrication once in a while. We usually use a silicone spray to lubricate the joints and working surfaces of these stands. It penetrates and lubricates without leaving a greasy mess.

LIGHTING EQUIPMENT

If you are like us, a lot of your film making takes place outdoors during the day, or indoors in well-lighted rooms. This kind of photography is called *available light* photography because it uses the

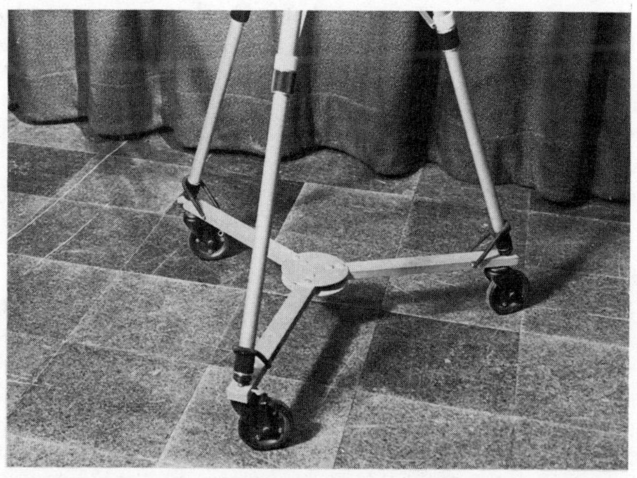

Fig. 4-8. A "dolly" is used for ease of movement in dolly and trucking shots.

light available (the sun, the room lights, etc.) as the main source of light. With the advent of XL cameras and fast film, available light film making is becoming the most popular kind of film making.

But, there are times when the available light is not bright enough to get an adequate exposure, or the light is not positioned correctly for you to shoot the picture you want. When this happens, you must add light, usually with specially designed lighting equipment. The specific techniques of lighting a scene will be discussed in Section III of this book. Here, we will only discuss the basic principles of lighting, how lighting equipment works, and show how different kinds of lighting instruments can be applied to work in different lighting situations. We will also make recommendations on lighting instruments and lighting kits.

Objectives of Lighting

The objectives of lighting are to improve exposure, to highlight the subject, to counter another lighting source, to reduce shadows, and to compensate for lighting "flaws" in the scene. Two kinds of light are used to accomplish these effects—*hard light* and *soft light*. Hard light is a narrow, sharp-edged beam of light usually used to accent the subject or to overpower another lighting source. Soft light is a broader, more diffused beam of light that is usually used to fill shadows, to even out light levels, and to increase the overall illumination for better exposure.

In the following explanation of lighting instruments, we will refer to two general types of instruments, the spotlight and the floodlight. Each type produces a specific kind of light. The spotlight produces a hard light and the floodlight, a relatively soft light. The limitations of any lighting instruments, however, are decided more by how they are used than by what they are called.

The Basic Elements

The elements that are basic to all lighting instruments are the reflector, the lamp, the socket, the support, the power cord, and the switch. (Some lights add a lens, in front of the lamp, to focus or diffuse the light.)

Reflector—The reflector is usually a piece of stamped sheet metal of a rounded or conical shape surrounding the lamp. It is usually finished with a uniformly dull or pebble-grained reflective surface. This reflector gathers the light rays coming off the back and sides of the lamp and reflects them outward. The amount and intensity of this reflected light depends upon a number of factors, including the placement of the lamp within the reflector and the wattage of the lamp being used. But, the shape of the reflector has much to do with the "brightness" of the light coming from it. In general, the spotlight is the most efficient producer of light, due, in part, to its use of a reflector that closely follows the shape of the lamp.

In the simple floodlight (Fig. 4-9), the reflector is the housing of the lighting instrument as well as the reflector. However, the more complex instruments have a separate metal or plastic housing. This housing usually includes a place for the lamp socket, an anchor place for the instrument support, and cooling fins or vents to dissipate the heat of the lamp. The use of this housing allows the reflector to be of a simpler and lighter design since the reflector does not have to function as the housing also. This design also allows the reflector to be made in the most efficient shape for good illumination.

Lamp Socket—The lamp socket is set in the center-back position or at the base of the lamp housing. It protrudes through and is sometimes a part of the reflector. The socket is positioned to give the maximum amount of light from this lighting instrument when used with the correct lamp. Lamp sockets range in size and type from the tiny socket for a small quartz lamp to the screw-base type used by the giant Mogul lamp, which resembles an enlarged household light bulb. Lamp sockets are usually made of a porcelain material and fitted with plated metal strips to provide the electrical contacts.

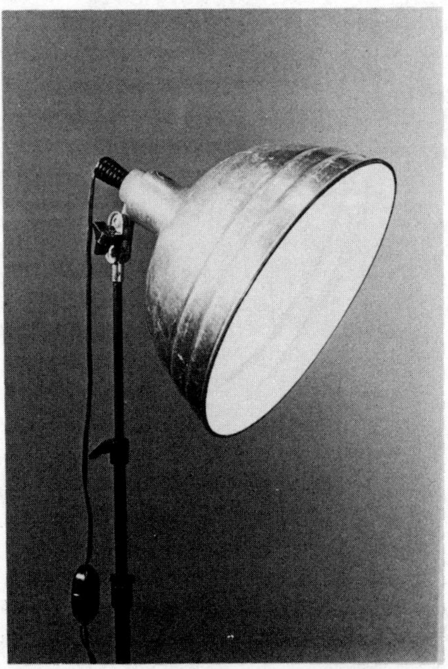

Fig. 4-9. A simple floodlight.

Lamps—There are two basic types of lamps used in motion picture lighting instruments—the conventional incandescent lamp and the tungsten-halogen (quartz) lamp. The conventional incandescent lamp (Fig. 4-10) has a glass envelope, a conventional base, is usually filled with a mixture of inert gases, and often looks like a household light bulb. (The Number 2 Photoflood is a good example of this type of lamp.) It operates like other incandescent lamps; when the current flows, the tungsten filament is heated until it glows or incandesces. As this filament glows, it deposits atoms of tungsten on the inside of the envelope causing the glass to blacken. Eventually, the filament is weakened by this process and the lamp "burns out."

The tungsten-halogen lamp is also an incandescent lamp and emits light in the same way as the conventional lamp. But the construction of the tungsten-halogen lamp is radically different. The envelope is made of quartz (hence its popular name, quartz light), and it is filled with an iodine or bromine gas. This gas helps to prevent the tungsten deposit problem found in conventional lamps. Consequently, the quartz lamp will remain "clean" longer and perform up to specifications (color temperature) for a greater length of time relative to its rated life than will an incandescent lamp of similar wattage and

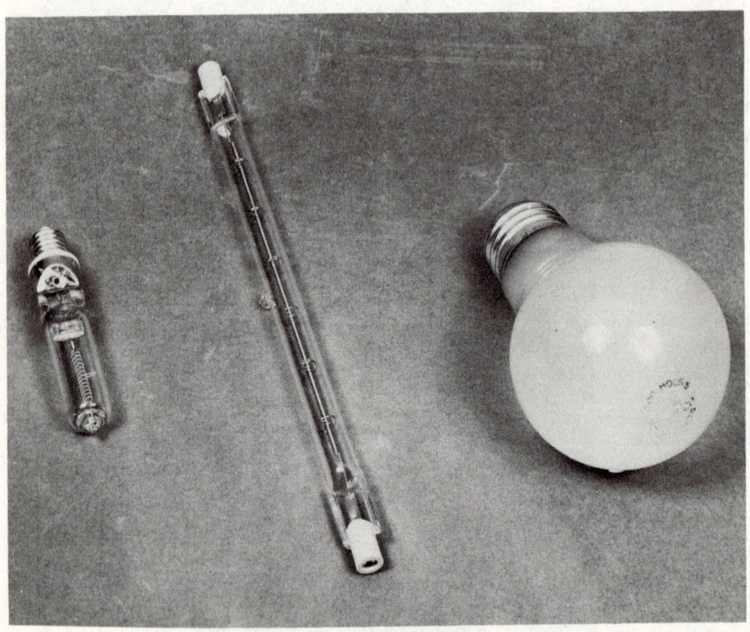

**Fig. 4-10. Tungsten-halogen and incandescent lamps
used for movie lighting.**

color temperature. The quartz lamp does burn hotter than the conventional lamp, however, and is more fragile in ordinary handling. Typical quartz lamps are the type with a miniature base and the double-ended lamp with its long envelope shown in Fig. 4-10.

Color Temperature

Color temperature is a system of measurement which describes the temperature, in Kelvins[1], to which a "black body" must be raised to emit that visible color of light. While this might sound confusing, it merely means that every visible light source possesses a certain color temperature (Chart 4-2). Color photographic emulsions are designed to be exposed correctly (for proper color rendition, that is) under a light of a certain color temperature.

Light sources that have *lower* color temperatures are referred to as being "warmer" than those that have *higher* color temperatures. Household incandescent lamps are warmer than photofloods, which, in turn, are warmer than sunlight. The term, warmer, refers here to how the color of the light from a warm source *looks*, not to its color temperature. Also, the color temperature of a lamp has nothing to do with its *operating* temperature; that is related to the kind of lamp it is, and how much power (in watts) it puts out.

There are lamps available with different color temperatures in order to complement the different emulsions of film stock. It is also possible to change the color temperature (and the visible color, of course) by using filters or gels in front of the lamps. The use of filters is

Chart 4-2. Color Temperatures of Typical Light Sources

Source	Color Temperature
Sun	5500 K +
Daylight fluorescent light	6500 K
Cool-white fluorescent light	4300 K
White fluorescent light	3500 K
Warm-white fluorescent light	3050 K
Type-B photoflood (incandescent)	3400 K
Movie lights and Lighting kits (incandescent and tungsten-halogen)	3400 K
Tv studio lighting	3200 K
Household incandescent light	2900 K
Mercury-vapor light	5900 K
Sodium-arc light	2100 K
Candle flame	1900 K

---

[1]The Kelvin scale is a temperature scale that uses the same divisions as the Celsius scale but where the zero point is established at -273 °C (absolute zero).

a common theatrical practice and it is one that is often employed by professional film makers. They use blue filters to "correct" incandescent light to the color temperature of sunlight so that the same lighting instruments can be used outdoors as well as indoors. Super 8 movie film is a Type-A film and it should be exposed under lights that have a temperature of 3400 Kelvin. So, we say that the color temperature of Type-A film is 3400. Since sunlight has a somewhat higher color temperature, upwards of 5400 Kelvin, a color-correction filter must be employed to get the right color when using Type-A film.

Chart 4-3 lists some of the popular incandescent lamps that are used in film and television production. The first group listed will fit into household light fixtures if the correct socket base is used. They are conventional-looking "light bulbs." The second group (the last ten listed) are reflector-type lamps. They are like self-contained spotlights. This group of lamps can be used for area fill-in and for directional lighting.

Chart 4-3. Some Popular Lamps for Movie Lighting

ANSI Code Number	Wattage	Type of Base	Color Temperature
BBA	250	Medium screw	3400 K
BCA	250	Medium screw	4800 K (Daylight)
BAH	300	Medium screw	3200 K
EBV	500	Medium screw	3400 K
EBW	500	Medium screw	4800 K
ECT	500	Medium screw	3200 K
DXR	1000	Mogul screw	3400 K
DXT	1000	Mogul screw	4800 K
DAN (R-20)	200	Medium screw	3400 K
BEP (R-30)	300	Medium screw	3400 K
EBR (R-30)	375	Medium screw	3400 K
DXH (R-32)	375	Medium screw	3200 K
EAL	500	Medium screw	3200 K
FAE (R-40)	550	Medium screw	3400 K

Various Types of Lighting Instruments

There are two basic types of lighting instruments used in film production—the spotlight and the floodlight. All other lighting instruments are merely variations of one of these basic types.

Movie Lights—The movie light, a very common sight in home-movie making until the XL camera came along, is one of the simplest and cheapest of the spotlights. It has a simple plastic or metal housing with an integral reflector of polished metal. Most movie lights have sockets that will accept high-intensity (600–650 watt) tungsten-halogen lamps. Movie lights usually are designed to be mounted on top of the camera, often in the opening where the filter "key" goes. This assures that they will be in position to give the most light and that they will automatically cancel out the filter when they are installed.

Spotlights—The regular spotlight is a more complex and expensive lighting instrument. It has a metal (or plastic) housing fitted with cooling slots or vents in order to aid in cooling the lamp socket. It has a separate reflector. The lamp socket is mounted on a slide so that it can be moved closer to or farther from the reflector. This is what allows the spotlight to be "focused." Moving the lamp closer to the reflector causes the beam of light to become brighter and sharper-edged. Moving the lamp away from the reflector makes the beam dimmer and more diffused. Some spotlights have lenses in front of the lamp to further enhance this focusing effect. Most modern spotlights use tungsten-halogen lamps since their smaller envelope and intenser light allow the lighting instruments to be smaller, lighter, and more efficient.

Floodlights—Floodlights are commonly divided into two subcategories—scoops and broads. *Scoops* are the simplest form of floodlight. They have stamped steel shells that double as reflectors and housings (see Fig. 4-9). These shells have a silvery coating on the inside and are painted or plated on the outside. In shape, they often resemble ice cream scoops. Their lamp sockets are at the base of the scoop and protrude through it. This places the lamp in the center of the reflector for good diffused illumination. Mounting brackets for the scoops are often fastened to the outside portion of the light socket. The cheaper scoops have their switches in the sockets, outside the housing. The more expensive scoops have line switches like regular professional lights. A variety of conventional incandescent and quartz lamps are available for these instruments.

The *broad* is a more complex floodlight (Fig. 4-11). In design and construction it resembles the spotlight but its lamp socket does not move and its reflector is usually wider than that of the spot. Since broads are not designed to focus light like the spots, they are often equipped with barndoors to control light spill. Most broads are designed to be used with tungsten-halogen lamps.

Light Supports

The most common means of supporting lighting instruments, on location, is the *light stand*. In the studio, lighting instruments are often hung from pipes, called *battens*. In either case, the light is usually fitted with a metal bracket, called a *yoke*, which is attached to both sides of the light housing (Fig. 3-26). The base of the yoke is a hollow shaft that can slip over the end of a light stand or can be

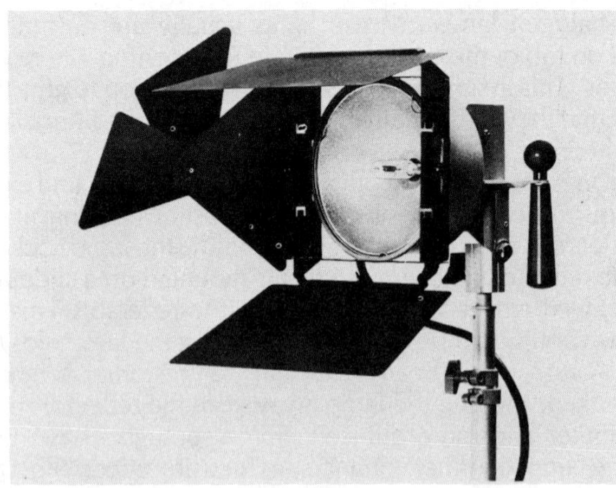

Courtesy Lowel-Light

Fig. 4-11. "Barndoors" help control light spill.

clamped, with an adapter, to a batten. When a light is mounted in a yoke, it can only be moved by turning the light in the yoke or by swiveling the yoke on the light stand. The yoke mount, however, provides a great deal of stability.

On some scoop-type floodlights, a ball joint and clamp arrangement is substituted for the yoke. The ball joint is fastened to the scoop and the clamp joined to it. This allows the light to be moved and set at many different angles relative to the mounting clamp. The clamp, itself, is a relatively versatile mounting bracket as it can be attached to almost any kind of edge as well as be mounted on a light stand. Clamp brackets of this type are cheaper but are somewhat less stable than the yoke and stand arrangement.

Light stands come in a variety of heights and styles but most have the following features: tripod legs with braces, adjustable extension sections with locking screws, and a 3/8-inch or 5/8-inch top section. The tripod legs give these stands some measure of stability when extended to full height. The braces allow the legs to be used in other than fully extended positions and still be stable. The adjustable sections allow a light stand to be raised to greater heights (from 2 feet 6 inches to 8 feet, for example), and still be folded up and stored in a fairly compact package. In light stands, we suggest you look for the following specifications:

1. A 7-foot minimum height.
2. At least a 4-section adjustment for height.
3. Positive locking screws that are easy to use.
4. Lightweight and of sturdy construction.
5. Maximum collapsibility for easy storage.

Lighting Accessories

Some common accessories for lighting instruments are barndoors, scrims, and filters. *Barndoors* are shutters made of thin sheet metal, that are attached by hinges to the front of the light housing (see Figs. 4-11 and 4-12). Their purpose is to control the spill of the beam of light from the instrument. They do this by cutting off the beam from either the sides or the top (or both).

The purpose of *scrims* is to diffuse the beam of light. Scrims are made of a wire screen set in a frame. They are usually mounted in front of the housing by means of special brackets or they can be attached to the barndoors.

Filters, which are used to change the color temperature of the light or to diffuse the beam of light, are usually attached in the same manner as are the scrims. Filters may be made of glass, plastic, acetate, or gelatin. The latter two types are more commonly used as filters for theatre lighting.

Lighting Kits

In the past few years, many lighting equipment manufacturers have come out with lighting kits that give you a combination of instruments, stands, and accessories. These kits, which usually come in a suitcase-like box, are very versatile for all kinds of location and studio work. There are two distinct types of kits, however. One uses very simple, but quite versatile, lighting instruments and a large assortment of accessories to adapt it to varying situations. The other uses more conventional lights (like spots and floods) along with barndoors and scrims to meet the same lighting conditions.

A good example of the "unconventional" approach to lighting kits is the first kit (Fig. 4-13). The basic light is a compact floodlight with built-in barndoors top and bottom. It has a very flexible beam pattern

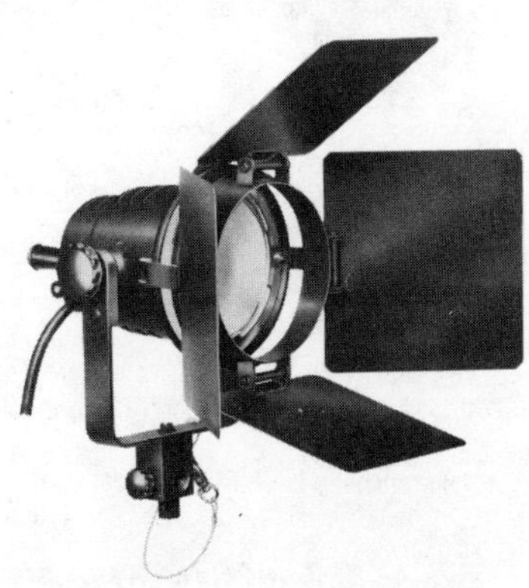

Fig. 4-12. A spotlight. Note yoke and removable barndoors.

Courtesy Smith-Victor

and an almost unlimited mounting ability. A typical kit provides the user with 3 lights, clamps, filter/gel frames, flags (for light diffusion or masking), and flex cables (for mounting the accessories). It allows a maximum of flexibility and portability in a lighting kit that still can put out 3000 watts of light. The manufacturer reasons that most location lighting situations can be covered with such a lighting kit.

The other kit (Fig. 4-14) is a more conventional approach to unit lighting. The kit that is illustrated provides over 3000 watts of light. These lights come with barndoors and adjustable floor stands. This kit is easy to set up and tear down. The manufacturer advertises this kit as a studio kit for the cine or tv photographer.

Lighting kits can give you enough power to light almost any location you are likely to use. They give you a selection of lamps and lighting instruments that makes them flexible enough to handle all the jobs they are called on to do. We have used both kinds of kits and have been satisfied with the results in most situations. The conventional kits were easier to use at first since we had had more experience with those kinds of lights. The "unconventional" kit offers so many possibilities that it is impossible to see them all right away, but its usefulness grows on you after awhile. When you think about lighting equipment, look into the kit concept. You might find, as we did, that it is exactly what you need.

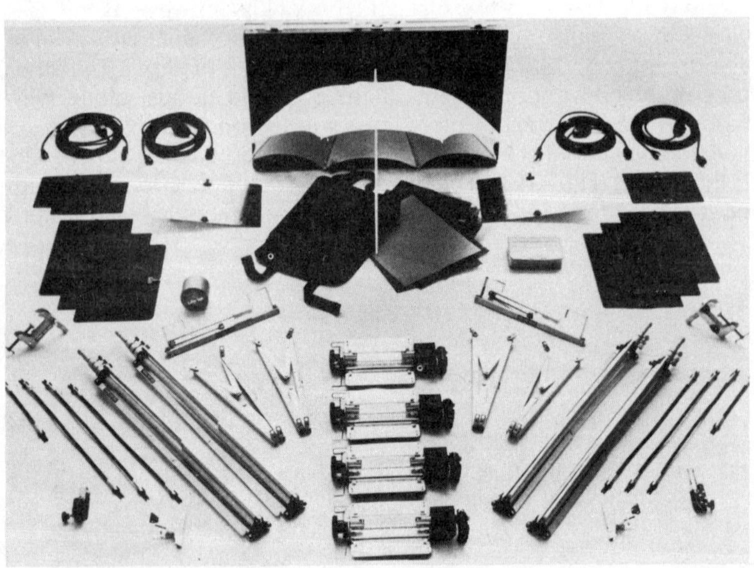

Courtesy Lowel-Light

Fig. 4-13. A wide variety of brackets, stands, hangers, and adapters are in this flexible kit.

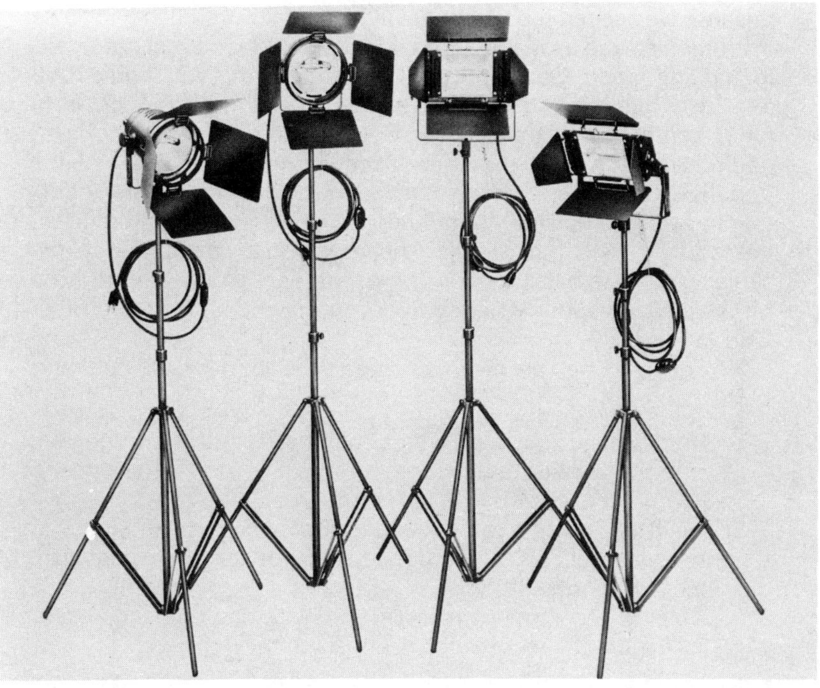

Courtesy Smith-Victor

Fig. 4-14. Two spotlights and two floodlights are in this kit.

A Word About Quality

As we have said before, when you are shopping for equipment look for good workmanship and solid construction. These qualities are especially important in lighting equipment. Many people mistakenly think that since they will not be using lighting equipment all of the time, they can get away with equipment that is cheaper and, usually, flimsier. We have found that it pays to buy quality lighting gear. If the equipment is reliable and sturdy, you will be able to use it for many years with only ordinary maintainence. Cheap equipment may give you adequate performance right now but it will prove more costly in the long run.

Our Recommendations

In some ways, it is difficult to make precise recommendations as to what are the best lighting instruments for your needs. We have used all kinds of lighting instruments in our film making. We used simple scoops when we began because that was all we could afford. In some of our late films, we used professional-type 2000-watt spotlights because we needed the additional light that they provided and those instruments were available. For each film, we found that our needs for lighting varied. Our conclusion is, therefore, that you should have a range of lighting instruments available. With the fast film stocks of today and the low-light cameras, you are more than likely to need additional light (fill light) in a given scene. Here is where the floodlight works well. On the other hand, when shooting in interiors that have a good overall illumination (like classrooms and offices), the spotlight, with its bright sharp beam, can help you "pick out" the subject from the background. The movie light works best in those on-the-spot situations where you do not have time to set up other kinds of lights.

However, to be specific, we suggest the following features for spotlights:

1. Sturdy metal housings with cooling slots or fins, a separate reflector, a solid yoke attachment, and provision for barndoors, scrims, and filters.
2. Tungsten-halogen lamps (600 watts minimum), mounted in porcelain sockets, and a simple provision for adjustment from spot to flood position.
3. A heavy-duty three-wire power cord with a built-in line switch.
4. Barndoors and scrims for each unit.

Then, for floodlights, we recommend that the scoops have:

1. Reflectors that are at least 12 inches in diameter, with mounting clamps or brackets.
2. Medium screw-base sockets (the household type) to permit use of 500-watt incandescent lamps.
3. A 6-foot minimum power cord with a built-in line switch.

and your broads should have:

1. Sturdy metal housing with cooling slots or fins, a separate reflector, a solid yoke attachment, and built-in barndoors.
2. Tungsten-halogen lamps (750 watts minimum) mounted in porcelain sockets.
3. A heavy-duty three-wire power cord with a built-in line switch.

CARE AND CLEANING OF EQUIPMENT

As stated earlier, your equipment will only perform up to its capability when it is clean and properly adjusted. Most lighting equipment needs only periodic cleaning and adjustment to work well. However, there are three areas of concern—the lamps, the cords, and the housing/accessories. As many lamps are "burned out" by careless handling as are actually burned out in use. All movie lamps, especially the tungsten-halogen lamps, are very fragile and must be handled with care. Observe the following rules and the lamps will enjoy a much longer life.

1. Let the lamps warm up to room temperature before you turn them on. A sudden surge of power through a cold lamp is likely to pop the filament and may shatter the envelope. This is especially true for conventional photofloods.
2. Let the lamps cool before you tear down the lights. Tungsten-halogen lamps are most vulnerable here. Their filaments are quite brittle when hot and can break easily. Let them cool for about 10 minutes. Our rule has been that if the housing is cool to the touch, the light is then cool enough to pack.
3. When tearing down lights, leave tungsten-halogen lamps in their instruments. They are difficult to remove and replace anyway, so this is no hardship. They should not be handled too much, either, as fingerprints on their envelopes can produce local hotspots that will cause the envelopes to burn out. Photofloods should be removed from their sockets, however. The large size of their envelopes makes them vulnerable to breakage. Store them in the paper sleeves in which they came when purchased.

Lighting instrument cords, switches, and extension cords should be checked after every shooting session for frayed wires, loose connections, and damaged plugs. All repairs should be made with soldered connections and then wrapped with electrical tape. If you are in doubt about any electrical connection, repair it or replace it. *Coil* instrument cords and extension cords. Do not wrap them around the object to which they are attached.

Check light housings for damage to yokes, reflectors, sockets, and moving parts. The majority of damage done to lighting instruments happens when they are being packed. Be sure you know how the lighting instruments fit in the carrying case. Do not just drop them in and slam the lid. If any parts do get bent or damaged, straighten them out or replace them as soon as possible.

Check photoflood lamp sockets occasionally for signs of arcing. This indicates weak contact tension and means the sockets must be replaced. Tungsten-halogen sockets will corrode at times, too. If they show signs of corroding, polish them with an emery cloth until they are shiny again.

Barndoors and scrims do not need much maintenance if they are handled carefully. Do not lubricate them as the oil will burn off during use and cause embarrassing smoke.

LIGHT METERS

One of the advantages that Super 8 cameras have had, since their introduction in 1964, has been the built-in light meter. A few years before Eastman Kodak Company invented the Super 8 format, camera manufacturers had begun to fit 8-mm cameras with automatic light-metering systems. When Super 8 came along, this technology was quickly incorporated into these new cameras by most manufacturers.

In the discussion of the metering system of the camera, we mentioned that one could use the camera as a light meter since, in fact, that is what the light-metering system is, in part. However, there are times when a separate light meter might come in handy. In this section, we will explain why you might need an external light meter, describe how they work, and give some suggestions as to which one would be the most valuable for your use.

The Purpose of the Light Meter

The purpose of the external light meter is the same as that of the meter portion in the metering system of your camera, namely to "read" the light in the scene and to "tell" you what f/stop you should set the aperture to. Within this general definition, light meters can be used to determine contrast ratio (the relationship of key to fill light), to get an average exposure setting for a shot with a wide range of light, and to determine exposures for small portions of a larger shot. All of these can be done with the camera's meter, of course. However, the separate external light meter is more portable than the camera, it can be programmed to compute a greater number of variables than can the meter on the camera (hence, it is a more flexible tool), and it is usually more accurate than the meter on the camera. Basically, it is handy and convenient.

The very fact that the external meter is hand held means that it is not tied to the tripod position. You can take it into the scene to read the light on the portion of the scene that you want. Or, you can move it to an off-camera position to check lighting ratios. The range of ASA settings for the average light meter (from 6 to 6400) is far greater than that of any camera. The same is true of the f/stop range and the shutter-speed scale. Finally, most external light meters are built more precisely and operate more accurately than do the camera meters. This is not to say that camera meters are unreliable. We merely recognize the fact that a machine like the light meter, built for a single purpose and costing from one-fourth to one-third as much as a Super 8 camera, is bound to be more accurate than a meter that is just an operating convenience.

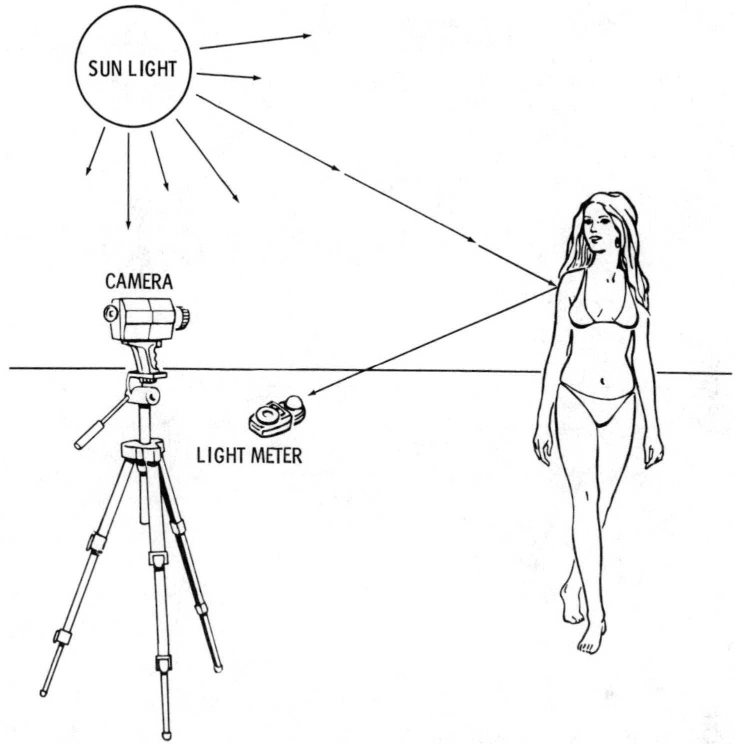

Fig. 4-15. Light reflected off the subject is measured by a reflected-light meter from the camera position.

Types of Light Meters

There are two main types of light meters, the reflected-light meter and the incident-light meter. The reflected-light meter is like the kind used in Super 8 cameras. It reads the amount of light that is *reflected from* the subject. Reflected-light meter readings are taken from the camera position (Fig. 4-15). The incident-light meter measures the light that is *falling* on the subject. Incident-light meter readings are taken from the subject position (Fig. 4-16).

How They Work

All light meters, regardless of type, are activated in one of two ways—either by a selenium cell or by a cadmium-disulphide cell. The selenium cell is a solar cell. It generates current from light energy in proportion to the amount of light that strikes it. In other words, in a bright light, it will generate a larger amount of current than it will in a dim light. This is its major problem. When using a selenium-cell light

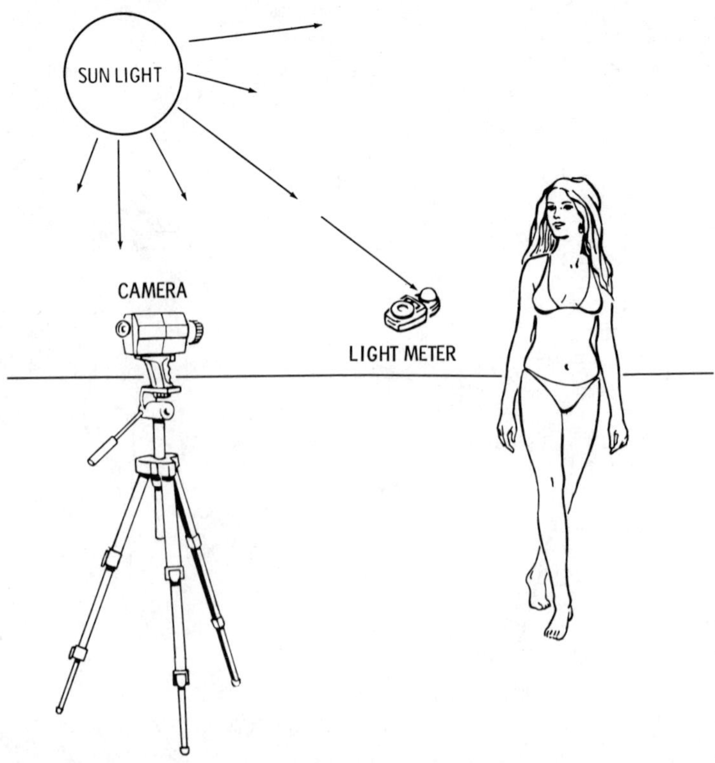

Fig. 4-16. The light falling on the subject is measured from the subject's position when using an incident-light meter.

meter under dim lighting conditions, you are less likely to get an accurate reading. (In fact, you may get no reading at all.)

The cadmium-disulphide (or CdS) cell is more sensitive to low light situations than is the selenium cell. The CdS cell is a light-variable resister powered by a battery. The more light it "sees," the greater is its resistance. Thus, the less light it "sees," the less resistance and the greater its current flow. Light meters using CdS cells are the kind most commonly manufactured today and they are likely to be the most accurate over the largest range of lighting conditions.

The average light meter looks like the sketch shown in Figure 4-17. It is a handy addition to film production, and is especially valuable in those special exposure situations. The particular meter illustrated happens to be both a reflected-light meter and an incident-light meter, a very popular combination. The procedure for using the meter is quite simple.

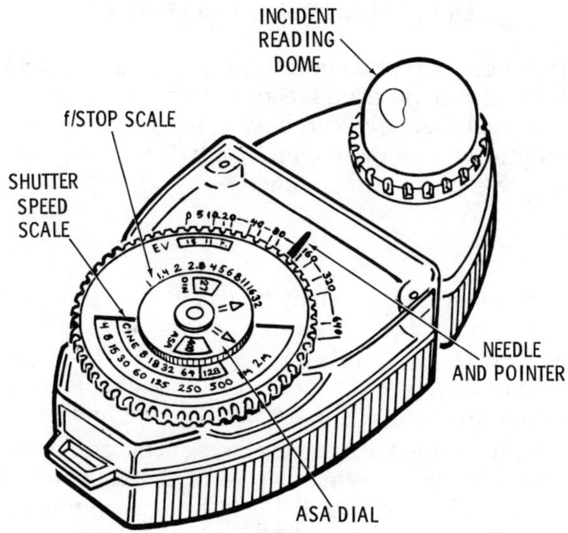

Fig. 4-17. Sketch of a light meter.

1. Dial in the correct ASA setting, for your type of film, on the ASA setting disk.
2. For a reflected-light reading, push the sliding diffuser to the right and point the meter toward the subject from the camera position.
3. Turn the computer ring until the indicator needle is lined up through the center of the white circle on the pointer.
4. Read the CINE scale for the proper fps reading and match it with the corresponding f/stop in the scale above it. Set your aperture for that f/stop reading.
5. For an incident-light reading, push the diffuser to the center and take your reading from the subject position toward the camera. Then, repeat Steps 3 and 4.

Additional details on using the light meter will be given later in Section III.

Which kind of external light meter is best for you? Our first choice would be an incident-reading meter activated by a CdS cell. Our second choice would be a good combination-type reflected-light and incident-light meter that uses a CdS cell. Even though they never need batteries, we feel that selenium-cell meters are a poor choice because of their inability to read dim light accurately. And, since your movie camera already has a reflected-light meter in it, it would be foolish to buy another reflected-light-only meter just for a possible external use.

MISCELLANEOUS EQUIPMENT

No chapter on tools and equipment would be complete without some reference to those extra pieces of film-production equipment that do not lend themselves to easy classification. The following discussion lists three of these pieces with explanations of their use and an estimate of their importance.

Reflectors

Reflectors are those large shiny boards that are used to fill in the shadows in a sunlit scene. They are usually made of fiberboard or stiff cardboard and covered with a reflective foil. This reflective foil comes in rolls as well, and is quite useful for illuminating the dark corners of rooms, hall, or the interiors of automobiles.

We have often made our own reflectors out of cardboard sheets or pieces of paneling by covering them with aluminum foil, dull side out. (The dull side will diffuse the light better than the shiny side.) One-quarter-inch plywood painted with aluminum paint (or flat white paint) will work as well, although plywood is heavier and consequently more difficult to hold for long periods.

Slate

We think that the slate (Fig. 4-18) is one of the most important pieces of miscellaneous film-making equipment. We record

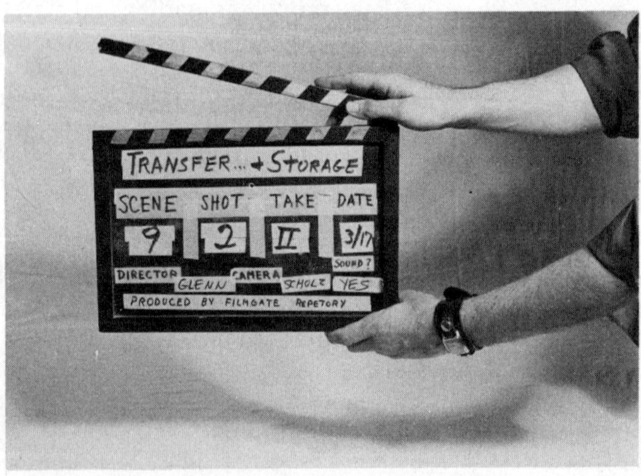

Fig. 4-18. A slate.

information about the shot on the slate (writing with marker pens on masking tape) and then the slate is filmed at the beginning of that particular shot. Later, when we look at the processed film, before or during editing, we can always tell which shot is which, by the notation on the slate.

During sync-sound film making, the clapstick, mounted on top of the slate, comes in very handy. At the beginning of each shot, we clap the stick just before the action begins. When we want to match the sound and picture from any given shot on the editing bench, all we have to do is locate that shot by its slate and then line up the picture of the clapstick with the sound of the clap. This makes sync-sound editing much easier and faster.

Tape

No item costs so little and yet is so indispensable to film making as tape. We regularly use three different kinds—masking tape, gaffers tape, and double-faced carpet tape. *Masking tape* is handy for short-term repairs of all kinds (except electrical). It is used for labeling (like with a felt-tipped pen on the slate), attaching signs, and 1000 other uses.

Gaffers tape (first introduced by Lowel-Light in 1959) is a 2-inch-wide silver-gray cloth adhesive tape. It can be used to attach lighting equipment to walls, hold shutters and barndoors on lights, tie up electrical cables, and generally do those jobs that are too heavy for masking tape but which do not need a permanent method of fastening. We have used *furnace tape* (also called duct tape) as a substitute for "real" gaffers tape. While duct tape is not quite as strong, its adhesive properties are very similar to those of gaffers tape. This kind of tape will remove paint if left on a surface too long.

Double-faced carpet tape is great for holding down those things that must be kept in place securely but unobtrusively. It is a strong plastic tape with adhesive on both sides. Merely cut it to length, peel off the protective coating, and mount it. Use it for holding down props, hanging pictures, and even securing carpets.

CHAPTER 5

Sound Equipment

Before we discuss the equipment needed to make Super 8 films with sound, we must understand what the purpose of a sound recording is and how it is accomplished by a magnetic-tape recording. The purpose of a sound recording is to take the vibrations in the air that we call sound and translate them into some form that can be stored and replayed at another time. A magnetic-tape recording is the most popular form of sound recording and is also one of the simplest forms. It works as follows. The sound waves are picked up by the microphone which changes them into electrical impulses. These impulses are transmitted to the recording head of the tape recorder where they are transferred as electromagnetic patterns onto the iron-oxide coating of the recording tape as it passes across the recording head.

In playback, the process is reversed. The electromagnetic patterns in the iron-oxide coating on the recording tape are "read" by a playback head as the tape passes across it. These patterns are turned into electrical impulses which are fed to a speaker. The speaker converts the electrical impulses into vibrations in the air which we then perceive as sound. (The actual circuitry of a magnetic-tape recorder may include an amplifier, a tone control, an automatic gain or level control, and other gadgets, but the process of recording and playback remains the same.)

Virtually all Super 8 sound movie systems use magnetic-tape recordings for their sound production and reproduction. There are two different systems in common use, the *single system*, which puts the sound right on the film, and the *double system* which records the sound using a separate tape recorder. Both these systems are synchronous sound-recording systems or sync sound systems. *Sync sound* means that the sound is always recorded in a specific and exact relationship to the picture. With sync sound systems, it is possible to play back and edit the sound and picture and always maintain the exact same relationship of sound to picture.

SINGLE-SYSTEM SOUND

Single-system sound (called sound-on-film) is the sync sound-recording system that utilizes a camera with a sound head, and a film cartridge with sound-striped film, to expose and record both the picture and sound at the same time. The sound-recording systems of these sound cameras work just like any other magnetic sound-recording system except that playback cannot be done in the camera. The picture-taking capabilities of sound-type Super 8 cameras are no different than those of silent-type Super 8 cameras. Essentially the Super 8 *sound camera* is a conventional Super 8 movie camera with another system added to it—a sound-recording system.

While there has been an eager acceptance of the concept of sound-on-film cameras in Super 8, there has been some controversy about the "correct" running speed for sound Super 8 film. When Kodak first introduced Super 8, they said that 18 frames per second would be the standard *silent* camera speed and that 24 frames per second would be the standard *sound* camera speed. However, when they brought out the first sound-on-film camera, the original Ektasound, it only ran at 18 fps. (Later models have been designed to run at both 18 and 24 fps.) Kodak now suggests that 18 fps should be considered the "amateur" sound filming speed and that 24 fps should be considered the "professional" sound filming speed.

The quality of sound-on-film sound recording seems slightly better at 24 fps according to our tests. This is probably due to the higher speed of the magnetic-recording stripe going past the sound head. A speed of 24 fps is also compatible with television film chains where Super 8 film can be transferred to videotape through the use of a 24-fps projector with a special shutter. Under normal recording conditions, though, we find it is almost impossible to tell the difference in sound quality between sound-on-film sound recorded at 18 fps and that recorded at 24 fps. Virtually all Super 8 sound projectors run at both 18 and 24 fps, so either speed will work in regular projection. Since this "speed-of-sound" problem is not likely to be resolved for some time, it is best to get a camera that shoots at both speeds.

The Sound System

The sound system in the Super 8 sound camera consists of a sound-recording head, a stabilizing flywheel and capstan, a microphone jack, an earphone jack, and the amplifier, volume, and tone controls. This system is usually monitored visually by some form of sound-level meter (sometimes a regular VU meter), and often has a "running" light or a "sound on" signal that is visible in the viewfinder and on the front of the camera.

The sound-recording head is located in the bottom of the film chamber in the film path, exactly 18 frames away from the film gate (Fig. 5-1). This 18-frame spacing is quite critical in Super 8 cameras as it represents the agreed-upon standard separation for both the recording and playback of sound in a Super 8 film. In order for sound film to be compatible from any camera to any projector, the distance between the sound and the picture must always be the same. Manufacturers of all Super 8 cameras and projectors have agreed upon this 18-frame interval as the standard for Super 8 sound equipment.

There might be some question in your mind as to why the sound is separated from the picture. It would be easier for editing if both the sound and picture were in the same place on the film. Then, when you cut through a picture you would also be cutting the corresponding sound. However, there is one major reason why the sound head is not located next to the film gate in *any* sound movie camera. Magnetic-sound recording only works when the sound strip or the recording tape is being drawn past the sound head at a steady speed. The speed itself is not so very important, either 18 fps or 24 fps are acceptable, as long as it is a *steady* speed. When the film goes through the film gate, it is stopped, exposed, and then moved on. This intermittent stop and start motion of the film, at the point of exposure, prevents an accurate sound recording. It is not until the film is well past the film gate that a steady speed can be maintained.

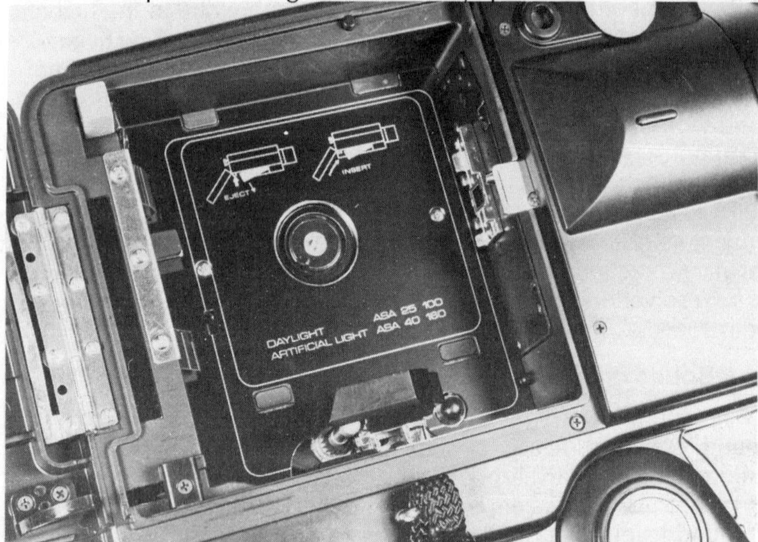

Fig. 5-1. Interior of a sound-on-film camera. Note the sound head under the silent-film cartridge pedestal.

Therefore, the recording of the sound and exposing of the picture *in the same place* on the film, at the same time, is simply not practical.

The *sound-recording head* is mounted on a pivot in the film chamber so that it can be swung down when the cartridge is loaded. The *stabilizing flywheel capstan* is also in the bottom of the film chamber. It is located in the film path behind the sound head. Its purpose is to keep the film running at a steady speed for good fidelity in sound recordings. The *microphone jack, earphone jack,* and *volume/tone controls* are usually located on the side of the camera body (Fig. 5-2). These jacks are usually the miniplug size like those found on cassette tape recorders. The *amplifier* is built into the camera body behind these controls. Unless there is some provision for *manual* control of the recording level, there will not be a real volume control on the camera. Instead, there will be two microphone jacks, one for regular sound recording and the other for "suppressed" sound recording. This suppressed microphone circuit is less sensitive to sounds, so it will pick up only the louder sounds and will not record "background" noises as readily.

All Super 8 sound cameras have some form of auto-volume control. This entire concept of recording without operator control of the volume was pioneered by the manufacturers of the cassette tape recorders of a few years ago. The system is called *automatic gain*

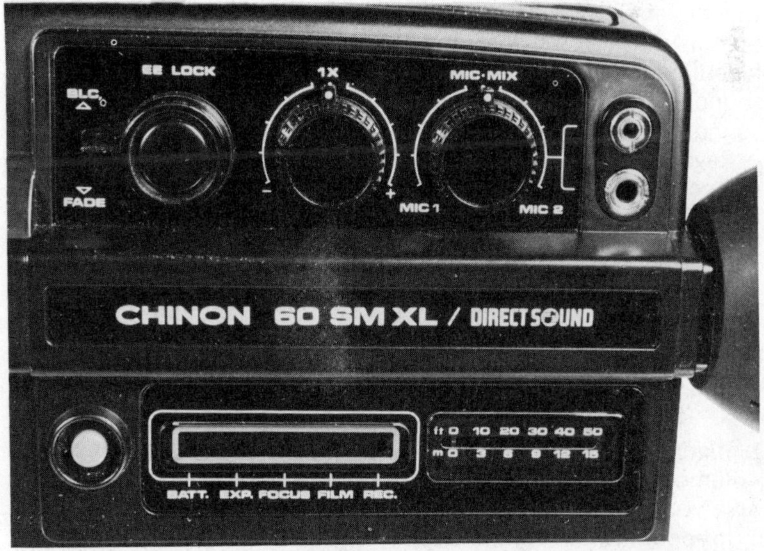

Fig. 5-2. Side panel of a sound-on-film camera showing the controls and jacks needed for SOF operation.

control (AGC) or *automatic level control* (ALC). AGC recording circuits are designed to maintain a certain level of recorded sound regardless of the actual level of the sound present during a recording. This means that the AGC circuit will "tone down" sounds that are too loud for the predetermined level and "boost" sounds that are too soft to reach that same level. AGC circuits do this through a process called "signal seeking." During recording, the AGC circuit automatically "seeks" the loudest sound present and takes that to be the base line for its sound level.

There is one major problem with an AGC circuit. The loudest sound on location may not be the "correct" sound for your film. If the background sound is of a higher volume than the correct (or wanted) sound, the AGC circuit will read the background sound as the base level and everything else will be at a lower volume. To compensate for this problem, camera manufacturers often include a second microphone jack that is designed to be less sensitive to all sound levels. With the microphone plugged into this "suppressed sound" jack and the microphone placed close to the desired source of sound, any unwanted noises can be kept in the background (or even eliminated).

Although most sound Super 8 cameras have some form of AGC circuit, volume controls are becoming popular again but, this time, for another reason. They are being used to fade sound in or out. In a manner similar to the manual aperture controls (and special fade buttons) that are on silent Super 8 cameras, and which can be used to fade the picture, manual volume controls can be used to fade the sound. In some cameras, these switches are coupled so that the sound and picture can be faded at the same time.

Regardless of what kind of volume-control system the camera has, some form of visual sound monitoring is usually provided. This monitor can be a conventional sound-level meter or a blinking light. The sound monitor is usually visible in the viewfinder. A *sound-level meter,* often called a VU meter (for volume unit) has a scale of numbers reading in decibels. When the sound is being recorded at the correct volume, the needle of the meter usually swings in the center of the scale. When used in conjunction with a manual gain (or volume) control on the camera, the VU meter can be a very accurate way of monitoring and controlling sound recording levels. A *blinking-light sound monitor* works like a VU meter in that as the volume of sound increases, the light gets brighter. The light does not give you the subtlety of readings that a VU meter does, however.

In addition to the components and circuits just described, the body of the Super 8 camera also undergoes some modifications when adapted for sound film making. The film chamber is made larger to accommodate the sound cartridge and a special pedestal is placed in the chamber to hold up the silent-film cartridge (all Super 8 sound cameras can use both types of cartridges). Also, the battery capacity of most sound cameras is greater than that of silent cameras because the *two* driving systems (film transport and sound stabilization) require more current. Some sound cameras even have a provision for connecting external battery packs that can provide power for long shooting sessions.

The Sound Film Cartridge

The Super 8 sound film cartridge is about half again as tall as the silent film cartridge. Its additional height is due to the fact that another opening must be made in the cartridge, 18 frames beyond the picture opening, to allow the sound head to contact the sound stripe in the right place (Fig. 5-3). Since the sound head contacts the sound stripe of the film on the inside of the film path, the sound cartridge must be taller to accommodate the sound head and the stabilizing capstan.

The film in this sound cartridge is like ordinary silent Super 8 film except that it has two stripes of an iron-oxide-coated material on its base side (Fig. 5-4). The widest of these two stripes (the one placed opposite the sprocket holes) is the *sound stripe*. It is the medium that your sound-on-film camera will record on. The narrower stripe is called the *balance stripe*. It can be used for mixing sound or for recording stereo sound. The actual purpose of the balance stripe is to give the film equal thickness on both edges so that it will lie flat in the film gate during projection and so that it will stack evenly on the film reels. However, it is made of the same material as the sound stripe and, consequently, can be used for recording.

Other than a taller case, the Super 8 sound cartridge is very much

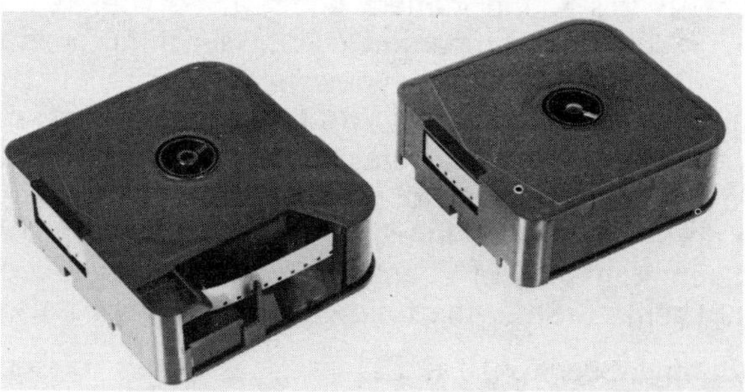

Fig. 5-3. Compared to a silent-film cartridge, the sound-film cartridge is taller and has two openings in the case.

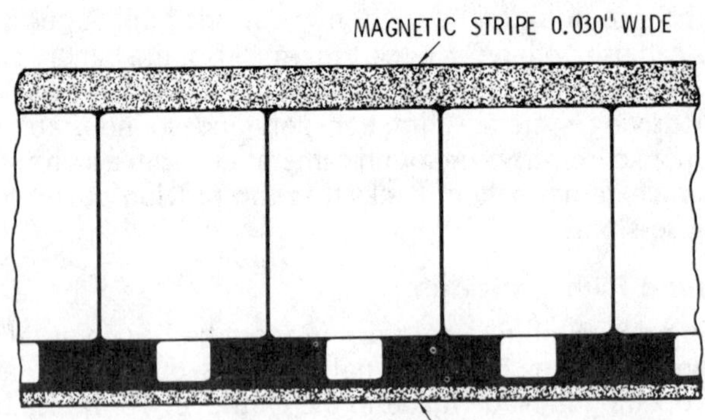

**Fig. 5-4. Typical Super 8 sound film showing the sound stripe
and the balance stripe.**

like the silent Super 8 cartridges. It holds 50 feet of film (or 200 feet in
the large loads). It has coding notches in the usual places and is used
in the regular way. The film, too, is like silent Super 8 film stocks. If
you are shooting Kodachrome 40 sound film, it can be processed just
the same as regular Kodachrome 40 and at the same price. At the
moment, not all color film stocks are available in sound cartridges.
No black and white film stocks are available. But this situation is
bound to change as more people start to use sound-on-film in film
making. Check with your local film supplier before making a final
decision about sound film stock.

Our Recommendations

The market is loaded with good single-system cameras. So, we
suggest you decide the following question first, before you purchase
a camera. Is this sound camera going to be your one and only
camera, or will it be a companion to your silent film camera? If it is to
be your only camera replacing your present silent film camera, you
will probably want it to have at least those features that you already
possess in your present camera. If you can afford to make it a
"second" camera, then look for special features in it that your current
camera does not possess. In either case, reread our recommendations, given at the end of Chapter 3, about picking a good quality
camera. Then, consider the following specifications also:

1. Running speeds of 18 and 24 fps are essential. You should get at
    least one other speed (preferably slow motion) and, of course,
    single-frame exposure ability. Remote run operation is also a
    must and radio-control capability is nice. Even if you cannot
    afford a radio-control unit now, you can always buy one later.

2. You should have a sound monitor that is visible in the viewfinder. The VU meter is best here, but even a blinking light will help give you some clue as to what the sound is doing.
3. Manual control of the sound volume, or manual override of the AGC is nice to have. Either will give you that additional measure of control over the sound and will allow you to make creative choices. They are handy for sound fades, too.
4. A boom for mounting the microphone is handy. While the microphone should not be permanently attached to the camera (this would really limit your microphone placement), the unattachable microphone can make it impossible for you to be a one-person camera unit. Besides, a boom mounting looks much more professional than a microphone that is mounted with gaffers tape.
5. Check the convenience of the controls. Since you are dealing with an additional set of controls for the sound-recording system, you must pay even more attention to how well the controls are laid out. Find the camera that feels comfortable and is easy to use.
6. Finally, test the lightweight and compact-size cameras. We have handled several enormous Super 8 sound cameras in the past year. Some of them weighed four pounds. For ease of operation a lighter and smaller camera is better.

DOUBLE-SYSTEM SOUND

Double-system sound, as the name implies, uses two separate systems to take the picture and record the sound. Unlike the single-system method, where the entire process is controlled by one sound-on-film camera, double-system sound requires a camera and a tape recorder. Usually the double-system sound equipment consists of a silent-film camera and an audio tape recorder. The camera shoots silent film; the tape recorder uses 1/4-inch magnetic tape, or cassette tapes. They are synchronized by an electric signal (or pulse); usually, one pulse for every frame of film exposed. This sync pulse is sent by cable to the tape recorder that is recording the sound. In the tape recorder is a special sync pulse circuit, which receives the pulse from the camera, and records it on the tape at the same time that the tape recorder is recording the sound track. (The two input signals, sync pulse and sound, are not in conflict. The sound track is recorded on one edge of the magnetic tape while the sync pulse is recorded in the middle of the tape.)

For playback, after the film is processed, the film is threaded onto a projector that has a pulse-per-frame switch on it. The tape is then played on a tape recorder that has a special sync pulse circuitry. They are connected together through a device called a *pulse resolver*. This resolver "reads" the sync pulses from the tape and the frame pulses from the projector, and coordinates the speed of the tape to match that of the projector. In this way, the film and the sound remain in the same synchronous relationship that was established when they were shot and recorded.

Magnetic Film

This system presents some problems when editing the sound with the picture, however. Since you cannot "see" the sound on tape, you cannot tell exactly where it is for editing purposes. The sound must be transferred to some medium that is easy to edit. This medium is *magnetic film*. Mag film, as it is called, is the same width as regular Super 8 film, has the same sprocket holes, and is made of a similar base material. Instead of emulsion, however, it is coated with an iron oxide, like audio recording tape. Fig. 5-5 shows a regular reel-to-reel tape recorder that has been modified for use with mag film.

The sound from the original tape is transferred, in synchronization, to this mag film by means of a special recording machine called a *dubber*. This machine, like the resolver, reads the sync pulses on the tape, translates them into a frame relationship and then transfers them in sync to the mag film. The result is a piece of mag film that has a length that is equal to the picture film, with the sound recorded in sync in a frame-for-frame relationship. After the sound track has been transferred to mag film, it can be played back in sync with the picture

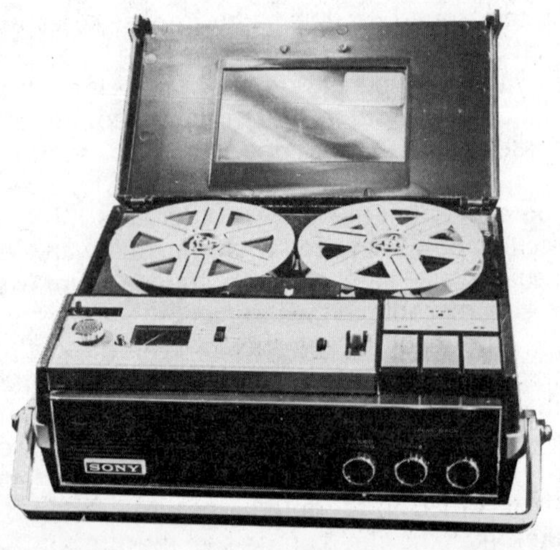

Fig. 5-5. A regular reel-to-reel tape recorder that has been modified for use with magnetic film.

in two ways. The mag film and the picture can be threaded into a special double-system projector which will play them simultaneously, or they can be run through a *sync block* on an editing bench.

A double-system projector is a unit which looks like (and sometimes is) two projectors built side by side. One side is set up conventionally for film. The other side is set up for sound playback. The two sides are threaded with film and mag film, respectively. When the previously determined sync marks are lined up, the projector motor (s) is started and you have picture and sound in sync.

The Editing Bench

The editing-bench method of playing back sound is used more often for actual editing than it is for playback. The sound-editing bench has a sync block, film viewer, and sound reader (Fig. 5-6). As in the double-system projector, the picture and mag films are each threaded through the sync block and aligned to the sync marks. The picture film is threaded through the viewer and the mag film through the sound head. When they are both drawn through the viewer and the sound head at the same time, they give a playback of the picture and the sound, in sync. Motor-driven sync blocks are the most common transport mechanism for these benches.

The Recorder

The recorder that we use for our Super 8 sync sound recording works on a principle similar to the pulse-synched tape recorder but

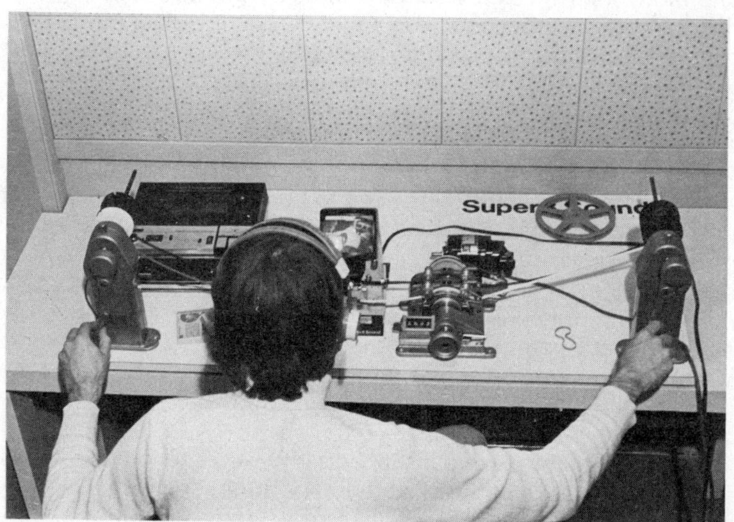

Fig. 5-6. A Super 8 sound-film editing bench.

with two differences. Before you shoot with this setup, you either set the speed of the recorder or match the filming speed of your camera (either 18 fps or 24 fps). The camera and tape recorder are connected with the usual pulse cable. When the camera and recorder are started, the recorder will sense the sync pulses from the camera, and will allow the operator to alter the speed of the recorder to keep an accurate frame-for-frame synchronization. The second difference is somewhat more important. This recorder records the sound directly on mag film. This means that you can play it back in sync as soon as the film is processed. No transfer of sound from tape to mag film is needed. And, direct editing of the sound and picture is possible, again, without dubbing.

Advantages and Disadvantages

The advantages of double-system sound over single-system sound are the ability to get a higher-quality sound recording on the original track, the fact that you can play back your sound "takes" directly after shooting in order to check the sound, and the ease of editing that comes with having separate picture and sound recordings.

The higher sound quality that you get with the double-system sound comes from the single-purpose recording machines you are using. Contemporary sound cameras may record a good quality sound for single-system sound systems, but it is not high quality when compared to tape recorders. Tape recorders have better sound heads, smoother and more constant-speed tape-transport systems, and more sophisticated electronic circuitry than do the sound-on-film cameras. The second advantage, of an immediate playback of sound, is possible only with double-system sound recording. Since the recorder can be run separately from the camera, one can hear the sound playback right away, without disturbing the picture or the synchronization.

Finally, the flexibility of editing that comes with using double-system sound must be experienced to be appreciated. It is just not possible to make the same kinds of sound and picture combinations using the single-system method as it is with the double-system method. And, by using a mag film recorder as your original sound recorder, the frame-for-frame editing of sound and picture can be easily and accurately accomplished. Single-system sound, with its built-in 18-frame displacement of sound from picture, makes any editing, that is more than just the simplest kind of editing, extremely difficult and time consuming.

However, there are two distinct disadvantages to the double-system approach. You must use two machines (camera and tape recorder) which means a doubling of equipment and probably a doubling of cost. For the average film maker, the single-system camera will certainly be cheaper and more portable. And, even with the most sophisticated sync pulse system available in the double-system cameras and recorders of today, it is still possible for the sound and picture to get out of sync. This can never happen with the single-system camera since the sound is going right on the sound stripe, even if it is 18 frames downstream from the picture.

Our Recommendations

At the present time, we can make only one recommendation about double-system sound and that is the Super 8 Sound System. Their recorders, which use mag film, are well made and consistently accurate. Their sync system is almost foolproof and they have a line of accessories that will enable you to operate as professionally as the 16-mm folks.

MICROPHONES

Good sound quality begins with a good microphone. All sound-on-film cameras come with their own microphones. Some cameras even have them built in. While you can get acceptable sound quality with these original equipment microphones, you would be better off at least trying a higher quality (and more expensive) replacement microphone.

Sound Pickup Patterns

The first thing to do is to determine what pattern of sound pickup you need (Fig. 5-7). There are three basic patterns—omnidirectional, cardiod, and unidirectional (or shotgun). Each kind has its specific use but the omnidirectional and cardiod patterns are the most useful and are the most common replacement microphones.

An omnidirectional microphone is likely to be the pattern of the microphone that is supplied with your sound-on-film camera. It collects sounds from nearly every direction, so it is also likely to pick up sound that you do not want as well as those sounds you are trying to record. The omnidirectional microphone is good for recording background sounds, however, and will give a lively "presence" to the sound location.

Most modern sound-on-film cameras come equipped with a cardiod-pattern microphone. This picks up the sound from a heart-shaped pattern, mainly in front of the microphone. The cardiod microphone has the most useful all-around pattern for voice recording because of this directional characteristic. It is also relatively insensitive to high-frequency sounds from behind it so it will not pick up much camera noise.

Unidirectional or shotgun microphones are quite selective in their

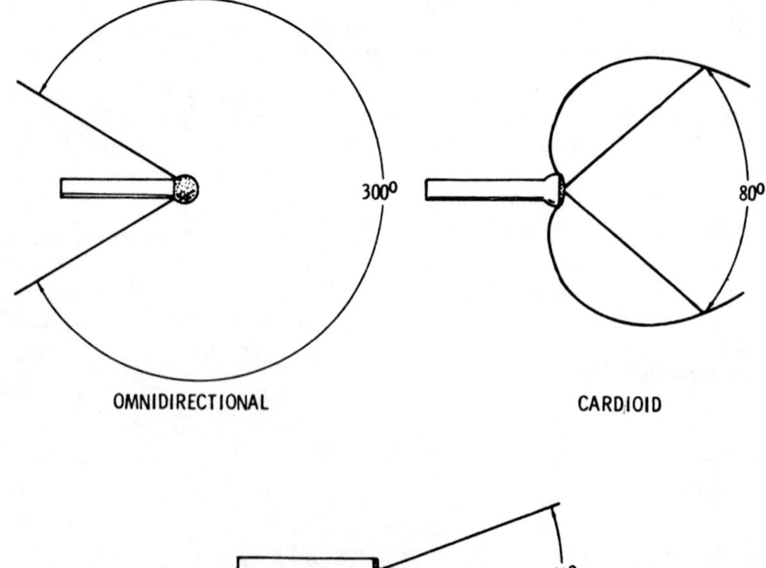

Fig. 5-7. Microphone pickup patterns.

pickup range. They only hear ''in front'' of them and, then, in a decreasing range relative to frequency. They are especially limited in their reception of high-frequency sounds. Shotgun microphones are most useful when it is necessary to isolate a specific sound source from a background of noise (we have used them to record the marching band at football games, for example), but they do not reproduce a full range of sound very accurately.

Dynamic or Condensor Types

After you have chosen your pickup pattern, you must decide whether the microphone should be of the dynamic type or of the condensor type. The basic difference between the two types is:

1. The dynamic microphone is powered by a current generated in the diaphragm of the microphone itself. This current (the electric signal carrying the sound information that was picked up by the microphone) is boosted by the amplifier in the camera and then put on the sound stripe.
2. The condensor microphone is self-powered, usually by a small battery. This makes the signal it sends to the recorder much

stronger and less in need of amplification before being recorded. The result is that the condensor microphone is the more sound sensitive of the two types.

There are drawbacks to condensor microphones, however. Their increased sensitivity to sound makes them more susceptible to handling "noise" and to other electronic interference. They are also much more expensive than dynamic microphones of similar quality. The dynamic microphone is cheaper, more rugged physically, and more able to take sound overloads without damage.

Our Recommendations

It pays to obtain the best microphone that you can afford, and it is important to use the best microphone for the job. If you can only afford one good microphone, buy a dynamic microphone with a cardiod pattern. It will probably be the best all-around microphone to use for voice recording on location. A good-quality omnidirectional condensor microphone would be handy for background sounds and for location music recording. If you are doing much post-production sound dubbing, a cardiod-pattern condensor microphone will work best here. Shotgun microphones are too specialized for all-around film work.

CARE AND CLEANING OF EQUIPMENT

Sound-recording equipment is like camera equipment in one respect. You can maintain it and keep it clean but there is very little you can do to adjust or repair it. There are several areas of general maintenance, however, such as the sound-recording heads, the electrical connections, and the power supply.

The Heads

The sound recording and playback heads should be kept as clean as possible. Swab the head surfaces with an audio head cleaner. It is also a good idea to demagnetize the heads every six months or so. This prevents stray magnetic fields from building up in the heads and causing noise in the recording signal. The drive or pinch rollers should be cleaned periodically, using a cotton swab dipped in denatured alcohol.

Electrical Connectors

All connections and connectors (jacks and plugs) should be clean and corrosion free. They should snap together tightly and positively. Replace any that are worn out or of doubtful quality. Microphone cables should be checked after every recording session for frayed wires or damaged connectors, and should be repaired accordingly.

The Power Supply

Batteries and battery chambers of portable recorders should be cleaned regularly. Do not store the machine with the batteries in it. Always use alkaline or rechargeable batteries for the power supply. As a further precaution against dead or faded batteries, we usually date each battery by writing the purchase date on it with a felt marker. Then, we can tell at a glance just how old the batteries are and can decide whether or not to replace them.

General Maintenance

Keep your equipment clean and dry. Do not lubricate cameras, lights, or tape recorders, as this will probably do more harm than good. Keep things in good repair and they will give you good service and long life. Finally, have the more complex pieces of equipment checked and serviced at regular intervals by a trained serviceman. He may be able to spot any problems that would prove troublesome later. Like seeing the doctor regularly, your equipment should also be given preventative maintenance.

CONCLUSION

In our descriptions, discussions, and recommendations in the last three chapters on tools for film making, we have tried to be as general as possible. We did not leave out specific brand names or pieces of equipment to confuse you, but rather to leave you with the impression that no one system or camera, tripod, or lighting instrument is the best one. We have sampled most of the current crop of film-making equipment and, of course, we have our personal preferences. But since new products come out every month, we feel it would be foolish to make specific recommendations. A better unit might come along tomorrow.

In equipment, as in most consumer purchases, you get what you pay for. When choosing equipment, weigh your needs against what you can afford and, then, look for the best bargains. When in doubt, buy the better quality item. Chances are it will last longer and work better for you.

CHAPTER 6

Preparation

After you have become fully familiar with the tools of a film maker, there are several steps that you must take between the planning of a film and the production of a film. There are two distinct, though related, areas in these steps, that we have chosen to place in a general category entitled *preparation*—organizational preparation and physical preparation. *Organizational preparation* includes budgeting, choosing the filming location and obtaining permissions, selecting the cast, rounding up a crew, and writing the shooting schedule. *Physical preparation* includes checking the equipment and getting ready to go on location.

These preparation processes can be as simple as those for your home movies, which may require $10.00 for film and processing, your camera and tripod, your family, and a sunny day. Or, they may be as complicated as a recent project of ours. We filmed a centennial celebration that involved using a full-time crew of four for six days, two cameras, full sound gear, using the town as the cast, and recording the events of the celebration as the script, for a cost of about $8,000. Nevertheless, the process of preparation is similar for each case.

ORGANIZATIONAL PREPARATION

Drawing up a budget for the film is the first step in organizational preparation. It is important to develop some idea of the cost of the finished film before it is made. This is especially important if someone else is supplying the money (i.e., a sponsored film). However, it is a wise practice to budget all your film productions, even your home movies.

Budgeting a Film

The basic budget (see Fig. 6-1) should include the cost of raw film, processing, printing, editing, sound recording, sound striping,

```
                    Tentative Budget, Transfer & Storage


     Estimated time of film:  20 minutes.  At a 4:1 ratio, 28-30 cartridges
     of film are needed.

          1.   30 cartridges of Kodachrome  40  @ $9.00 each,
               processing included . . . . . . . . . . . . . . . . . $  270.00

          2.   Cut original footage to 500' for workprint;
               one-light workprint, 500' @ $0.16/ft. . . . . . . . .     80.00

          3.   Edgenumbering workprint & original, 1000' @ $0.02/ft.    20.00

          4.   First trial-timed answer print, 350' @ $0.48/ft. ..    168.00

          5.   Release prints (2) 700' total @ $0.39/ft. . . . . . .   273.00

          6.   Sound stripping, 700' @ $0.11/ft . . . . . . . . . .     77.00

          7.   Black leader for A&B rolls . . . . . . . . . . . . .     14.00

          8.   Fog filter . . . . . . . . . . . . . . . . . . . . .     23.50

          9.   Gas & oil for double-decker bus (estimate)  . . . .    100.00

          10.  Mag Film for Recording, 4 - 5" reels @ $5.00 ea.  .     20.00

          11.  Miscellaneous (other mileage, expenses, rentals, props.
               & costumes, editing materials not on hand, etc.)  .    200.00


                                          TOTAL          $1,045.50
```

**Fig. 6-1. Tentative budget for a double-system sound movie
with some laboratory special effects.**

equipment rental, props, costumes, transportation, postage, telephone, cast, and crew. A more sophisticated budget would include itemized costs for script writing, producer fees, laboratory services, and others.

In order to determine raw stock and processing costs, often the two largest items in a Super 8 film budget, you must know what your *shooting ratio* is going to be. Shooting ratio is the relationship between the amount of film that you expose and the amount you incorporate in your final edited film. For example, if you shoot 5 rolls of film (250 feet) and end up with 1 roll (50 feet), your shooting ratio is 5 to 1. While it is impossible to accurately gauge your need without having had some experience with the type of film that you want to make, it is possible to state some guidelines for the various types of film production. Silent dramatic films can be shot on a ratio as low as 1½ to 1, though a more reasonable estimate would be 3 to 1. Sound dramatic films should be budgeted at a shooting ratio of 5 to 1 to allow for the inevitable reshooting of scenes because the sound was wrong. Documentary footage, that is done in news-film style, can run as high as 15 to 1. Sports footage is often shot at a ratio of 30 to 1 because the important action may happen at any moment.[1] With experience, you will become more capable of estimating exactly how much film you need.

Budgeting for a Sponsored Film

Although the budgeting process is the same for any kind of film, the presentation of the budget to the client is as important an item as the writing of the budget was itself. Three important points to remember are:

1. Never underestimate the production costs.
2. Always obtain some compensation for yourself and your helpers.
3. Do not be intimidated by a client's reaction.

It is less embarrassing to confront the sponsor with a realistic estimate of the total cost at the outset than it is to have to ask for more money after the project is underway. It is wiser to discourage a potential sponsor with a large estimate before you start than to anger him with additional expenses during production.

Secondly, most sponsors realize that their film is not being made simply for your amusement. They expect to pay you for your work. In fact, they might be suspicious of anyone who does not ask for compensation for his or her labor. Calculate the value of your own time and include it in the estimate. Above all, don't be intimidated by the client's reaction when you present your budget. Most people are unaware of the cost of motion-picture productions. If you have made an honest estimate, stick to it. You are the expert here. Do not let the client bully you into making a film for less than it costs you to produce it.

Location Preparation

We have often written specific scenes in our film that were to be played in certain locations because we were struck by the beauty of the place or intrigued by the camera angles available. Location preparation, the second step in organizational preparation, involves the selection of locations, obtaining permission to use them, and estimating the shooting conditions at each location.

---

[1] We recently watched an ABC "American Sportsman" camera team film muzzle-loading events almost constantly for six hours. They were covering a muzzle-loading shoot put on by the extras who were on location for Columbia Pictures' "The Mountain Men." The completed segment, when broadcast, lasted no longer than 10 minutes.

Choosing Locations—This might be the easiest job. Unless you have special needs, you can usually find most locations within your neighborhood, town, or county. To help us find locations, we keep notes on interesting areas that we drive through, visit, or camp in, while we are traveling. When we need a certain location that is not in our town, we check through our notes and often find just what we have been looking for.

Our main rules for picking a location are, in order of importance:

1. Physical conditions—conditions approximating the scene we had visualized when we read (or wrote) the script.
2. Proximity—some place that is close enough so we will not have to spend hours traveling just to get there.
3. Lighting, sound, and traffic/crowd conditions—conditions that are easy to deal with.

It should be obvious why we put the greatest emphasis on the physical site itself. One of the biggest advantages that movies have over plays and novels is that movies can actually show you the place where the action is happening. One cannot imagine "Jaws" without the beach, or "Stagecoach" without Monument Valley. (Think of how many films use locations for their names: "Casablanca," "The Old Man and the Sea," "The Snows of Kilamanjaro," "Boys Town," "The Big Country," etc.) So your first consideration in choosing a location is to find one that corresponds with the visual image you want your audience to have from that scene.

Our second rule is also obvious. Being part-time film makers, we cannot afford to travel long distances just to shoot one or two scenes. Unless a distant location background is absolutely essential, we try to stay within easy driving distance of all our locations.

The lighting, sound control, and traffic/crowd conditions are of lesser importance to us. We can usually bring in additional lighting, dub the sound in, and work around the traffic, if the location meets our first two requirements.

Obtaining Permission—Obtaining permission to use the locations might be more difficult but don't ignore this step. Some places, like New York City, require permits for outdoor filming. Check with local authorities to be sure. If it is essential to film in public places, check with the local police department to make sure they are at least aware of what you are going to do. That way, if anyone does complain, you will have already cleared it. Permission to film in nonpublic places, such as homes or businesses, should be obtained from the owners or managers. We have found that most people will be happy to let you shoot in their places as long as their regular activity is not disrupted.

When asking for permission, explain carefully what will be going on, how long it will take, and how many people will be involved.

Always request permission far enough in advance of the shooting date so that the people at the location can make any adjustments to their own schedule that are necessary to accommodate you. Oral permissions are usually sufficient for location work. Be sure to include the names of the persons who gave you permission in your credits and invite them to the premier showing of your film.

Estimating the Shooting Conditions—When permission to use the various locations has been obtained, three conditions should be checked at each location:

1. Lighting and power.
2. Sound.
3. Traffic and crowds.

Of these three conditions, lighting is the most critical, especially at interior locations.

Even with XL cameras and fast film, the lighting levels in many homes and businesses are almost always too low for good exposure. In most cases, the lights are the wrong color temperature, or are poorly placed for filming. Since you want to work with the minimum of lighting equipment on any location, the first thing you must do is determine where the scenes will be played and, then, decide on how much light is going to be needed (or how much will have to be added). The easiest way to figure this out is by using a light meter, either the camera meter or a separate one. If the lighting level is adequate for good exposure (we suggest at least one stop higher than your lens rating, i.e., f/2.2 if your lens is f/1.2), then check the type and placement of the existing light fixtures. Their color temperature should be compatible with the type of film you are using. The fixtures should be placed so the light is directed toward the main action area in the scene.

If you are going to have to add light to the scene, scout the location for electrical outlets and, if possible, check the fuse box for the amount of power in each of the circuits. Remember, a 500-watt lamp draws about 4.5 amps of current on a regular 110-volt circuit. So three of these lights will come close to peak load on the average 15-amp household circuit. After you have made these checks, you can plan your portable lighting to utilize the available outlets and power at the location.

An evaluation of sound conditions is also quite important. Unwanted sounds and disturbing background noises can be a real problem when shooting with live sound. When checking out the location, identify, and plan ways to work around any sound disturbances that you might discover.

Traffic and crowd conditions are your final location problem. When you scout your location, be sure you make a realistic estimate of traffic. Do not expect the inner-city freeway to be as deserted at 7:30 Monday morning as it was at the same hour on Sunday. Some crowd situations cannot be avoided (sports events, for example), so you must work around them. Simply consider the possibilities of crowd disruption, estimate how it will affect the efforts of you and your crew, and plan accordingly.

A final word about locations. Try to leave them in better shape than you found them. Dispose of your trash properly and replace anything you moved or took down. Take only pictures, leave only footprints.

Selecting the Cast

As we do with locations, we often write our scripts with certain individuals in mind as the main characters. This simplifies our casting problems. If you haven't done this before, here are a few suggestions for your casting. Attempt to get actors and actresses who "look the part" as you have envisioned it. The actor who looks the role is more likely to be believable to the audience. This is particularly true when the age of the character is a factor. Age makeup for film is more difficult to create realistically than similar makeup for the stage. Therefore, if you need an older character, choose an older actor. Second, do not be afraid to pick amateurs for your leading roles. Movie acting, with its short takes, its stops and starts, is such a different form of acting than stage acting that many amateurs will often appear as natural as professionals. Of course, the gifted actress can provide the role with more dimensions than a beginner and still make it look natural. And the trained actor may respond to direction more readily, since he has experienced it before.

There are several places to recruit performers for your films. The local community theatres, television stations, or college theatres are all good spots. Or you can simply use your relatives, friends, and neighbors as your performers. Only a few of the people we have approached have ever declined to act in our films. In fact, most of them have been anxious to get the experience of being on the screen, and many volunteer to work in our next film.

If you plan to show your film publicly, it is a wise practice to require all persons cast in the film to sign a form similar to the Standard Release Form shown in Fig. 6-2. If you are filming on location and persons in the background become part of that scene, simple verbal permission from them will suffice.

After the film has been cast, but before any shooting is done, meet with all the actors and read through the scenario. At this time, set forth your own conceptions of the individual characters and how they relate to the total film. Encourage the actors to give their ideas too. We have found that sometimes the actors will come up with inspiring ideas that illuminate the character much better than we

```
                        Standard Release Form

     (YOUR NAME)              (YOUR ADDRESS)

                                 Date: _______________________


        I hereby give my permission to ________(Your Name)__________ ,

     his agents, successors, assigns, clients, and purchasers of his

     products to use my photograph (whether still, motion, or television)

     and recordings of my voice, and my name, in any manner whatsoever.



                         Signed      : ______________________________

                         Address     : ______________________________

                         City & State: ______________________________
```

Fig. 6-2. Standard release forms for the cast of the movie.

could. Whatever you do at this meeting, this is the time to tell the cast what the film is going to be about and how it's going to be done. Sometimes, we will even go through the blocking of a scene just to give our performers an idea of what they will have to do.

The Crew

Although the automatic nature of Super 8 cameras makes solo film making a distinct reality, help is likely to be needed at some point. We know that if we are shooting live sound, using a number of lights, or filming a complicated piece of action, we will need a crew. Some typical crews (and their tasks) are:

1. Simple silent film or sound-on-film:

   Director—Runs camera, follows script, directs action.
   Assistant—Sets up lights, runs slate, keeps log, holds microphone.

2. Scripted film with double-system sound:

   Director
   Camera Operator
   Sound Person—Handles microphone setup, monitors sound.
   Lights/slate/script

<table>
<tr><td>3. Complicated live action or documentary film.</td><td>Director
Camera Operator
Camera Assistant—For dollying, focus shifts, complex camera movements.
Sound
Grip—Does set up of lights and sound.
Lights
Slate/script/props/continuity</td></tr>
</table>

These crews are not the absolute minimums (or maximums), of course. Many film makers can do everything themselves. We did our first two films by ourselves; we even acted in the second one. One of the reasons that Hollywood film makers utilize such large specialized crews is that they are working on a tight schedule and time wasted means money lost. Time is one commodity that is plentiful for amateur film makers; therefore, you can afford to work alone and still obtain good results. However, it is convenient to have someone available to hold lights or reflectors, monitor the sound, check the scripts, fill in the log, etc.

Usually, we have selected our crews from students or from among film-making friends. If you need specialized help in lighting, sound, or what-have-you, choose someone who practices a similar skill in his own job or hobby. Technical theatre people are often very knowledgeable in both lighting and sound. Many still photographers possess substantial knowledge of lighting conditions,. lenses, and film stocks. Tv station personnel often are quite knowledgeable about camera operation and sound recording.

We have found it best to assign one person to each crew position for an entire film production. This assures consistency in each operation from day to day. But, if the person's primary purpose in working for you is to learn about all phases of film making, let him perform as many different jobs as possible. In any case, after the crew is selected, make sure each member knows his/her job and understands how much time it will entail. Let them know, too, that crew work can be tiring, tedious, and even boring, but tell them that the help (and perhaps the special skill) they provide is greatly appreciated. Be gentle with your crew. If they are not being paid, you really cannot afford to yell at them. Buy them lunch and a cool beer after a long, hot, shooting session and they will come back for more work.

The Final Organization

Planning before production is the key to good film making. Here are two final steps in organizational preparation that you should take—make a breakdown of the shooting script and draw up a shooting schedule.

The *Breakdown* is a list of the shots in the shooting script in the order in which you will actually shoot them. As you know, few films are ever shot entirely in sequence. Unless you can afford to take the time, or are able to use a different location for each successive shot (or scene), you will be better off shooting out-of-sequence, too.

The order in which you decide to film the shots can be determined by analyzing the shooting script for camera positions that can be used for more than one shot. Plan to shoot the Master Shot first, of course. Then, group the rest of the shots that will require the same, or roughly the same, camera position and lighting setup. For example, in "The Bandits," the first shot is the Master Shot of the entire scene. But the camera position for this shot will also work for Shots, 10, 11, 14, and 17. Grouping the shots in this manner will minimize camera setup time. Our Breakdown for this film reads:

BREAKDOWN FOR THE BANDITS

Camera Position	*Shot(s)*
One	Master Shot, 10, 11, 14, 17
Two	2, 9, 16
Three	3, 5, 7
Four	4, 6
Five	8
Six	12
Seven	13, 15

Notice that we put the camera position from which we take the most shots first in our Breakdown. We always schedule the most used position first. If you study the shooting script, you will also notice that we move the camera into the location by stages, with each different setup.

There is nothing formal about this list, it's just a note to yourself. Since you have already planned the camera positions in the shooting script, it is a fairly simple matter to group them in such a Breakdown.

Once the Breakdown is completed, you can devise a *Shooting Schedule* (Fig. 6-3). The Shooting Schedule is a list of times and places, scenes and shots, cast and crew, that tells you where and when each shot will be filmed, and who and what will be needed. The length and complexity of the schedule will vary with the size of the production. The cardinal rule here is to plan for enough time to allow for the careful setup and filming of each shot.

The elements which should be considered when drawing up a Shooting Schedule are:

1. The size of the cast and crew.

Shooting Schedule--Thanks a Lot, Goldie.

This schedule is adjustable according to weather and other acts of
God, but we will try to follow it as closely as possible. If we can,
we will get ahead on the MWF shooting schedule--the week-end
schedules are pretty firm, I believe. The crew and the cast
involved should meet at my office (B2) 15 minutes before the
scheduled shooting time, except for Saturday and Sunday, when you
will be needed all day. All MWF shooting will begin at 3:00 p.m.
   CREW: We will need everybody except Lights for every set-up.
Lights will be needed only in the interior shots.
   CAST: We will need you only when a scene involving you is to be
shot. Check with me or Charlie if you're not sure. You are re-
sponsible for your own costume (Cherie--can you come up with a
white nurse-type uniform and weird little cap?) Your costume should
be the same for all scenes taking place in the same "day"--and
should be appropriate for the action in that scene.

	Sequence	Scene	Shot(s)	"Day"
Wed., Sept. 29--Outside Campus Shots:	III	1	2,3	2
	III	2	4	2
Fri., Oct. 1--Interior Campus:	III	2	1,2,3, 5,6	2
Sat., Oct. 2, 8:00 a.m.--Laundromat	VIII	2	1a,1,2	13
9:30 a.m.--Interior, Lee's Apt.	VI	3	1,2,3	8
	VII	3	1,2,3,4	11
1:00 a.m.--Farmhouse	V	1	1,2,3	5
	V	2	1	5
	V	2	2,3,4,5	5
Late afternoon, Oscar's car:	VI	1	1,2,3, 4,5	7
Sun., Oct. 3, 8:00 a.m.--Supermarket	IX	1	2-6	3
	VIII	1	1-5	12
10:00--gas station:	II	1	2,2a	2
	II	1	1	2
1:00--Tony's, Interior	I	2	1-7	1
	VII	2	1	10
3:00--Hospital	X	1	1-6	15
Mon., Oct. 4--Interior, Union	IV	2	1-4	4
Wed., Oct. 6--Exterior, College Hill	I	1	2,3,4	1
Fri., Oct. 8--Interior, Sabin 102	VI	4	4	9
Sat., Oct. 9, 11:00 a.m., Their Apt.	IX	1	1	14
exterior	XI	1	2	16
1:00 p.m., Their Apt., interior	IX	1	2,3,4	14
	IX	2	1,2	15
	XII	1	1,2	16
Unscheduled as yet: Oscar's House, exterior	VI	1	1	6
Oscar & Lee in parking lot	VIII	1	1	12
Class in Sabin 102, w/Lee	VI	4	2	9

Fig. 6-3. Sample shooting schedule.

2. The locations on which the work will be done.
3. The relative skills of yourself and your crew in setup and filming.
4. Travel time to and from locations.
5. The weather.

Obtain the individual schedules of cast and crew in advance so that you can plan shooting with a minimum of inconvenience to them. Schedule the members for a block of time, such as Sunday from 9 A.M. to Noon, or all day Saturday.

Location shooting presents another scheduling problem if the location is not near by. Usually, we choose a central point of departure and plan to meet there at an appointed time. Before we leave, we explain the day's shooting. Then, we all leave together, in a minimum number of vehicles.

We choose the order of shooting locations in the same way that we picked our shooting order in the breakdown script. The first location will be the one that has the greatest number of shots or the one that is the furthest away (or most difficult to get to). That way, we get the biggest part of the work done as soon as possible. Plan to spend at least 30 minutes on setup at each new location. When you are using additional lighting, add another 15 or 20 minutes. For live-sync sound, add the same amount of time. After you have done one or two setups, you will be much better able to estimate the amount of time that you will need on future locations.

Weather can be an enormous problem to the film maker. We have had to wait as long as three weekends to film on a specific location since it rained each Sunday. Your best bet is to plan alternate interior scenes for rainy days so that you will not lose all that time. Also, it is sensible to check the long-range weather forecast. Your local airport weather service is usually the most accurate source of weather information. After the Shooting Schedule is completed, make a copy for each cast and crew member. If possible, place an assistant in charge of the schedule. This person should have all the telephone numbers of the cast and crew as well as those of the people to be contacted on location. If schedule changes have to be made, this person can handle them. If delayed while filming, be sure to call ahead to your next location to make sure they know you will be delayed. Keep to the schedule if possible; it will make film making easier for all concerned.

Film Days

Even though you have been careful to explain to cast and crew the concept of shooting out-of-sequence and have provided them with a shooting schedule, there still may be some confusion as to what *time* in the *film* a given scene actually takes place. This is especially true for actors and actresses who are used to creating a role on stage in sequence. We try to solve this problem by including a list of "film days" in our shooting schedule. "The Bandits" film we have been using as an example takes place in one "day" so there should be no confusion in anyone's mind as to when the events are taking place.

But, if we were shooting a film in which the action seemed to take place over a period of three or four days, then we would have to label those shots or scenes which correspond with the particular "day" on which they are supposed to take place. If the third scene was shot first, the cast would have to act as if the first two scenes had already taken place. These problems are part of continuity, a subject we will cover in more detail in the section on Production. Nevertheless, it is a good idea to figure out the "film days" in your script to help yourself keep track of the actual sequence of the show.

PHYSICAL PREPARATION

Now that you have the organizational details prepared, you are ready for the simpler, but equally important, task of making the physical preparations. There are two areas that require specific preparation—*equipment* and *personnel*.

Equipment

First of all, round up the equipment you are going to need. The following list is a checklist of necessary equipment. (If you are doing a very simple film, some of these items may be left out. Use your judgment).

1. Camera and tripod.
2. Sufficient film for one session of shooting.
3. Spare batteries for the camera.
4. Reflectors for sunlight fill-in.
5. Lens-cleaning tissue and cleaner.
6. Brushes for cleaning camera, swabs for cleaning film gate.
7. Tape measure.
8. Lighting instruments with correct color-temperature lamps.
9. Spare lamps, for Item 8.
10. Heavy-duty (14-gauge) 3-wire extension cords with three-prong adaptors.
11. Circuit tester for checking outlets.
12. Light meter.
13. Small tool kit, including hammer, nails, pliers, soldering iron, knife, screwdriver, adjustable wrench, C-clamps, electrical tape, and solder.

14. Masking tape, gaffers tape, and carpet tape.
15. Notebook for keeping shooting log.
16. Slate or chalkboard.
17. Marking pens.
18. Props and costumes.
19. Sound equipment, including tape recorder(s), sync cables, microphone(s), mike boom, mike stand, mike extension cables, and tape or magnetic film.
20. Still camera loaded with color-print film, or a color "instant" camera.
21. Small first-aid kit.

Some of these items are so obvious that they need no explanation. Others require a bit of explaining since they might seen unnecessary. For instance, many Super 8 film makers are used to going to the corner store and buying another cartridge of film when the first one runs out. That is okay if you're shooting at home. But, if you are any distance at all from a town, it is a real waste of time to have to hold up the shooting while someone goes for film. And, if you are using something other than Ektachrome G or Kodachrome 40, the local store may not even stock it. Buy your film in bulk and take enough along to cover each day's shooting.

The same argument can be made for stocking spare batteries. Most Super 8 cameras use AA batteries in groups of 2, 4, or 6. We have found that these batteries will last through about 25 cartridges of film. But we usually replace them after shooting 20 cartridges in silent cameras and after shooting 10 cartridges in sound-on-film cameras. That way we are assured of getting the correct running speed on every cartridge and, consequently, the best exposure and sound quality, too. Carry spare batteries.

We always carry two tape measures, a 10-foot pocket tape for use with close shots and a 100-foot reel-type tape for use with long shots. The camera person carries the shorter tape while the other is carried in the tool box. The longer one has come in very handy when we wanted to plot depth of field at a certain focus setting.

Spare lamps are probably more essential than spare batteries. Most lamps, especially the tungsten-halogen variety, do not give much notice before they burn out. Incandescent lamps do darken somewhat before they go but even that is not a reliable indicator. We like to carry a minimum of one spare lamp for every three we have in use. Also, we try to bring one extension cord for every two lighting instruments on the theory that one light will always be closer to the regular outlet than the other.

We always slate our shots in production. We have found that this practice makes it easier to identify the shots on the editing bench. We have a regular slate but a chalkboard or any other erasable surface will do fine.

A still camera is very handy for taking pictures of setups, backgrounds, placement of props or persons within a scene, or as a record of dress and costume for continuity purposes. Use print film instead of slide film so you will be able to carry the prints around easily. (We sometimes use a Polaroid camera which serves the same purpose.)

Once you have all the equipment assembled, check it out thoroughly. Clean the camera lens, the film chamber, and the battery contacts. Check the batteries on a reliable battery tester (even if they are new). Make sure all your tripod and light stands work smoothly and lock positively. Try all the lighting and sound equipment before you leave home. Nothing is more aggravating than to arrive on location only to discover that an extension cord is shorted out or that the tape recorder will not record. When you have finished your checkout, pack everything carefully in carrying cases.

Personnel Preparation

There are three parts to personnel preparation—preparing the cast, preparing the crew, and preparing yourself. You only need to spend a little time on these preparations to make your film making go smoothly.

First, give everyone a copy of the shooting schedule. Make sure that they note when they are supposed to be someplace, where that place is, and how long they will be there. We usually have one mass meeting with the cast and crew to explain the shooting schedule and to discuss any problems any one of them might have with it.

Next, meet with the cast separately and read through the script. At this time set forth your concept of the film (and of the individual characters). Encourage the cast to think about what they are going to be doing when they play that role, and remind them to learn their lines. This is also a good time to discuss how each shot is going to be set up and how the actors might be blocked. Be sure to give each cast member a copy of the script with his or her part marked out.

It is a good idea to go through the script with the crew as well. But, it is more important that they know what their assignment is and how they should do it. We have found that it is simpler to assign a task or a series of tasks to one person and have that person do those jobs for the entire production. That way you only have to explain the job once or twice before you start filming. After that, the person will be repeating the actions a number of times and, hopefully, getting better each time.

Put each crew member in charge of a specific piece(s) of equipment, especially those pieces they work with. Giving them this responsibility means you will not have to worry about whether or not the lights were taken down at the last interior shot. Someone on the crew will make certain they were, as it will have been part of his job.

Your job in all this is to coordinate the work of your cast and crew. In addition to your copy of the shooting schedule, you should have a list of the telephone numbers of your cast and crew. In case there is any change in the schedule, you can notify them at once. You should arrange the transportation for your group. But don't insist on driving. You have more important things to do.

SECTION III

Production

CHAPTER 7

Concepts and Techniques

There are several concepts and techniques that you should understand before you start actual film production. These concepts are Composition, Depth of Field, Exposure, and Blocking. The techniques are Focusing, Lighting, and Sound Recording. Some of these concepts have been defined in previous chapters and several of these techniques were touched on during our discussion of the tools of film making. But, because they all relate directly to film production, we will review them and expand on some. Thus, your knowledge and understanding of these techniques will be complete.

THE COMPOSITION CONCEPT

The basic elements of composition (line, mass, and space) and the rules of composition (balance and harmony) apply to motion pictures just as they apply to other visual media. The major difference between movies and the other forms is that movies can show movement while the others can only imply it.

There are four basic shot compositions in film making—the Static Camera-Static Subject shot, the Static Camera-Moving Subject shot, the Moving Camera–Static Subject shot and the Moving Camera-Moving Subject shot. All of these shots are limited by the same two factors, *field of view* and *camera angle*.

Field of View

The field of view, or the frame in which you will compose the shot, is determined by two things—the focal length of the lens being used, and the distance of the camera from the subject.

Each focal-length lens has its own *angle of acceptance*. This is the area that the lens "sees." The rule is that the shorter the focal length, the wider the angle of acceptance and the longer the focal length, the narrower the angle of acceptance (Fig. 7-1). This angle of

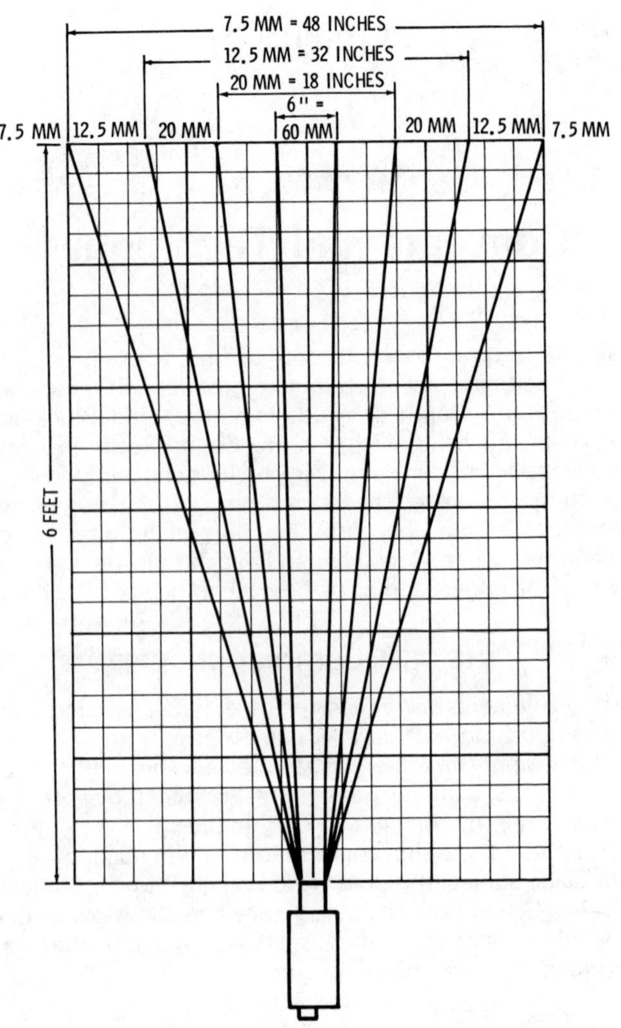

Fig. 7-1. The "angle of acceptance" varies with the focal length.

acceptance, when set at a specific distance from the subject creates what we call the *field of view*. A given focal-length lens will have various fields of view at various distances from the subject. This can readily be seen if you halve the distance that is shown in Fig. 7-1. (For example, a 7.5-mm lens has a field of view of about 26 inches at 3 feet.)

The field of view is expressed in terms of camera distance from the subject (closeup, medium shot, long shot). This is because in the olden days, when movie cameras had only fixed focal-length lenses, and there were not many different focal lengths available, changes in the field of view were effected by moving the camera toward or away from the subject. With modern zoom lens cameras, this situation has changed. Now, we often zoom in for a closeup shot or zoom out for a long shot while our camera-to-subject distance remains the same. However, just because we tend to change the field of view by using these variable focal-length lenses should not keep us from remembering that there are still two ways to change the field of view—changing the focal length and changing the distance from subject to camera.

There is a difference, however, between the field of view obtained by zooming in for a closeup and the field of view obtained by moving the camera in close for a closeup. The fields will be the same size but they will look different. Any field of view that is obtained by zooming the camera lens, whether to telephoto or to wide angle, changes the perspective of the field more than does the same size field of view that is obtained by using a normal focal-length lens (12.5 mm) and moving the camera. Zooming to a telephoto shot, for example, makes the field of view look compressed (Fig. 7-2). There is less apparent distance between the foreground, subject, and back-ground. A zoom to a wide-angle shot gives the opposite appearance; there appears to be much more distance (than actually exists) between the foreground, the subject, and the background (Fig. 7-3).

Is it better to use a normal focal-length lens and move the camera to get a certain field of view, or is it better to vary the focal length of the zoom lens, without moving the camera, to get the same effect? If your concern is for a "normal" look in the shot, moving the camera is the best solution. You will find, however, that the changes in perspective, caused by zooming within the range of focal lengths that are close to normal (9 mm-20 mm), are so slight that they will go unnoticed by you and your audience.

The distortion that accompanies extreme telephoto and extreme wide-angle focal lengths can be used to advantage. The long focal length appears to flatten the subject against the background. This can be used to deemphasize the importance of the subject or, in a shot with a subject moving toward or away from the camera, it can make it look like the subject is not making any progress. The extreme wide-angle shot appears to make the subject stand out from the background. This could be useful for isolating the subject from the scene or, with the same kind of moving subject, allow the subject to appear to move a great distance in just a few steps. Personally, we have found ourselves using the normal and wide-angle focal lengths more and more often. The telephoto is good for extreme closeups, handy when we cannot get close to our subject, and fun to play with,

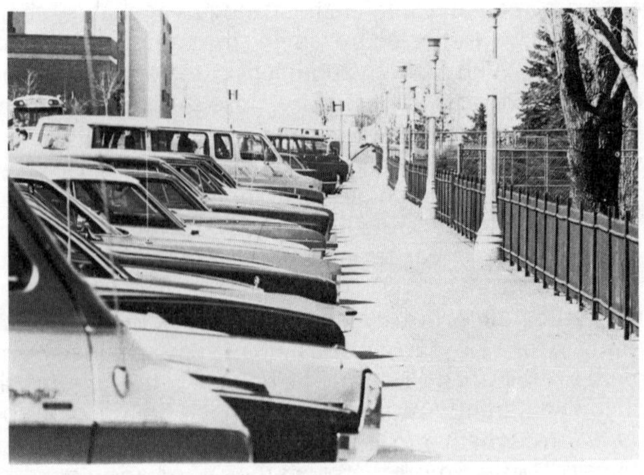

Fig. 7-2. Long focal lengths appear to compress distance.

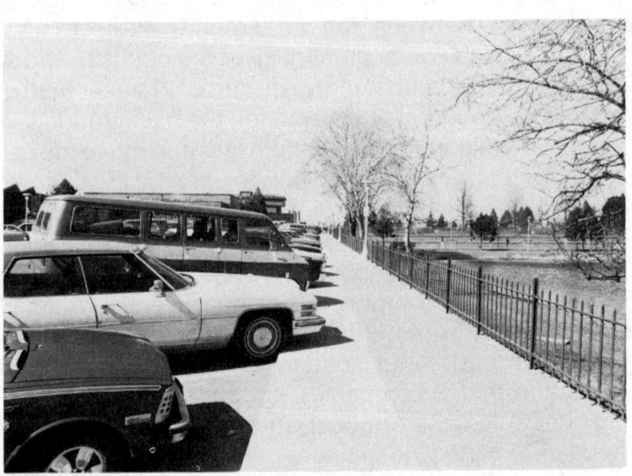

Fig. 7-3. Depth exaggeration of a wide-angle shot.

but we have come to prefer the shorter focal-length lenses for much of our shooting.

What size field of view should you have for each shot? The general rule is that the long shot is used for giving the whole picture (the Master Shot). The medium shot is often used to add details that we cannot see in the longer shot, details like expressions on faces and closer looks at settings or backgrounds. The closeup is commonly used to point up subtleties of expression, small details, and emotional reactions.

When you planned your script, you visualized the story in a series of shots, and you planned your shots with specific fields of view in mind. On location, check these concepts against the realities of the situation and adjust your fields of view accordingly. Just remember that each field of view should give the audience the exact information that you want them to have about that shot.

You will have noticed, too, that the change in field size also causes a relative change in figure size as long as the subject to camera distance stays the same. This is an inverse relationship, the larger the field of view, the smaller the size of the figure, and vice-versa. Your choice of field of view might ultimately depend on how much of the subject you want us to see, or how much you want the subject to dominate the picture.

Camera Angle

When we visualize a shot for purposes of drawing the storyboard or for blocking the action, we usually think of it in terms of the position of the camera with regard to the field of view. This positioning is called the *camera angle*, and it is the way we look at the field of view. Our choice of camera angle is controlled by our *point of view,* or rather by the point of view we want the audience to have in the shot.

A point of view has two aspects—*objective* and *subjective*. The objective point of view is the one used most often by film makers. It is the all-seeing observer viewpoint, the one that enables the audience to know more about the film (the plot) than anyone in it. The subjective point of view is that of a person in the film. By their nature, subjective point of view objects are limited in what they are able to see; consequently, they are less reliable indicators of what is "really" happening. They are valuable, however, in letting us see things the way that the characters might see them. In film production, it is possible to change from an objective point of view to a subjective point of view and back again, from shot to shot. In practice, it is advisable to make a broad use of the objective point of view and a sparing use of the subjective point of view, since the objective point of view is somewhat easier for the audience to relate to and understand. In addition, the subjective point of view often does not look as "real" to the screen audience as the objective point of view does.

The term, camera angle, probably comes from the discovery that a picture could be more revealing or more expressive (and, therefore, more interesting), if photographed at some angle to an axis instead of from a straight-on view. In a two-dimensional medium like photography, shooting pictures from a camera position off the axis to the subject lends depth to what is otherwise a flat image. Camera angles can make the action appear more dynamic, they can allow the shot to convey more information about what is going on (both on and off screen), and they can make the shot more interesting visually. Camera angles also expand the point of view when used with (intercut with) other camera angles of the same subject.

Camera angles are expressed as arrangements of the camera on the horizontal and vertical planes in relation to the subject. In describing each of these angles, we relate them to the direction in which the subject is facing or to the direction in which the action is moving. Common angles on the horizontal plane are the straight-on angle, the side view, and the quartering angle (Fig. 7-4). Each angle reveals a different facet of the subject. The quartering angle is the most versatile of these three as it can be almost any angle between the straight-on view and the side view (which is 90° to the subject). On the vertical plane, there also are three commonly used angles—the high angle (where the camera looks down on the subject), the eye-level angle (where the camera is the same level as the subject), and the low angle (where the camera looks up at the subject). High angles give the most godlike views, and low angles are the more menacing views.

The so-called *reverse angle* is merely the opposite side of any previous camera angle. It means the camera is now looking at the field of view from the other side of the frame, and is looking at the previous camera position.

Through repeated use, and because of our acceptance of visual conventions, certain camera angles have become associated with certain kinds of meanings and emotions. Here are some general rules about the application of camera angles to different shots.

> *Horizontal plane*—Straight-on angle shots, especially those taken from eye level, tend to be the dullest picture visually and the weakest dynamically. These angle's are popular for I.D. photos and are about as flattering. Camera angles that are perpendicular to the action (side views) tend to make the action look like it is moving faster. They are good for chase scenes. Quartering angles (Fig. 7-6) tend to create and

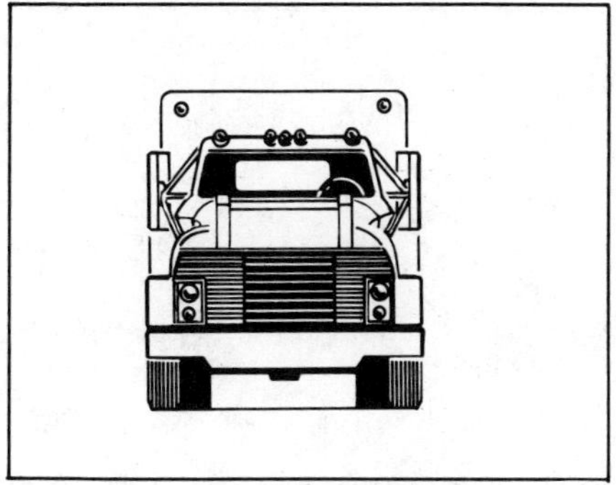

(A) Straight-on view.

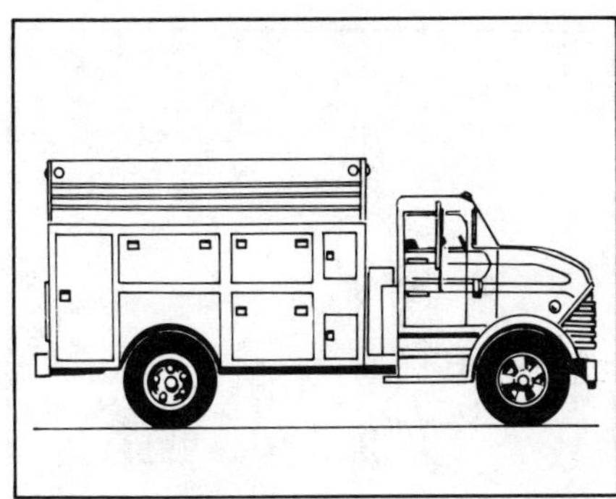

(B) Side view.

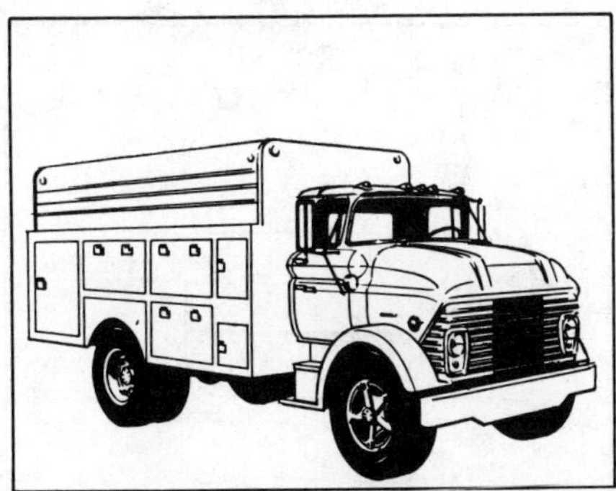

(C) Quartering view.

Fig. 7-4. Camera angles on the horizontal plane.

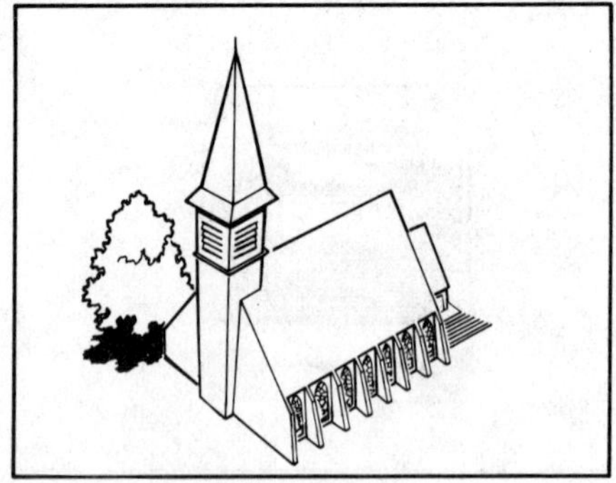

(A) High-angle view.

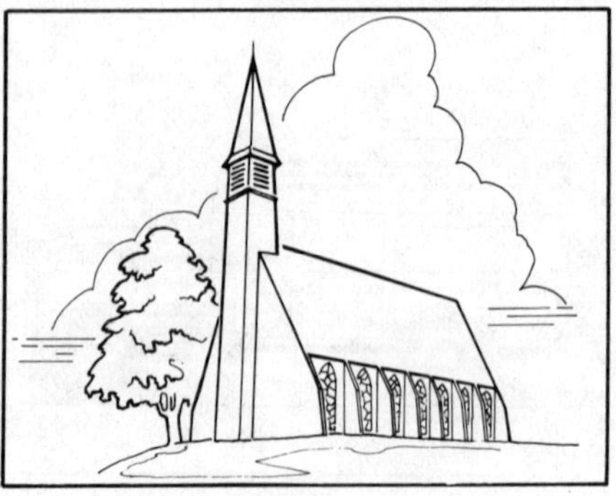

(B) Low-angle view.

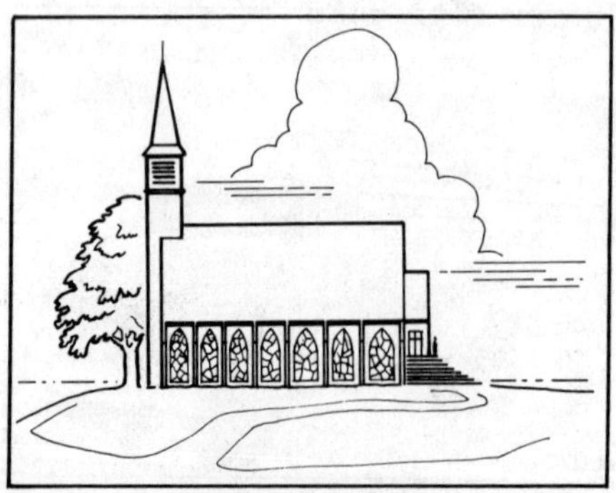

(C) Eye-level view.

Fig. 7-5. Vertical plane camera angles.

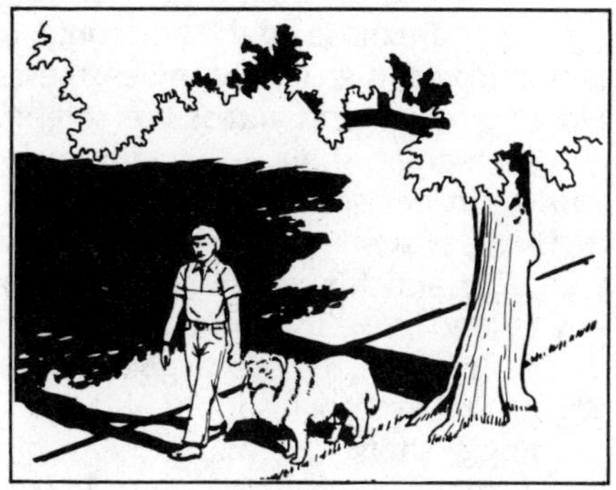

(A) High level.

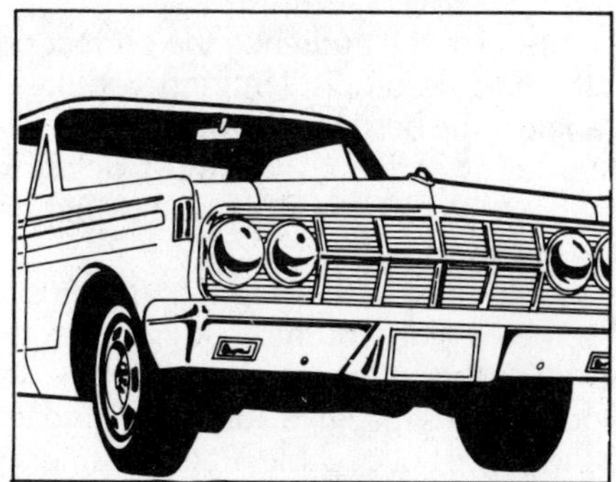

(B) Low level.

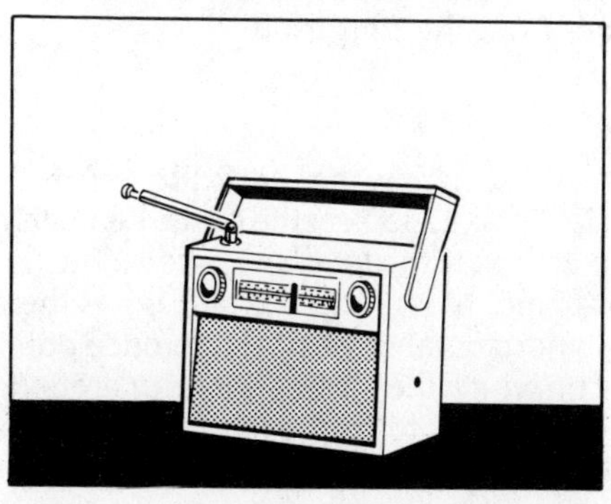

(C) Eye level.

Fig. 7-6. Quartering angles.

enhance the feeling of depth in the frame. The most interesting angles are those *off* the horizontal or vertical axis. When combined with high or low angles, these off-axis angles create dynamic movement across the screen.

Vertical plane—High-angle shots, especially of long shots, give more information per shot than do eye-level or low-angle shots. High-angle shots are good for Master Shots, for showing groups, and for following the action on a broad scale. They tend to make the subject(s) look smaller and less powerful. Eye-level angles are a good "normal" point of view. They are fine for conversations and other more intimate shots. Low-angle shots can make the subject look more powerful and menacing. In action shots, low angles make the action appear almost overwhelming.

How does one choose the best camera angles for the field of view? Here are three suggestions:

1. The angle must give the audience the correct point of view. If you want them to be omniscient and godlike, then the most revealing angle is the best one. If you want the shot to appear in a subjective point of view, you must determine where the character whose eyes you are "using" would be in relation to that field of view.
2. The angle should present the action in the most dynamic way. Since the screen is flat, you must suggest depth by the use of angles and, since the action takes place in two dimensions, you should choose angles that give additional impact to the action.
3. The angle should be believeable. Put the camera where it needs to be. Although the audience will probably accept almost any camera angle, don't use an angle just for the sake of using the angle. This will only call attention to your camera placement and detract from the film itself.

Composition

Now that we have seen how the shot is limited (by field of view and camera angle), let us take a look at the basic elements of composition before we try to compose the four basic shots. The three elements of composition are Line, Mass, and Space. *Line* is the element that is used to establish horizontal or vertical reference points in the frame. It is the element on which the masses are set or around which they are grouped. Line is also used to set the limits of the frame and to define the foreground and background. *Mass* is another name for the objects with which you compose within the frame. Mass can be a single object, a group of objects, or any combination of the two. Mass may be entirely contained within the frame or it may be only partially in it.

Space is the area around the mass(es). It can also refer to any area of indistinct visual appearance, i.e., a background.

In an attempt to create balance and harmony in pictorial composition, certain rules have evolved for the use of each of these elements. The rules for Line (Fig. 7-7) are:

1. Horizons should be parallel with the bottom of the frame if the camera angle permits. Where no actual horizon line exists, one can be implied by the horizontal or vertical aspect of the mass(es) in the frame. If a vertical line is used to imply a horizon, it should be parallel to the side of the frame.
2. The function of the frame line is to separate the actual field of view from the rest of what is there. The frame line may be used to contain the action or to allow it to spill out of the frame.
3. Foreground lines add depth to the shot but place a visual barrier on the near side of the frame.
4. Background lines also add depth as well as providing a sense of perspective to the frame (and place a limit to the far side of the frame).

The rules for Mass are divided into two parts, those that deal with the size and those that deal with placement. The rules of *size* are:

1. The relative size of the mass(es) in the frame is determined by the field of view. For a given camera-to-subject distance, a wide-angle field of view will allow the large frame to dominate

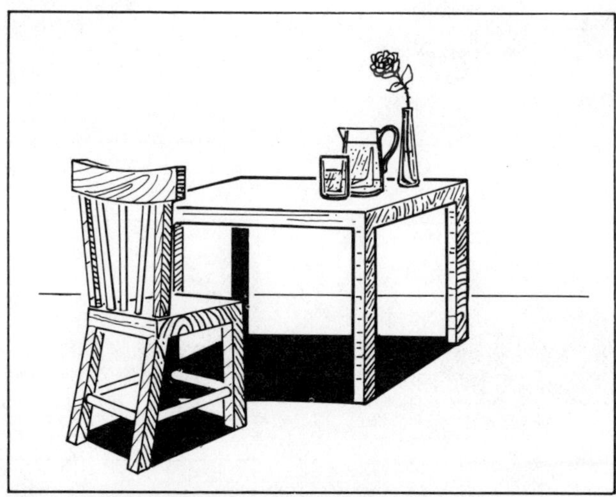

Fig. 7-7. There should either be a recognizable horizontal line or a vertical reference to help establish one.

the mass. A telephoto field of view will allow the same mass to dominate the small frame.
2. The larger the mass, the larger the field of view will have to be to show it effectively.
3. If the mass fills the field of view, it becomes both the mass and the space around it (or both foregound and background).

Once the mass size is determined, the mass must be arranged and balanced in relation to the frame. Thus, the rules of *placement* (Fig. 7-8) are then considered. To make a balanced composition, arrange the masses harmoniously. To increase tension, leave the composition unbalanced.

1. The bulk of large masses should be placed in the lower half of the frame to avoid the top-heavy look.
2. A single mass looks better when placed slightly off-center rather than when placed directly in the middle of the frame.
3. Masses may be placed partially in or partially out of the frame.
4. The location of large masses should be balanced by the opposite placement of small masses in a teeter-totter fashion.

Space refers to the area (Fig. 7-9) in the frame surrounding the mass(es). The general rules regarding space are simple:

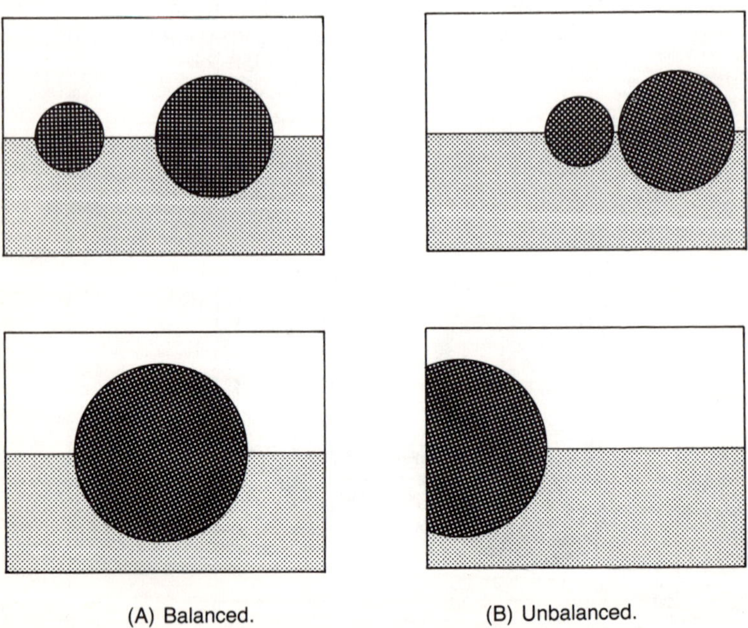

(A) Balanced.   (B) Unbalanced.

Fig. 7-8. Rules for placement.

1. Mass should not appear cramped by lack of space at the side or at the top of the frame.
2. There should be breathing space or moving space in the frame around the mass. More space should be allowed on the side of the frame toward which the mass is facing or in the direction in which the mass will move.
3. Space can be used to balance mass in the same way that mass can be used to balance mass.
4. Space can function as mass. When the field of view is so large

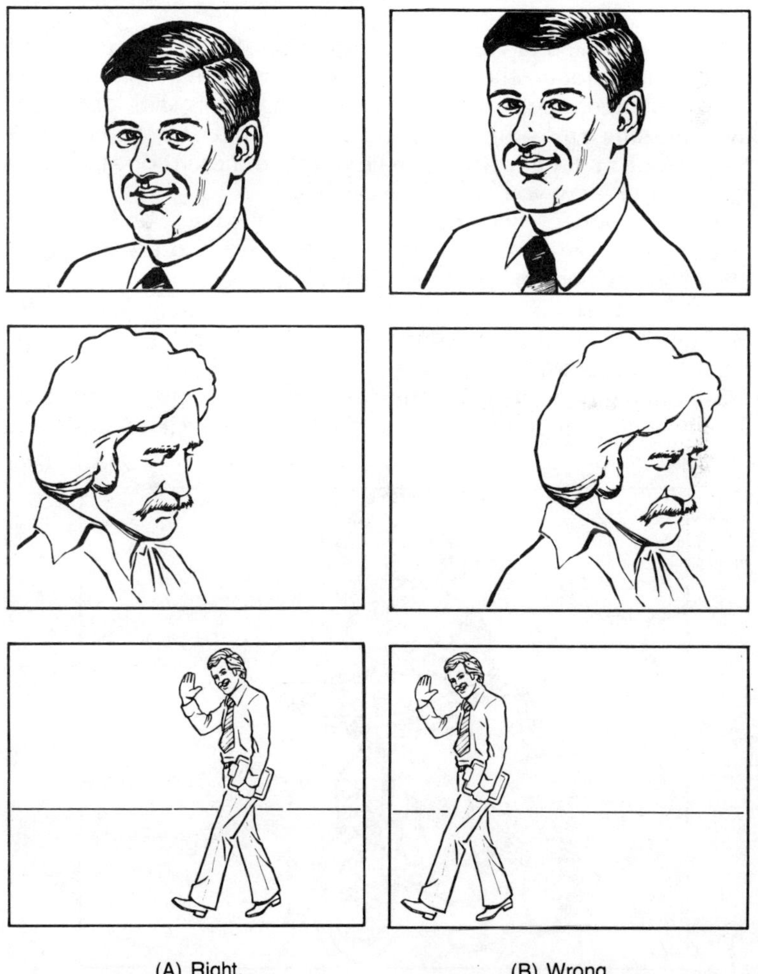

(A) Right.   (B) Wrong.

Fig. 7-9. Allow room for the subject to move about in.

and the relative size of the mass so small, the space itself becomes the dominant mass.

Composing the Shots

There are four basic shot compositions that you can use in your film making.

Static Camera-Static Subject—In many ways, this may seem to be the easiest shot composition, but because of its static nature, the audience will pay more attention to the elements of composition in this shot and will probably be more critical of their arrangement (Fig. 7-10).

Choose the field of view that gives the best figure size. Now find the best frame for that field. Next, pick a camera angle that will give some feeling of depth and one that will make this shot look more dynamic. Since the subjective point of view is often expressed in this type of shot, be certain that the angle you have chosen corresponds to the point of view you want to establish.

Place the horizon line near the middle of the frame and level the picture. If no horizon is visible, you might want to use a vertical object somewhere in the frame as a visual indication of "level." Place the masses in the field of view so that they look naturally positioned. Do not squeeze them against the edge of the frame. Give them head room and breathing room.

If the foreground seems particularly prominent, place objects at the lower edge or at the bottom of the frame to break up this area.

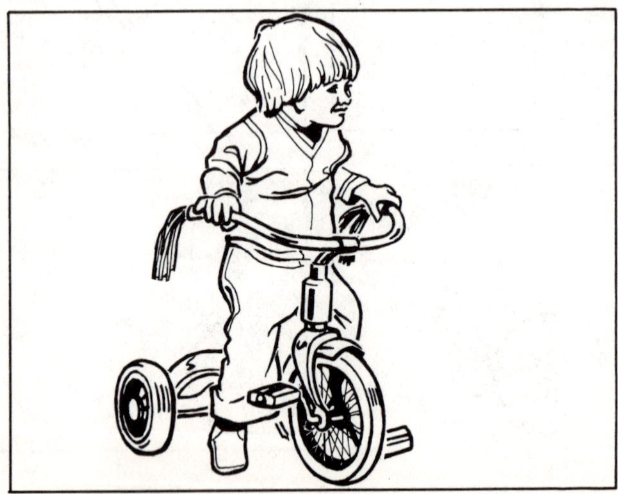

Fig. 7-10. A static camera/static subject composition.

These foreground objects, which will often be out of focus, will also enhance the illusion of depth in the shot.

Static Camera-Moving Subject—Here the problems of space and balance are compounded by the movement within the frame (Fig. 7-11). But by a careful choice of field of view and of camera angle, these and other problems can be overcome.

First, the field of view must be large enough to contain the majority of the movement. The camera angle can be either high or low but it should be off-axis to the movement since this will create a more dynamic picture. (Remember that a corner-to-corner movement looks more like action on the screen than does a movement from side to side.) Also, if you use a straight-on angle shot to the action, the figure size in the shot will vary greatly with a relatively small movement of the subject.

Try to have the movement in this shot go with the lines in the picture, not against them. At the beginning of the shot, give the subject some space to move into. Try to keep the composition as balanced as possible even though the major mass(es) may be moving.

Moving Camera-Static Subject—This kind of shot is a little more complicated since both the camera angle and the field of view can change at the same time. Pans, tilts, and trucking shots all alter the camera angle in some way, while dolly shots and zooms change the field of view. (The zoom, of course, is not a moving camera shot. The camera remains stationary while the elements inside the lens move.

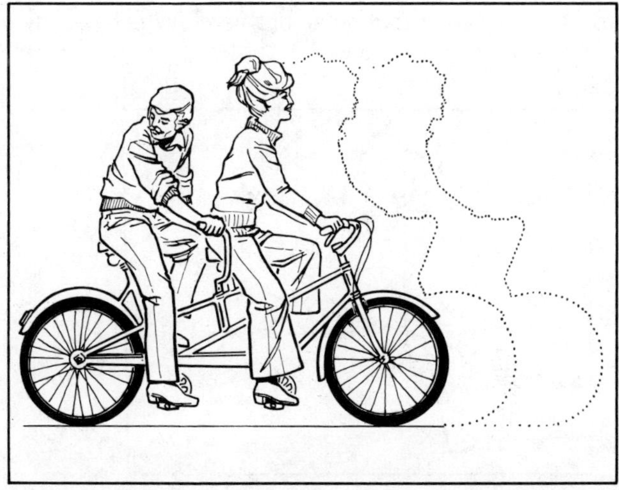

Fig. 7-11. A static camera/moving subject composition.

But, we will deal with its composition problems and possibilities in this section.) Since the field of view and the angle can change, compose for the end of the shot and keep the subject framed (Fig. 7-12).

There are two compositional difficulties with pans—the extreme angles one might encounter at the start and finish of the pan, and the problems of keeping the camera level. The first may be overcome, to some degree, by having your subject or the action be at the same distance from the camera throughout the arc of the pan (see Fig. 7-12). This can be done by careful camera placement. If this proves impossible, then, panning from a near object to a far one, or vice versa, would be the next best solution. The second problem can be compensated for by changing the level of the tripod during the actual pan. In pans of short arcs (less than 30 degrees), this "level" problem is of little consequence.

In both pans and trucking shots, there should be sufficient space around the mass(es) at the beginning and at the end of the shot. These start and finish compositions of moving shots should be as carefully arranged as are static camera shots. The tilt shot has the same camera angle problems that the pan shot has only they are in a different plane. The solution is the same; make sure that the distance of the subject(s) from the camera remains roughly the same throughout the arc of the camera movement. Do not try to imitate the movements of the eye too closely when using moving camera shots. Even though they may be realistic eye movements, excessive panning and tilting will look "mannered" on the movie screen. (The head-to-toe glance is very difficult to show naturally.)

The dolly shot has a particular problem. When you move the camera toward or away from the subject, the camera angle is

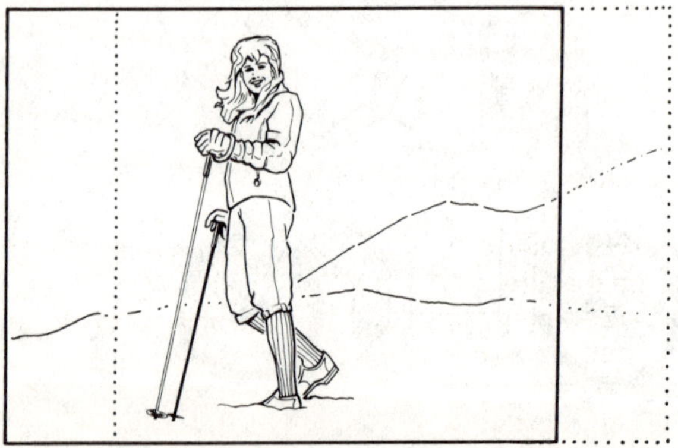

Fig. 7-12. A moving camera/static subject composition.

constantly changing as the field of view decreases or increases. This means that the relationships of the masses within the field of view are also changing. The best you can do here is to compose for the end of the shot. Keep the masses balanced and maintain an adequate space around the subject.

Although they both alter the field of view, the zoom shot differs from the dolly shot in that the zoom shot does not change the camera angle. Instead, it selects a section of the field of view and concentrates on it (zoom in), or shows us the field surrounding the original field of view (zoom out). As we observed earlier, zooming does cause some apparent changes. Zooming in appears to compress the subject against the background while zooming out does the opposite. The altering of the field of view may also contribute to this compression; as the size of the field decreases, the frame may "compress" the subject. The zoom out could effect a similar expansion.

Some of the composition problems that come with this field of view change are like those of the dolly shot. You should compose for the end of the zoom shot, using space and balancing your picture as you would a static shot. Although dolly shots accomplish the same field of view change as the zoom shots, the zoom shot is probably more versatile for rapid and radical changes in the amount of space that surrounds the subject or the action. And, the zoom shot does not have the camera angle changes to deal with that the dolly shot does.

Moving Camera-Moving Subject—This can be the most difficult shot composition since the field size, figure size, and camera angle might all be changing at the same time. Framing is critical here (Fig. 7-13) and, also, you should try to maintain a sense of horizon. In this shot, the main concern should be to keep the action within the frame. The field of view is not as important as long as it encompasses the space around the subject.

For the sake of audience orientation, keep the horizon as level as you can. This is especially important in dolly and trucking shots. Use space carefully to keep from "crowding" the subjects or the action. "Lead" the subjects within the frame in pan shots and give them room to move into in trucking shots.

Zooming shots offer some unique possibilities in this type of shot. Zooming with the direction of the action causes it to appear to slow down or stall. Zooming against the direction of the action will make it appear to speed up. For example, if you zoom out as a person is walking toward the camera, the apparent progress of that person will be slowed. On the other hand, if you zoom in while the actors are walking toward the camera, they will appear to close the distance very rapidly.

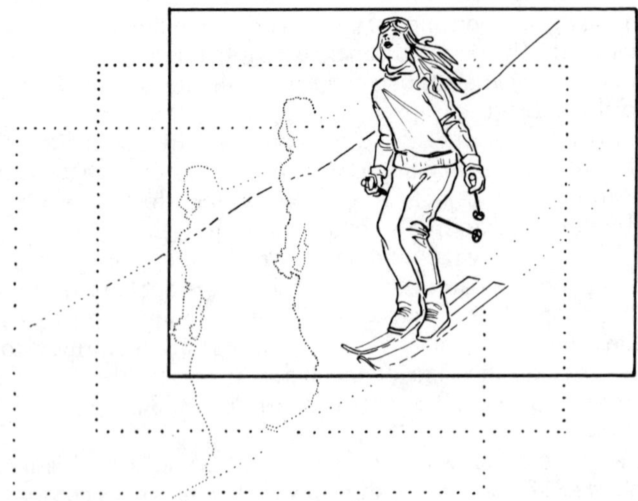

Fig. 7-13. A moving camera/moving subject composition.

Conclusion

The rules and suggestions we have given you in this section are not absolutes, of course. It might be possible to violate all of them and still produce an understandable movie of some charm and beauty. But, you must know the rules before you can break them creatively. Learning to compose motion-picture shots quickly and artfully is not difficult. It just takes time and practice.

FOCUSING AND DEPTH OF FIELD

With any lens, except a fixed-focus lens, there is an adjustment on the lens barrel that is used to allow an object (located at a distance in front of the camera) to be put in focus with the film plane of the camera. This adjustment is called the focus ring. For every object-to-film plane distance, there is a particular focus setting. This setting is called the hyperfocal distance. It varies with the focal length of the lens, the f/stop, and, of course, the camera-to-subject distance.

Focusing

The actual focusing of a Super 8 camera with a zoom lens is quite simple. After you have composed your shot, pick your focus point (the object that should be in the sharpest focus). Then, zoom in to full telephoto (the longest focal length on the zoom ring), and turn the focus ring until that object comes into focus in the viewfinder. Now you can zoom out to the desired field of view. Because you have focused at the longest focal length of the zoom lens (where the focus is the most critical), your subject/object will be in focus at any other focal length in the zoom range.

This choice of focus setting works fine if the camera-to-subject distance remains the same throughout the shot. And, it provides an adequate solution for those shots in which only one subject or object needs to be in focus. But what happens if the subject moves toward the camera or the camera moves away from the subject? And, what should be the *object of focus* if both the subject and the background must be sharply focused?

Depth of Field

The answer to these problems lies in the concept of *depth of field*. Depth of field is the invisible area ahead of and behind a given focusing point. In this area, the subject appears to be in focus even though it is closer than (or farther away than) the actual focusing distance. This field exists around *all* focusing points. Its spread of coverage is roughly one-third in front of the focusing point and two-thirds behind it.

Depth of field is affected by three things—the focal length of the lens, the size of the aperture (f/stop), and the focusing distance of the camera (i.e., the focus point). Focal length works in an inverse relationship here; the longer the focal length, the shallower the depth of field, and the shorter the focal length, the greater the depth of field. The inverse relationship applies to f/stops and depth of field combinations, too. Larger apertures give shallower depths of field than do smaller apertures. On the other hand, the relationship of focusing distance to depth of field is a regular one. The closer the focus point, the shallower the depth of field, and vice-versa.

Since computation of depth of field involves these three variables in a rather complex relationship, we usually figure depth of field from prepared tables. Depth of Field Tables 7-1 through 7-7 cover most apertures and focal lengths, and they are scaled for the distances at which you will most likely be shooting with your Super 8 camera.

How To Use Depth of Field Tables

After you have set up the camera, and determined the field of view and the camera angle, focus on the subject or object that you want to be most prominent in this shot. Now note three things: the focal length of the lens (in mm, read the zoom ring), the focusing distance (in feet or meters, read the focus ring), and the aperture size (in f/stops, read the camera light meter). In the depth of field tables, find the focal-length lens table that corresponds closest to the focal-length setting just recorded. Look down the left-hand side of that table to find the focusing distance closest to the distance the camera is set for.

Go across on that line to the f/stop column that matches the f/stop displayed on the camera meter. The "From" and "To" boxes (on the distance line) in that column will give the depth of field for the shot that you have set up.

For example, if our focal length is 32 mm, our focusing distance is 10 feet, and our f/stop is f/4, our depth of field would have a From distance of 8 feet 6 inches and a To distance of 12 feet 2 inches. These distances are approximate, of course, but they are accurate enough to allow planning for movement of the subject or the camera within a 3-foot range before the subject or object would go out of focus. Actually, if the subject moved out of the Depth of Field, nearer than 3 feet 6 inches or farther than 12 feet 2 inches from the camera, it would not go abruptly out of focus. The From and To distances indicate the limits of sharp focus. After passing these points, the subject would go gradually out of focus. (Any "limiting" markers could have been used instead of From and To. For example, the markers Near and Far are used in Table 7-8 to designate the depth of field limits.)

Perhaps when we did our computation, our tables did not include a table for a 32-mm focal-length lens. Since we know that longer focal lengths have shallower depths of field, we would choose the next longer focal length of 36 mm (Table 7-8), thereby ensuring that if we erred, it would be on the side of caution. Also, say we were shooting at 9 feet. Since 9 feet was not a distance on the 36-mm table, we have to find a focusing distance that is close to 9 feet to continue our computation. We chose the next longer distance setting, which was 10 feet. This choice would seem to contradict our previous line of reasoning. You know that the greater the focusing distance, the greater the depth of field. If we could not find the exact focusing distance on the table, we should seemingly go to the next *shorter* focusing distance to be sure to not underestimate our depth of field. However, our thinking in this situation is that if the focusing distance is *1 foot or less* than the next higher number on the distance scale, we can use that *higher number* for our computation. If the focusing distance is *more* than 1 foot away from the next higher number on the scale, go to the next *lower number* on the scale and use that line in your computation.

Once we have the correct table and distance line chosen, it is easy to find the f/stop column and note the depth of field. If we had an f/stop reading that was not on our depth of field tables, we would have reverted to our first rule—err on the side of caution. Pick the next lower f/stop on the scale (a larger aperture will give less depth of field), and compute from there. The same rule applies if the camera light meter does not stop exactly on one of the f/stop markings. Read it as the next lower f/stop and you will be all right.

Table 7-1. Depth of Field Table (Focal Length = 8 mm)

Focusing Distance		f/1.2	f/1.4	f/2	f/2.8	f/4	f/5.6	f/8	f/11	f/16	f/22	f/32	f/45
5 feet	From	3.47	3.32	2.92	2.49	2.06	1.66	1.30	0.99	0.74	0.55	0.40	0.29
	To	8.88	10.04	17.27	∞	∞	∞	∞	∞	∞	∞	∞	∞
7 feet	From	4.33	4.10	3.50	2.90	2.33	1.83	1.40	1.05	0.78	0.57	0.41	0.29
	To	18.10	23.69	∞	∞	∞	∞	∞	∞	∞	∞	∞	∞
10 feet	From	5.32	4.98	4.12	3.31	2.59	1.98	1.49	1.10	0.80	0.58	0.42	0.30
	To	81.41	∞	∞	∞	∞	∞	∞	∞	∞	∞	∞	∞
15 feet	From	6.47	5.96	4.77	3.72	2.84	2.12	1.56	1.14	0.82	0.59	0.42	0.30
	To	∞	∞	∞	∞	∞	∞	∞	∞	∞	∞	∞	∞
20 feet	From	7.25	6.62	5.18	3.97	2.98	2.20	1.61	1.16	0.83	0.60	0.42	0.30
	To	∞	∞	∞	∞	∞	∞	∞	∞	∞	∞	∞	∞
30 feet	From	8.25	7.44	5.67	4.25	3.13	2.28	1.65	1.18	0.85	0.60	0.43	0.30
	To	∞	∞	∞	∞	∞	∞	∞	∞	∞	∞	∞	∞
∞	From	11.37	9.89	6.99	4.94	3.49	2.47	1.74	1.23	0.87	0.61	0.43	0.30
	To	∞	∞	∞	∞	∞	∞	∞	∞	∞	∞	∞	∞

Table 7-2. Depth of Field Table (Focal Length = 10 mm)

Focusing Distance		f/1.2	f/1.4	f/2	f/2.8	f/4	f/5.6	f/8	f/11	f/16	f/22	f/32	f/45
5 feet	From	3.90	3.78	3.43	3.04	2.62	2.18	1.77	1.40	1.07	0.81	0.60	0.44
	To	6.94	7.36	9.16	13.97	54.57	∞	∞	∞	∞	∞	∞	∞
7 feet	From	5.02	4.82	4.27	3.68	3.07	2.49	1.97	1.52	1.14	0.85	0.62	0.45
	To	11.51	12.73	19.28	70.67	∞	∞	∞	∞	∞	∞	∞	∞
10 feet	From	6.40	6.08	5.23	4.36	3.54	2.79	2.15	1.62	1.20	0.88	0.64	0.46
	To	22.78	28.12	112.84	∞	∞	∞	∞	∞	∞	∞	∞	∞
15 feet	From	8.14	7.62	6.33	5.10	4.01	3.07	2.31	1.71	1.25	0.90	0.65	0.46
	To	95.21	464.78	∞	∞	∞	∞	∞	∞	∞	∞	∞	∞
20 feet	From	9.41	8.72	7.07	5.58	4.29	3.24	2.40	1.76	1.28	0.92	0.66	0.47
	To	∞	∞	∞	∞	∞	∞	∞	∞	∞	∞	∞	∞
30 feet	From	11.16	10.21	8.02	6.15	4.62	3.42	2.50	1.81	1.30	0.93	0.66	0.47
	To	∞	∞	∞	∞	∞	∞	∞	∞	∞	∞	∞	∞
∞	From	17.76	15.46	10.93	7.73	5.46	3.86	2.73	1.93	1.36	0.96	0.68	0.48
	To	∞	∞	∞	∞	∞	∞	∞	∞	∞	∞	∞	∞

Table 7-3. Depth of Field Table (Focal Length = 15 mm)

Focusing Distance		f/1.2	f/1.4	f/2	f/2.8	f/4	f/5.6	f/8	f/11	f/16	f/22	f/32	f/45
5 feet	From	4.44	4.37	4.16	3.89	3.56	3.18	2.77	2.33	1.91	1.52	1.18	0.90
	To	5.70	5.82	6.25	6.98	8.36	11.60	25.61	∞	∞	∞	∞	∞
7 feet	From	5.96	5.83	5.45	5.00	4.47	3.89	3.28	2.69	2.14	1.66	1.26	0.94
	To	8.47	8.74	9.75	11.65	16.09	34.81	∞	∞	∞	∞	∞	∞
10 feet	From	8.00	7.77	7.12	6.36	5.52	4.66	3.82	3.04	2.36	1.79	1.33	0.98
	To	13.31	14.00	16.78	23.35	52.29	∞	∞	∞	∞	∞	∞	∞
15 feet	From	10.91	10.49	9.33	8.06	6.77	5.51	4.37	3.38	2.55	1.90	1.39	1.01
	To	23.96	26.29	38.22	106.57	∞	∞	∞	∞	∞	∞	∞	∞
20 feet	From	13.34	12.71	11.04	9.31	7.62	6.07	4.71	3.58	2.67	1.96	1.43	1.03
	To	39.92	46.87	105.69	∞	∞	∞	∞	∞	∞	∞	∞	∞
30 feet	From	17.15	16.12	13.53	11.02	8.73	6.75	5.11	3.80	2.79	2.03	1.46	1.05
	To	119.64	215.32	∞	∞	∞	∞	∞	∞	∞	∞	∞	∞
∞	From	39.97	34.79	24.60	17.39	12.30	8.69	6.15	4.34	3.07	2.17	1.53	1.08
	To	∞	∞	∞	∞	∞	∞	∞	∞	∞	∞	∞	∞

Courtesy Chinon U.S.A. Inc.

Table 7-4. Depth of Field Table (Focal Length = 20 mm)

Focusing Distance		f/1.2	f/1.4	f/2	f/2.8	f/4	f/5.6	f/8	f/11	f/16	f/22	f/32	f/45
5 feet	From	4.67	4.63	4.49	4.31	4.07	3.79	3.44	3.05	2.62	2.19	1.78	1.40
	To	5.37	5.43	5.63	5.94	6.45	7.34	9.11	13.81	51.22	∞	∞	∞
7 feet	From	6.37	6.29	6.04	5.71	5.31	4.83	4.28	3.69	3.08	2.50	1.97	1.52
	To	7.75	7.88	8.31	9.02	10.24	12.68	19.12	67.76	∞	∞	∞	∞
10 feet	From	8.77	8.61	8.14	7.56	6.87	6.08	5.24	4.37	3.55	2.80	2.15	1.62
	To	11.62	11.91	12.93	14.73	18.32	27.95	109.14	∞	∞	∞	∞	∞
15 feet	From	12.39	12.08	11.18	10.11	8.91	7.63	6.34	5.11	4.02	3.08	2.32	1.71
	To	18.99	19.77	22.77	29.00	47.28	436.12	∞	∞	∞	∞	∞	∞
20 feet	From	15.61	15.12	13.73	12.16	10.46	8.73	7.08	5.59	4.30	3.24	2.41	1.76
	To	27.79	29.50	36.74	56.24	225.68	∞	∞	∞	∞	∞	∞	∞
30 feet	From	21.10	20.21	17.81	15.24	12.66	10.21	8.02	6.15	4.63	3.43	2.51	1.81
	To	51.83	58.12	95.02	929.57	∞	∞	∞	∞	∞	∞	∞	∞
∞	From	71.06	61.86	43.74	30.93	21.87	15.46	10.93	7.73	5.46	3.86	2.73	1.93
	To	∞	∞	∞	∞	∞	∞	∞	∞	∞	∞	∞	∞

Courtesy Chinon U.S.A. Inc.

Table 7-5. Depth of Field Table (Focal Length = 25 mm)

Focusing Distance		f/1.2	f/1.4	f/2	f/2.8	f/4	f/5.6	f/8	f/11	f/16	f/22	f/32	f/45
5 feet	From	4.78	4.75	4.66	4.53	4.37	4.15	3.88	3.55	3.17	2.75	2.32	1.90
	To	5.23	5.26	5.38	5.56	5.84	6.27	7.02	8.43	11.78	26.88	∞	∞
7 feet	From	6.58	6.53	6.35	6.12	5.82	5.44	4.98	4.45	3.86	3.26	2.67	2.12
	To	7.46	7.53	7.78	8.16	8.77	9.80	11.76	16.37	36.78	∞	∞	∞
10 feet	From	9.18	9.06	8.73	8.29	7.75	7.09	6.32	5.49	4.62	3.78	3.01	2.33
	To	10.98	11.14	11.69	12.58	14.08	16.96	23.83	55.80	∞	∞	∞	∞
15 feet	From	13.22	12.99	12.31	11.46	10.44	9.27	8.00	6.71	5.46	4.32	3.33	2.52
	To	17.32	17.73	19.18	21.69	26.61	39.19	118.11	∞	∞	∞	∞	∞
20 feet	From	16.95	16.58	15.48	14.16	12.63	10.96	9.23	7.55	6.00	4.65	3.53	2.63
	To	24.37	25.19	28.22	34.01	47.93	113.77	∞	∞	∞	∞	∞	∞
30 feet	From	23.63	22.90	20.86	18.52	15.99	13.40	10.90	8.63	6.66	5.04	3.74	2.75
	To	41.06	43.44	53.35	78.74	240.78	∞	∞	∞	∞	∞	∞	∞
∞	From	111.03	96.66	68.35	48.33	34.17	24.16	17.08	12.08	8.54	6.04	4.27	3.02
	To	∞	∞	∞	∞	∞	∞	∞	∞	∞	∞	∞	∞

Courtesy Chinon U.S.A. Inc.

Table 7-6. Depth of Field Table (Focal Length = 32 mm)

Focusing Distance		f/1.2	f/1.4	f/2	f/2.8	f/4	f/5.6	f/8	f/11	f/16	f/22	f/32	f/45
5 feet	From	4.86	4.85	4.79	4.70	4.59	4.44	4.25	4.00	3.70	3.34	2.94	2.51
	To	5.13	5.15	5.22	5.32	5.47	5.70	6.05	6.64	7.68	9.89	16.16	456.44
7 feet	From	6.74	6.70	6.59	6.43	6.23	5.96	5.61	5.19	4.68	4.12	3.52	2.92
	To	7.27	7.31	7.45	7.66	7.98	8.47	9.28	10.74	13.79	23.06	469.96	∞
10 feet	From	9.48	9.41	9.18	8.88	8.49	8.00	7.38	6.66	5.85	5.00	4.14	3.33
	To	10.57	10.66	10.96	11.42	12.14	13.33	15.46	19.99	34.11	∞	∞	∞
15 feet	From	13.86	13.71	13.23	12.62	11.84	10.89	9.79	8.55	7.26	5.98	4.79	3.74
	To	16.33	16.55	17.30	18.47	20.43	24.04	32.05	60.57	∞	∞	∞	∞
20 feet	From	18.02	17.76	16.98	15.98	14.75	13.31	11.69	9.97	8.26	6.64	5.20	3.98
	To	22.45	22.87	24.32	26.71	31.02	40.19	69.11	∞	∞	∞	∞	∞
30 feet	From	25.76	25.23	23.67	21.77	19.55	17.09	14.50	11.95	9.56	7.46	5.69	4.26
	To	35.89	36.98	40.92	48.19	64.36	122.47	∞	∞	∞	∞	∞	∞
∞	From	181.92	158.37	111.98	79.18	55.99	39.59	27.99	19.79	13.99	9.89	6.99	4.94
	To	∞	∞	∞	∞	∞	∞	∞	∞	∞	∞	∞	∞

Courtesy Chinon U.S.A. Inc.

Table 7-7. Depth of Field Table (Focal Length = 48 mm)

Focusing Distance		f/1.2	f/1.4	f/2	f/2.8	f/4	f/5.6	f/8	f/11	f/16	f/22	f/32	f/45
5 feet	From	4.94	4.93	4.90	4.86	4.81	4.74	4.64	4.50	4.33	4.10	3.82	3.48
	To	5.05	5.06	5.09	5.13	5.19	5.28	5.41	5.60	5.90	6.38	7.22	8.84
7 feet	From	6.88	6.86	6.81	6.74	6.63	6.50	6.31	6.06	5.75	5.35	4.87	4.33
	To	7.11	7.13	7.19	7.27	7.40	7.58	7.85	8.27	8.94	10.10	12.37	18.15
10 feet	From	9.76	9.73	9.62	9.47	9.27	9.00	8.64	8.19	7.61	6.93	6.15	5.30
	To	10.24	10.28	10.40	10.58	10.84	11.24	11.85	12.83	14.54	17.91	26.66	86.10
15 feet	From	14.47	14.40	14.16	13.84	13.41	12.85	12.13	11.25	10.19	9.00	7.72	6.42
	To	15.56	15.65	15.93	16.36	17.00	17.99	19.62	22.49	28.36	44.96	260.78	∞
20 feet	From	19.07	18.94	18.54	17.99	17.27	16.35	15.20	13.83	12.27	10.57	8.84	7.18
	To	21.01	21.17	21.70	22.50	23.73	25.73	29.19	36.06	54.05	183.38	∞	∞
30 feet	From	27.96	27.68	26.82	25.69	24.25	22.47	20.35	17.96	15.40	12.82	10.36	8.15
	To	32.35	32.74	34.03	36.03	39.31	45.11	57.00	90.90	571.22	∞	∞	∞
∞	From	409.33	356.34	251.97	178.17	125.98	89.08	62.99	44.54	31.49	22.27	15.74	11.13
	To	∞	∞	∞	∞	∞	∞	∞	∞	∞	∞	∞	∞

Courtesy Chinon U.S.A. Inc.

Table 7-8. Depth of Field Table (Focal Length = 36 mm)

Focusing Distance		f/2.7		f/4		f/5.6		f/8		f/11		f/16	
		ft.	in.	ft.	in.	ft.	in.	ft.	in.	ft.	in.	ft.	in.
4 feet	Near	3	10	3	9¼	3	8¼	3	6¾	3	5⅛	3	2⅝
	Far	4	2	4	3	4	4⅜	4	6½	4	9½	5	3¼
6 feet	Near	5	7¾	5	5⅞	5	3¼	5	0⅞	4	9½	4	4⅝
	Far	6	4⅝	6	7⅛	6	10½	7	4	8	0⅛	9	5⅜
10 feet	Near	9	0⅝	8	8	8	2¾	7	7¾	7	0⅜	6	2¼
	Far	11	1¾	11	9¾	12	8¾	14	5⅛	17	3⅝	25	10¾
15 feet	Near	12	11⅝	12	2⅛	11	3⅞	10	3	9	2	7	9½
	Far	17	9¼	19	6	22	2	27	10⅝	41	2	198	9⅞
25 feet	Near	19	9⅞	18	0⅜	16	2⅝	14	1⅛	12	1⅜	9	9¾
	Far	33	9⅞	40	8⅛	54	5⅝	110	1	∞		∞	
∞	Near	94	5¾	63	11⅝	45	9¼	32	1	23	4¼	16	0¾
	Far	∞		∞		∞		∞		∞		∞	

Courtesy Eastman Kodak Co.

Increasing and Decreasing Depth of Field

So far we have only determined the depth of field for a given shot. The background or foreground can be emphasized with changes in the depth of field (Fig. 7-14). How can we increase the depth of field to allow for camera or subject movement? There are three options: We can alter the focal length of the lens, change the f/stop, or change the focusing distance (or a combination of all three).

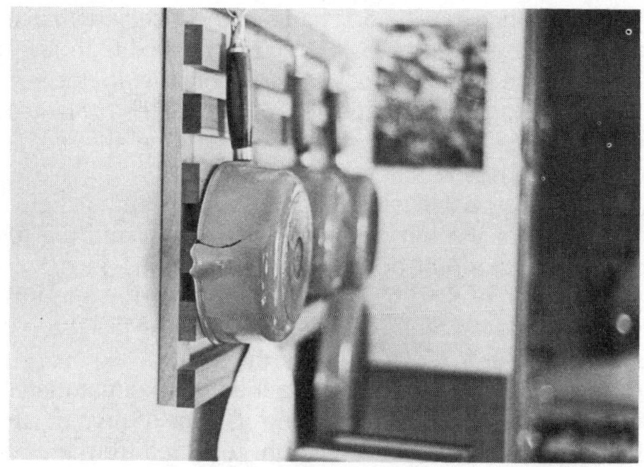

(A) Short depth of field.

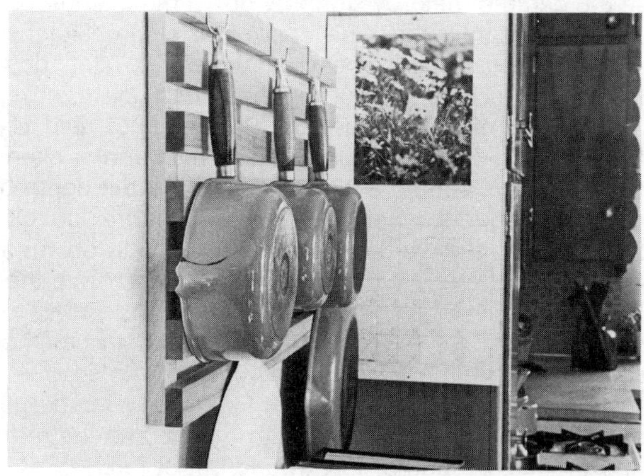

(B) Increased depth of field.

Fig. 7-14. Increasing or decreasing the depth of field.

Taking our previous shot as an example, let us say that we need to increase the depth of field to at least 10 feet. Looking at the tables will show us that if the focusing distance and f/stop remain the same, we would have to go from a 36-mm focal length to at least an 18-mm focal length to achieve that increase in depth of field. But if we alter the focal length of the lens, we also change the field of view. In this case, we would have a *larger* field of view because of the *shorter* focal length lens. To return to the "look" of our original shot, we would have to move the camera toward the subject, thereby, altering the focusing distance as well. So changing the focal length of the lens to increase the depth of field is more complicated than just merely zooming out. One must also move the camera toward the subject or object being photographed or the field of view will be enlarged. And, this means that the focusing distance will now be different and this difference must also be taken into account.

Changing the f/stop will cause changes in the depth of field, too. If the focal length of the lens remained at 36 mm and the focusing distance at 9 feet, stopping down the aperture from f/4 to f/5.6 would increase the depth of field by 1½ feet. Stopping down to f/8 would increase it by almost 4 feet. But, merely changing the f/stop is not a good solution. The f/stop reading is the correct exposure for the scene. It is the exposure that is determined by the light meter of the camera, after it has been set to the correct film ASA value and then allowed to measure the amount of light reflected from the scene to the camera. Changing the f/stop to improve the depth of field would give us a shot that was exposed wrong (underexposed). If we want to increase the depth of field by stopping down the aperture, we will have to add more light to the scene or use a faster film. Either of these changes could cause the camera light meter to stop down the aperture and, thus, increase our depth of field.

Adding light to effect increases in the depth of field is rather difficult outdoors. So, changing the focal length and/or altering the focusing distance is a more effective way to handle depth of field problems there. Indoors, where it often may be more difficult to use the focal length or change the focusing distance to obtain a good depth of field, it is much easier to add light to change the f/stop readings.

Up to this point, we have only talked about the methods for increasing depth of field. Each of the solutions presented, if reversed, could operate to *decrease* the depth of field. It is often desirable to have only the subject or object in sharp focus, and the rest of the scene and the background or foreground out of focus. This can be accomplished by choosing combinations of focal length and focusing distance that give rather shallow depths of field. Again, changing the f/stop (opening up) will help here but this change is easier to accomplish indoors where you have some control over the amount of light.

Focus Shift and Follow Focus

If you cannot change the focal length or f/stop and still need a larger depth of field, there are two solutions, both of which involve changing the focus setting. One is called *focus shift* and the other is called *follow focus*.

Focus shift is commonly used in static camera shots. It consists of focusing on an object (at a specific distance in the field of view) for a portion of the shot, and then shifting the focus to another object (at another distance) for the remainder of the shot. This will give two separate depth of fields at the same focal length and f/stop. The main purpose of the focus shift is to allow focusing on near and far objects in the same shot without changing the field of view or moving the camera. It is often used in the "stacked-two" composition to shift the attention of the audience from one subject to another.

Follow focus is commonly used in moving camera shots or in shots where the subject moves quickly out of the depth of field setting at a given focus distance. Follow focus is done, as the name implies, by actually moving the focus ring to keep the subject in sharp focus. The follow focus technique is effective for use with dolly and trucking shots, and for use with the static camera when the subject is moving rapidly toward or away from the camera.

EXPOSURE

When the fully automatic exposure systems for 8-mm cameras were first introduced, it was thought that most film makers would soon forget how to set an exposure manually, or that people would actually forget the purpose of exposure. For most of your shooting in Super 8 format (and for much of ours, too), this is effectively true. We note the f/stop, as registered by our camera's light meter, in our shooting log, use it to compute the depth of field, and then forget about it. We are well aware that as long as the camera light meter is working correctly, we will get a good exposure on every frame we shoot. But, because proper exposure is so basic to all photography, you should know how to obtain it with or without your camera meter. And, you should know how different exposures, other than the correct one, will affect your film.

Exposure, you may recall, is dependent on three factors—the size of the aperture (or the f/stop), the amount of time the frame is exposed to the light (or the *shutter speed* of the camera, expressed in fractions of a second), and the sensitivity of the film emulsion to light (or the *film speed*). Of these three factors, the aperture size is the easiest to change in normal camera operation. We could also change running speeds and, therefore, shutter speeds every time we changed lighting situations. This is commonly done in still photography. But, in motion pictures, such changes would produce serious discontinuities when we tried to project our film. The speed of the action would not seem consistent from shot to shot. We could also change film speeds, and we do so on occasion, to take advantage of the greater sensitivity to light of a faster film stock. But, changing film emulsions is a crude way of making exposure adjustments. The simplest way to make an exposure adjustment is to do what your Super 8 camera does now, automatically. It determines the correct f/stop to use by taking into account the selected camera running speed, the film speed (from the notch on the cartridge), and the light that is reflected off the subject into the lens.

Using the Camera Light Meter

If the camera is willing to do this for us, why should we interfere? We sometimes need to override the automatic meter because of the very things that make it work well for us under "normal" lighting conditions. The automatic light meters on Super 8 cameras are *averaging meters* and they tend to be *center weighted*. An averaging meter is one that reads the light over the entire viewing area and registers the average of all the different readings. A center-weighted meter is one that averages the light readings but will put more emphasis on the light that it reads from the center of the field (often the area on which you focus). Both of these characteristics are worthwhile but they allow the camera to be "fooled" by some lighting situations.

For example, if you are photographing a scene that has strong contrasts between light and dark, the averaging light meter will read the scene and will give you the correct exposure for *no* part of it. A similar thing could happen if you were panning across a scene with wide contrasts between light and dark. The automatic meter would almost bounce as it sought to maintain the correct exposure. Or, perhaps you set up your shot so that the subject was not in the center of the frame. A center-weighted meter would give you a correctly exposed background but would not necessarily give you a correctly exposed subject.

Another characteristic of Super 8 camera light meters is their sensitivity to the brightest light in the scene. In an effort to develop movie cameras that will photograph under low light conditions, some camera manufacturers have designed their light meters to be very sensitive to small amounts of light. This is all right for normal use, but when you are trying to get the best possible exposure under production conditions, this feature can be self defeating. The classic backlight situation is one that illustrates this meter problem. If you photograph a subject against a background that is brighter than the subject (Fig. 7-15), your subject is likely to be underexposed. Shooting outdoors in the snow will illustrate this. The camera meter will key in on the brightest source of light in the scene, in this case, the background, and will expose it, not your subject, correctly.

Finally, overexposure or underexposure can give certain special effects to otherwise ordinary shots in your film. By manipulating the exposure control of your camera manually, you can create a variety of visual effects.

The usual way to manually set the exposure on a Super 8 camera is to set the light meter switch to manual and then dial in the desired f/stop. (On some cameras, you must find some view which will give you the exposure that you want and *lock* it into the meter.) But first, you will need to know what the correct f/stop must be in order to expose that special lighting situation correctly. There are four ways of determining the correct exposure. All of them involve using the camera light meter in a slightly different manner than it is used in normal filming.

First, you can use the camera as if it were a "spot" light meter. A spot light meter is one that scans only a small field of view (often less than 1° of included angle). This kind of meter is used by still photographers to measure the light falling on a very small area of a field of view. This allows them to calculate, very precisely, the correct exposure for any portion of the field. You can use the camera as a spot meter by taking it off the tripod and moving it closer to your subject until the object on which you want the correct exposure completely fills the viewfinder (Fig. 7-16). With the light meter on automatic, note the reading on the f/stop scale. Set the meter manually to that f/stop (or lock the meter at that reading), and then return the camera to the tripod. Now your subject will be correctly exposed.

This method works well in the backlight situation or when there is an extreme difference between the light on your subject and the light in the surrounding area. A word of warning, however. If you take the light reading off a person's face, remember to open up one more f/stop than the meter is reading. This rule applies to fair skin only. If the person's face is dark skinned, the meter reading that you get will give you the correct exposure.

Then, you may use the camera and make some calculations to get the average light reading in a scene. This average light reading will work well for a moving camera or for zoom shots in which the differing light conditions within the field of view could cause meter bounce. Here is how to take an average reading. With the camera meter on automatic, take a series of light readings throughout the field of view. Pay special attention to the reading at the end of the zoom or camera movement. What f/stop is most often noted in your readings? You can set the camera to that one. Or, you can calculate the average reading that will satisfy most of the light conditions in the

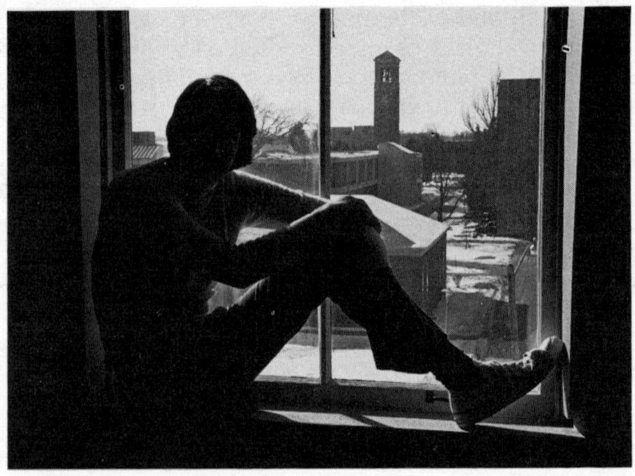

(A) Uncompensated. The camera meter reads the brighter background and exposes for it.

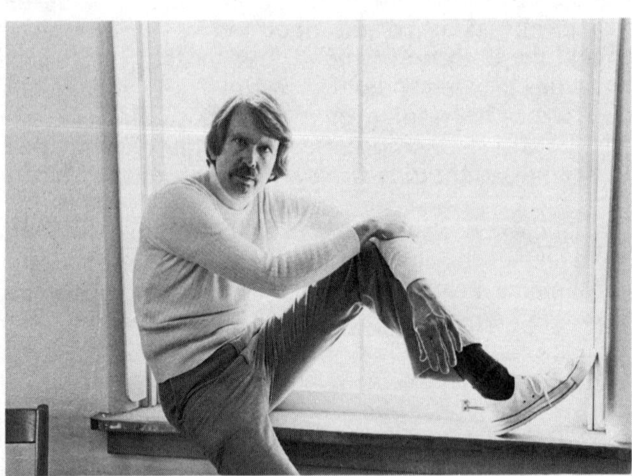

(B) Compensated. An exposure-meter reading is taken off subject so background is overexposed.

Fig. 7-15. Backlight situations.

scene. Whichever way you figure it out, set the aperture manually to this f/stop. When we are in doubt about the correct setting, we usually err in the direction of overexposure. Most film stocks are more tolerant of overexposure and look better that way than if they were underexposed.

The next method of determining exposure is the *gray card method* (Fig. 7-17). The automatic light meters in movie and still cameras are designed to read exposure in terms of the gray scale. It has been calculated that, if black is zero and white is 100, a reading of 18 (18% gray) would give a correct exposure to most objects under any kind of light. On automatic exposure, the camera light meter will read every object as 18% gray and expose it accordingly. When working under lighting conditions that might "fool" the automatic meter, we can reverse this process and use an 18% gray card to set the meter.

The gray card system works like this. Place the gray card in the shot so that it is lighted normally. With the camera meter on automatic,

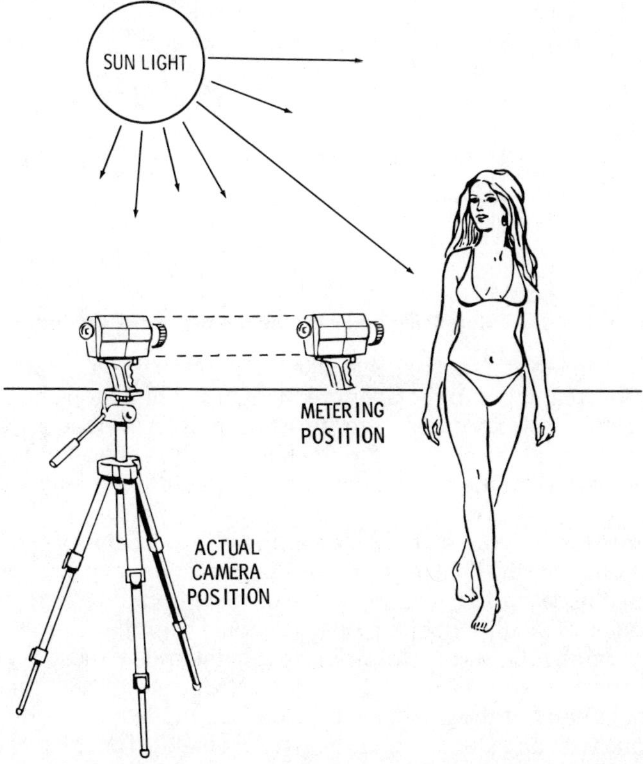

Fig. 7-16. Using the camera as a spot meter.

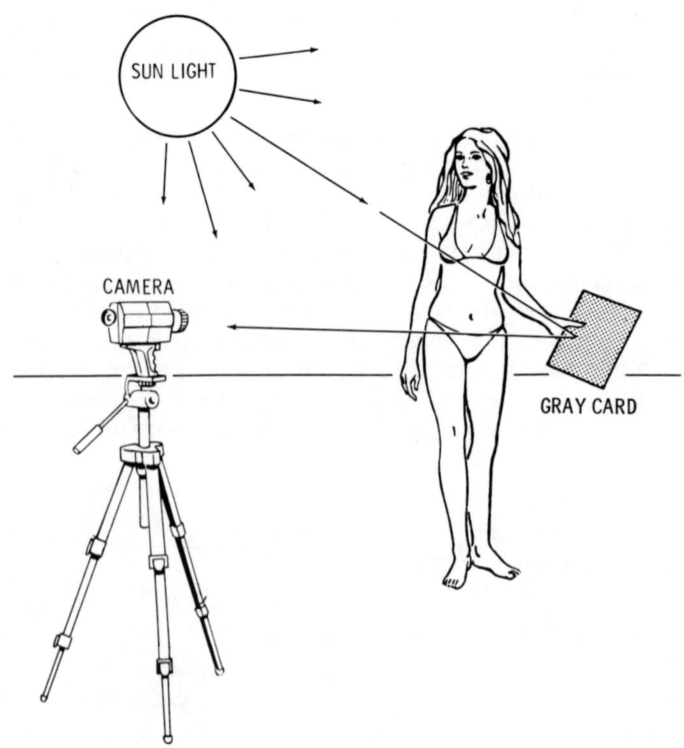

Fig. 7-17. Determining exposure by the gray card method.

use the camera as a spot meter to take a reading off the gray card only. Lock this reading into the aperture manually. This f/stop should be correct for most exposures since the gray card is an averaging system. We have found the gray card most effective with controlled-lighting situations and on the copy stand. It may be used under any lighting conditions, however.

If there is no gray card available, there is the palm-of-the-hand variation. Take the light reading in the same manner as just described but use the palm of your hand instead of the gray card. When you set the meter manually, open up one additional stop. Just as in the fair skin lighting rule, your palm will give a slight underexposure which you must correct.

Finally, any of the previous exposure-setting determinations can be done with an external or hand-held light meter. The light meter in your camera is probably pretty accurate under most lighting conditions. But a hand-held meter, being a special-purpose tool, is likely to be more accurate. And, it is often more convenient to use a separate light meter than it is to lug the camera around.

Special Effects

There are a variety of special effects that you can create by varying the exposure of your film from the correct exposure setting. Overexposing by 1½ to 2 stops will produce washed-out colors and gives a soft quality to the visuals. Overexposing by 3 to 4 stops causes a considerable loss of detail and looks very ghostly. (We have done this accidentally with some very interesting results.) Underexposure will create opposite effects. A bright sunny day, underexposed by 2 stops, will appear to be quite gloomy. And the famous movie-lighting trick of exchanging *day for night* can also be created by underexposure.

We have gotten good results in day-for-night shots using this technique. Shoot outdoors in bright sunlight or with a bright overcast. Use Kodachrome 40 or an equivalent speed color film. Take a meter reading of the scene with the camera on automatic exposure. Stop down 4 additional stops from this reading (3 stops for bright overcast). If your camera will not stop down that far, use a neutral-density filter to reduce the amount of light that the camera sees. Finally, take the color-correcting daylight filter *out.* The resulting effect should be a good imitation of nighttime. Two words of caution. A bright overcast will not produce the high contrasting shadows that bright sunlight does so you could lose the "moon-lit" effect. And, avoid shooting the sky if at all possible as the day-light sky will look too bright.

CHAPTER 8

Lighting and Sound-Recording Techniques

In the last chapter, we discussed the concepts that you should know and understand before you start to actually produce a film. We also mentioned that there are several techniques that you should understand. We discussed one of them—Focusing. In this chapter, we will discuss in detail the remaining techniques of Lighting and Sound Recording.

LIGHTING

Up to this point, we have ignored the source of the light that we were measuring. In general, when determining exposure, this is all right. But you should know how to compensate for existing outdoor lighting conditions in order to get a better exposure, and you must know how to light interior scenes.

There are two kinds of light under which you will shoot—available light and enhanced light. *Available light* includes sunlight, normal room light, firelight, etc. *Enhanced light* includes any lighting situation where you change the normal lighting conditions by adding more or different light(s). Both kinds of lighting have their own set of operating rules which must be followed if you want to get good exposures and natural looking shots.

Available Light

Sunlight is one particular kind of available light that has several rules all its own. In the first place, sunlight is so much brighter than any kind of artificial light that it creates a definite shadow problem in photography. Sunlight also changes color with the time of day and the seasons of the year, which can cause some color-balance problems. Finally, sunlight, even when filtered by a cloud layer, is usually too bright for some of the faster film stocks. Each of these conditions must be compensated for by special shooting techniques.

To avoid problems with shadows, one can always shoot with the sun at one's back or over one's shoulder. Then, if the sun is high enough, the shadows will tend to fall behind the subject or slightly to one side where they will not be very noticeable or bothersome. But, this kind of photographic lighting, like the straight-on camera angle, tends to give the picture a rather flat uniform look that is not very interesting visually. You certainly would not want to shoot all of your scenes that way. It is better to bring the light in from a quartering angle or even from the side. This kind of lighting makes the subject stand out from the background and enhances the lines and features of the subject.

To fill those deep sunlight shadows, use some simple reflectors placed opposite the sunlight side and aimed at the subject (Fig. 8-1).

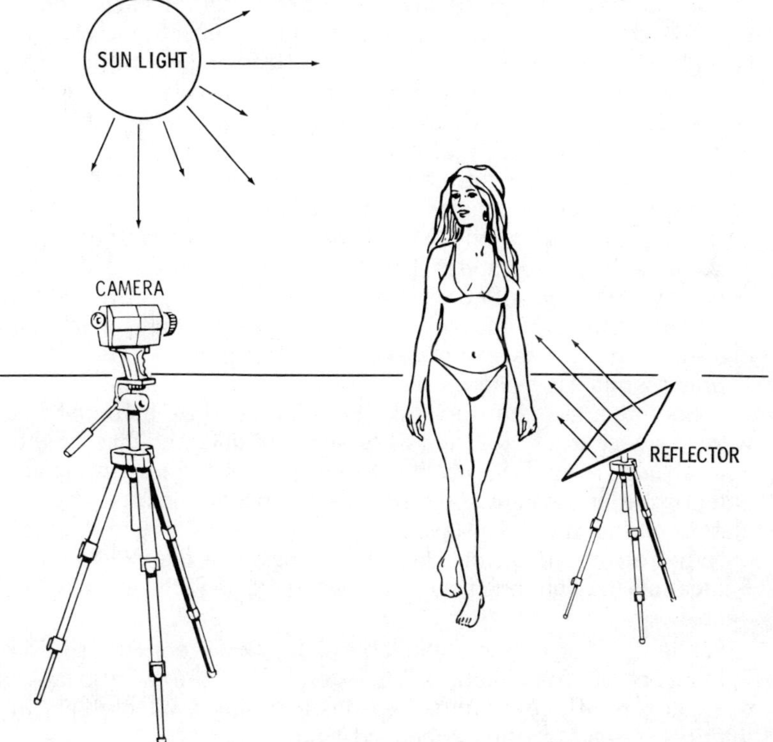

Fig. 8-1. Put reflector in a "fill" position opposite the sun side for better balanced light.

Use dull-painted or silvered sheets for this task. (While shiny reflectors might be more efficient, they also cause hot spots in the shadows.) Reflectors should never be used too close to the subject or the shadows will look "washed out." Although it is the goal of the reflectors to fill the shadows, our eye tends to look for a natural balance between the hot side of the picture (sunlight) and the cool side of the picture (shade). If this balance is upset with too much fill light, the picture looks wrong. A good rule for reflectors is:

> If you can see them working, they are probably reflecting
> too much light.

The changing color of sunlight can be compensated for by shooting at certain times of the day when the sunlight is the most color consistent. Between 9 A.M. and 3 P.M., the color is quite consistent throughout the year. During the summer, we have shot as early as 7:30 A.M. and as late as 4:30 P.M. without any problems at all. But, both very early morning light and late afternoon light tend to be more reddish than normal. If you prefer these effects, the angle of the light and the resultant long shadows make for interesting pictures. Dawn and sunset look somewhat alike as far as the color of the light is concerned, so one may be substituted for another when filming. The amount of light available at either dawn or sunset changes very rapidly, however, so the camera light meter must be kept on automatic or incorrect exposures will result.

Shots taken at high noon in May, June, and July present a particular problem to the photographer. The sun is almost overhead giving the *down lighting* effect of conventional interior lighting. This causes unflattering shadows under noses and chins. We usually avoid the high-noon shot by breaking for lunch at this time.

Bright sunlight can often provide too much light, particularly if you are shooting a fast film stock (like Ektachrome 160). If you do not want to switch to a slower film when shooting under bright sunlight, you can use a neutral-density filter to cut down on the amount of light entering the lens. A neutral-density filter is a neutral-colored piece of glass or plastic which is installed on the front of the lens barrel. It will cut down on the amount of light by the rating on the filter. (A Number 3 filter cuts the light one f/stop). It does not change the color of the light.

Sunlight is not the only available light, however. The existing lighting conditions in interiors (and exteriors at night) can also fall in this category. There are three reasons for using available light in interiors instead of using enhanced light:

1. To preserve the natural look of the scene.
2. It is less bothersome than setting up special lighting.
3. The faster lens and film stocks of today allow it.

While the second two arguments make sense from a production standpoint, the first point needs some additional explanation. There is no such thing as "natural" photography. The entire process of taking pictures, with any kind of camera, is one of extreme artifice. It always involves the intrusion of the business of taking the picture into the scene itself. And, it imposes the viewpoint of the camera on the audience. When we speak of preserving the "natural" look of light in a shot, what we really mean is, preserving the way that we imagine the scene should look when photographed with a minimum of intrusion. There is much to be said for this "natural" look, and it is often worth shooting with only available light in an attempt to capture its effects.

When working with available light, the placement of the subject is very critical to getting a good picture (Figs. 8-2 and 8-3). If you are shooting against bright backgrounds (windows, white walls, lights), it is better to place your subject so that he or she is partly lit by that background. Strong backlit shots are also very interesting. Remember to take the light reading off the subject. Or, you might want to place the subject near some bright source of light in the room. While some manipulation of the camera, subject, and light might be necessary, you can create a well-exposed scene and still keep the natural light look. Many available light situations are too dim for the use of standard speed film, so using fast film is your best solution. There will be some increase in "grain," so pay close attention to the focus and depth of field to maintain maximum image sharpness.

Another drawback of available light photography is that the color of the light might be wrong. Fluorescent-lighted interiors, like offices and classrooms, are often bright enough for good exposures using XL cameras and slow film, but the color is off when the film is exposed with the filter out. Putting the filter in cuts the speed and it will not always compensate for the blue-green cast of the light. Tungsten-lighted locations, like homes or older businesses, often give a pronounced yellowish tone to pictures that are taken there even when the filter is correctly left out. There are several ways of dealing with this color-balance problem without changing the light. Special filters can be obtained to correct almost any color imbalance. They do cut down on the incoming light, however, sometimes by as much as two stops.

Choosing a different film stock might also help to alleviate a color problem. Ektachrome 160 G does look correct when photographed under fluorescent lights and supposedly needs no filter under any lighting conditions. Do not use this film stock under tungsten light, however. Its yellowish cast makes it look like the filter was left in by mistake. Ektachrome 40 has a nice mellow look under the color temperatures of ordinary household lamps. It could serve as a good

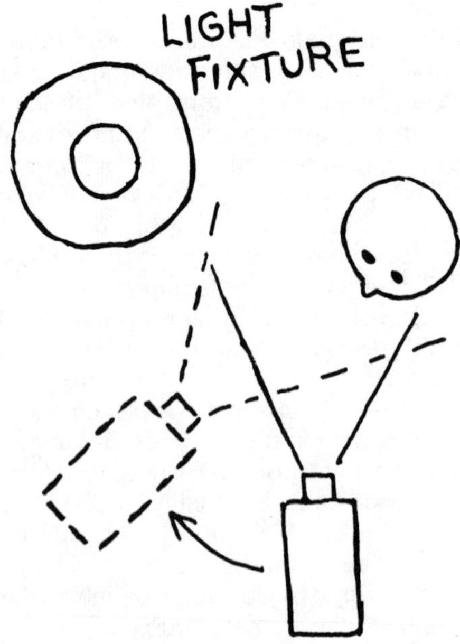

(A) Arrangement of subject, lights, and camera.

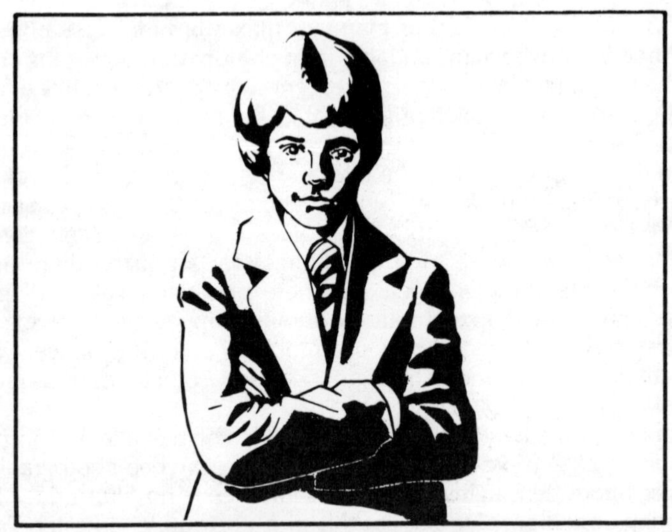

(B) View of subject through viewfinder.

Fig. 8-2. Placement of subject using available light.

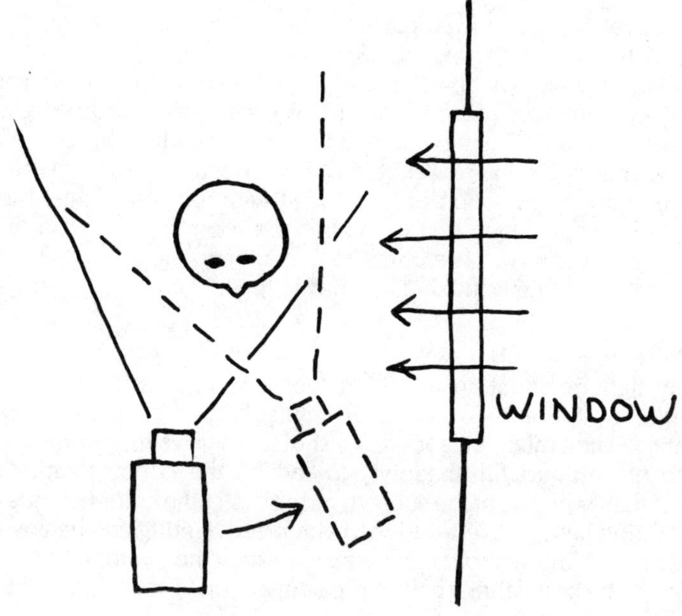

(A) Using sunlight from window.

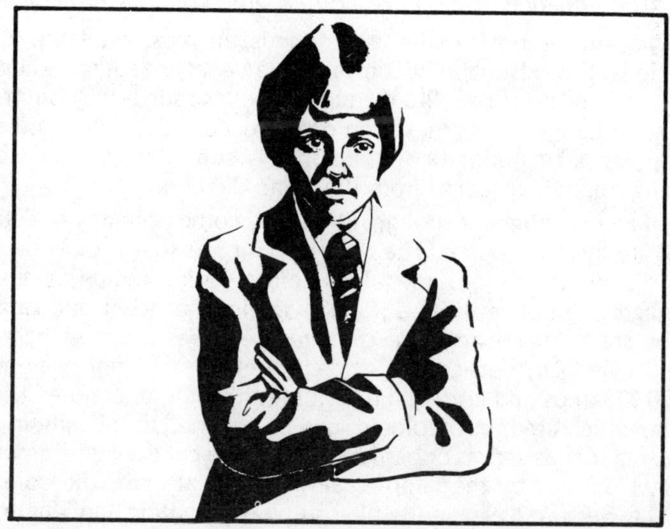

(B) View of subject through viewfinder.

Fig. 8-3. Placement of subject for best exposure.

alternative to your normal camera stock when filming under that yellowish light.

The other way to deal with the color problem is to ignore it. Your audience perceives rooms lit with fluorescent lights to be slightly blue-green anyway. They probably will not notice the off-color lighting unless you intercut shots that are correctly lighted. The same is true of their perception of interiors lit with tungsten lights. Most people will not notice that the colors are a bit warmer than they should be. Again, be careful not to call attention to the lighting by intercutting correctly lit shots with this footage.

Enhanced Lighting

Any lighting situation in which the normal or existing light is changed by the addition of other light(s) is an *enhanced lighting* situation. Light might be added to a shot to improve the exposure or depth of field, to fill shadows, to reduce the contrast ratio, to emphasize or highlight the subject, or to correct the color balance of the existing light(s). Well-designed enhanced lighting can be any or all of these things without appearing to destroy the "natural" look of the shot. The best lighting calls the least attention to itself, i.e., it is the most natural looking.

When enhancing sunlight, there are two rules to remember:

1. Sunlight only comes from one direction.
2. The enhanced light must be the same color as sunlight.

The first rule is not as silly as it sounds. In most available light situations, the existing light comes from a variety of sources, hence from as many directions. But outdoors, when the sun is the dominant source of light, it all comes from one direction. So, when you are enhancing an exterior or interior that is sunlit, make sure your lighting appears to come from the same direction.

Reflected sunlight or sunlight fill-in may come from any direction opposite the sun source. The only limitation is that it must be the same color as the source. The correct color temperature for "sunlight" lamps is 4800–5500 Kelvin. Incandescent and quartz lamps are available in these color temperatures for most lighting instruments. Or, you could put dichroic filters in front of normal (3400 K) lamps and correct the light to sunlight temperature. These filters, which are bluish-colored, can be attached to the light in the same manner as scrims or barndoors. They do cut down the amount of light put out by the lamp somewhat but, at least, the color is correct. Be sure to leave the filter in when shooting sunlight or its enhanced light.

Most of your enhanced lighting (and, from this point on, we'll just call it lighting) will be done under artificial light, either tungsten or fluorescent, and most of it will be done inside buildings. The problems of lighting are:

1. Raising the overall level of illumination in order to get an exposure or to increase the depth of field.
2. Correcting the color balance, especially when shooting under fluorescent lighting, or with a mixed daylight and artificial light.
3. Reducing the contrast ratio by filling in the shadows.
4. Emphasizing the subject and/or separating the subject from the background or foreground.

There are a number of ways these problems can be solved, or at least partly solved, by the application of a specific lighting design. These designs take their names from the arrangement of the lighting instruments on the set or their relationship to the subject being photographed. The most common lighting designs are:

1. *Augmented existing lighting*—Replacing the ordinary household lamps in the ceiling fixtures and floor lamps with higher-wattage photoflood lamps.
2. *Bounce lighting*—Using two or three floodlights angled up toward the ceiling in order to reflect light on the shot.
3. *Direct floodlighting*—Aiming floodlights at the subject or the shadows, usually from either side of the camera position.
4. *Key-Fill-Backlight*—Using spotlights in specific positions with specific wattage lamps in each (or, scrimmed to reduce brightness).

We will go through each lighting problem later and will examine the possibilities of applying each of these lighting designs.

One of the most common problems in lighting is that of not having enough light for a good exposure. Even with the fast films of today, there are a number of interiors like hallways, living rooms, clubs, basements, and garages that simply are not well enough lighted to shoot good pictures. Or, if they have enough light for an adequate exposure, there isn't enough to get a good depth of field. The simplest solutions to these problems are *augmented existing lighting* and *bounce lighting.*

To augment the output of existing lighting, replace the household bulbs with photoflood lamps of a higher wattage. A 100-watt table lamp bulb can be replaced with a 250-watt photoflood. A 200-watt ceiling fixture may be replaced with a 500-watt photoflood. If a floor lamp is available, the main bulb in it can often be replaced with a Mogul-base 1000-watt lamp. All of these changes are temporary, of course, and the original household-type bulbs should be returned to their sockets as soon as you are done shooting. When putting higher-wattage lamps in ceiling fixtures, we usually leave the lamp covers off so that they do not overheat. Of course, you should check the circuits into which the existing fixtures and lamps are wired to be sure that you are not overloading them. Using higher-wattage lamps in existing fixtures is usually effective in raising the light levels *in those areas that are lit by those fixtures*. But doing this may compound the problems of contrast between the light and dark areas.

Bounce lighting is a better solution for raising the light level in every part of the room. Bounce lighting is light that is reflected or bounced off the ceiling onto the subject instead of shining directly on the subject (Fig. 8-4). Use high-wattage floods or scoops for

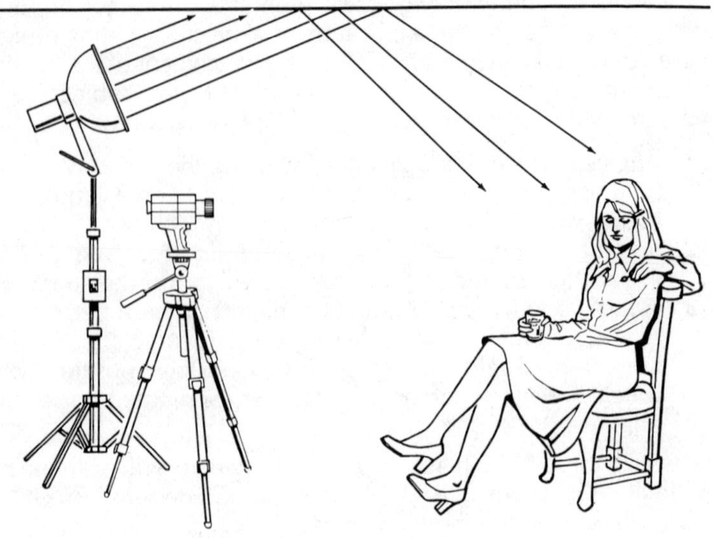

(A) Bouncing light off ceiling onto subject.

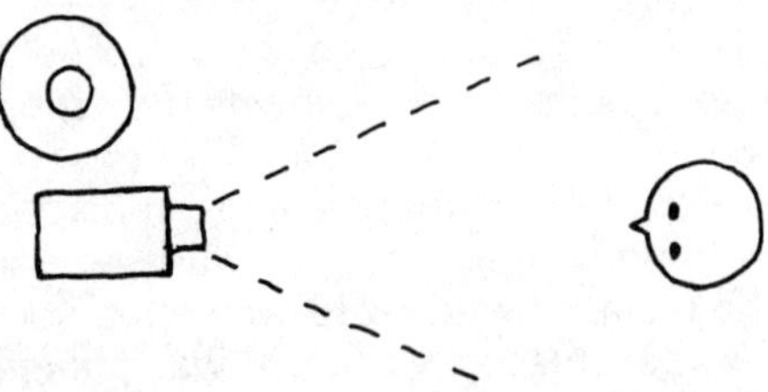

(B) Arrangement of lights, camera, and subject.

Fig. 8-4. Raising the overall illumination is easily accomplished using bounce lighting.

maximum effect in bounce lighting. The lighting instruments should be placed behind or to either side of the camera field of view and angled up toward the ceiling. (We sometimes turn them straight up toward the ceiling.) The soft even light that is reflected off the ceiling will tend to fill shadows as well as raise the light level. Two words of caution here. Be sure the ceiling is white or some other neutral color; otherwise, the color that is reflected will tint your subject. Second, do not place the lights so close to the ceiling that they scorch the plaster or paint. Most interior paints have a fairly good resistance to heat, but a 500-watt or 1000-watt floodlight can get mighty warm.

It is also possible to raise the overall light levels with direct floodlights but this method is tricky, especially if you are trying to avoid shadows and still keep a fairly natural contrast ratio. We suggest that, with the limited number of lighting instruments you will probably have, that you stick with bounce lighting as your best solution to this first problem.

Correcting color balance can be a serious problem when shooting in mixed light situations. It seems that every modern building we have shot in recently has had a mixture of tungsten, fluorescent and, sometimes, even capacitive-discharge lighting. Daylight, coming through windows or doors, can also give color-balance problems. There are two good solutions. Overpower the existing mixed light with your own tungsten lighting equipment, or add correctly colored light to augment the existing dominant light source.

While bounce lighting can help to overpower existing lighting, *direct floodlighting* and *key-fill-backlight lighting* are the best designs to use. Direct floodlighting is, as the name implies, shining floodlights directly on the subject or scene (Fig. 8-5). The lights should be even with the camera or slightly ahead of it and should be equally distributed on either side. They should be raised as high as possible and aimed down toward the subject. In some instances, merely flooding the shot will not produce the effect you want. You can get more concentrated light by hanging the floodlights from the existing lighting fixtures and using the floods as the main source of light in the room. This has proved quite effective for us in halls, stairwells, and other confined places.

A rule of thumb for exposure, when overpowering existing light, is to make the total of your new light twice as bright as the existing light. For example, if your existing light gave you a light-meter reading of f/2.8, you would have to add enough light to get an f/4 on the same meter, to have doubled the light. Or, you can use your added light as the main source and shut off the existing light. We have done this with our ceiling-mounted floods, but a better way to do it is with the key-fill-backlight design (Fig. 8-6). Key-fill-backlight is a classic interior lighting setup. It works very well for this problem because it

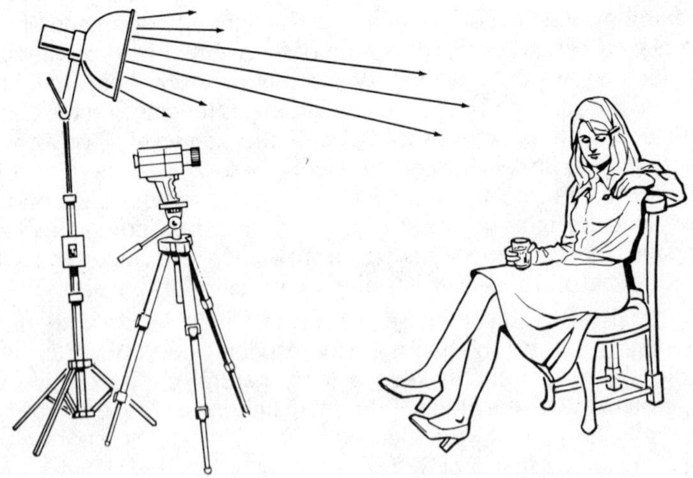

(A) Floods are good for filling in shadows without complex
lighting setup.

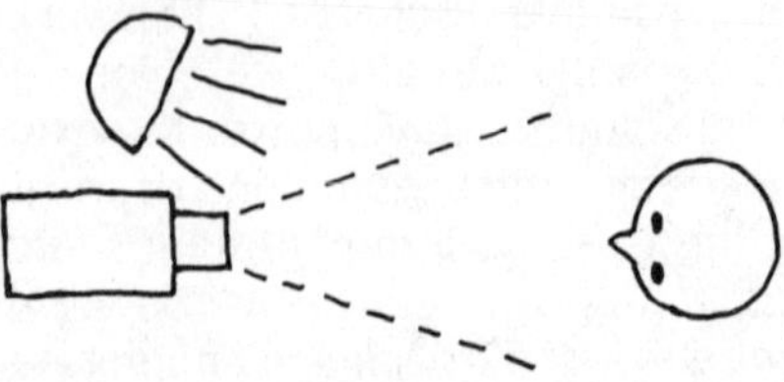

(B) Arrangement of light, camera, and subject.

Fig. 8-5. Direct floodlighting.

can be used as the main source of light and still maintain some
semblance of "natural" looking light.

It works this way. The *key light* is the main source of light in the
shot. It is placed to one side of the camera (usually 45° off an axis
drawn from the camera through the subject). The key light is raised as
high as it will go and it is aimed down toward the subject (usually at a
45° angle). The key should be the brightest light in the setup either by
having the highest-wattage lamp or by being closest to the subject.
The lighting instrument used for key lighting is usually a spot.

The *fill light* is set next to the camera on the opposite side from the
key, and at the same height as the camera. The job of the fill light is to
fill in and even out some of the harsh shadows that the key light
creates. Under normal circumstances, the fill light should have about
half the lighting power of the key light. Floodlights are commonly

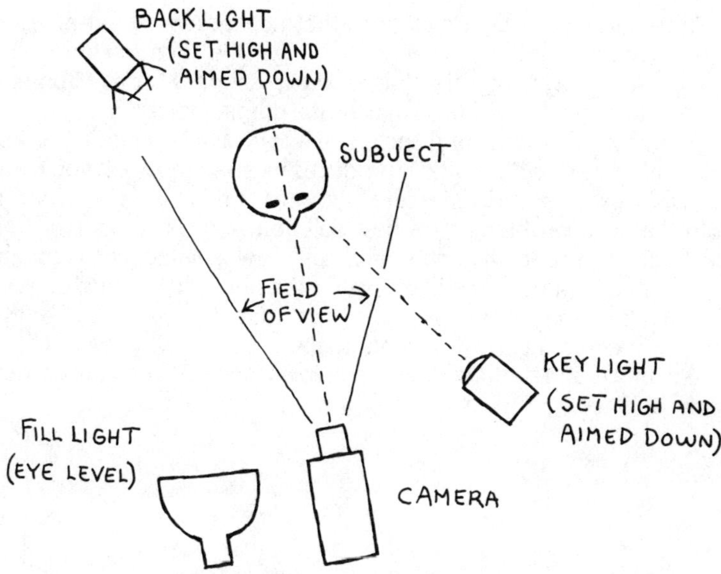

**Fig. 8-6. The classic 3-light arrangement of key, fill, and backlight
gives good depth and modeling.**

used for fill lights but spotlights that are suitably defocused may work
just as well.

The *backlight* is placed on the other side of the subject opposite the
key light. It, too, is raised high and aimed down at a fairly steep angle.
Its purpose is to illuminate the back of the subject and provide some
separation of the subject from the background. The backlight should
be about the power of the key light. Because of its location, nearly
opposite the camera lens, the backlight may tend to flare into the
lens. This can be controlled by using a lens hood on the camera, a
barndoor on the light, or both. If is not possible to alter the wattages of
the fill lights (making them less than the key light), their effective
outputs can be reduced with scrims.

The difference between the amount of light put out by the key and
fill lights is called the key-fill ratio. Generally, a 2-to-1 ratio is used.
This is where the key light is twice as bright on the subject as is the fill
light. This ratio can be attained by having a higher-wattage lamp in
the key light, scrimming the fill light to reduce its output, or by
moving the key light closer to the subject than the fill light is. Any of
these methods will have the same effect. The same rules apply to any
set of key-fill ratios. The main reason to use the key-fill light design in
this situation is because it allows a natural-looking shot with enough
light for good exposures and correct color balance.

There are mixed light situations that do not lend themselves to being overpowered by additional lighting. One such mixture is the daylight-incandescent mix that is prevalent in houses. Sunlight coming through the windows may be the dominant light in the room, but it is often less than useful because it is at the wrong angle, it comes from only one direction, and it produces harsh shadows. If you try to use the existing incandescent light as fill you will have a color-balance problem. The best solution here is to shut off the existing incandescent lights and use color-balanced (sunlight temperature) lamps to fill in and augment the sunlight. Use floodlights either bounced or aimed directly, or replace the incandescent lamps with blue photofloods. Either way, you will be able to utilize the sunlight, fill the shadows, and still keep the correct color balance.

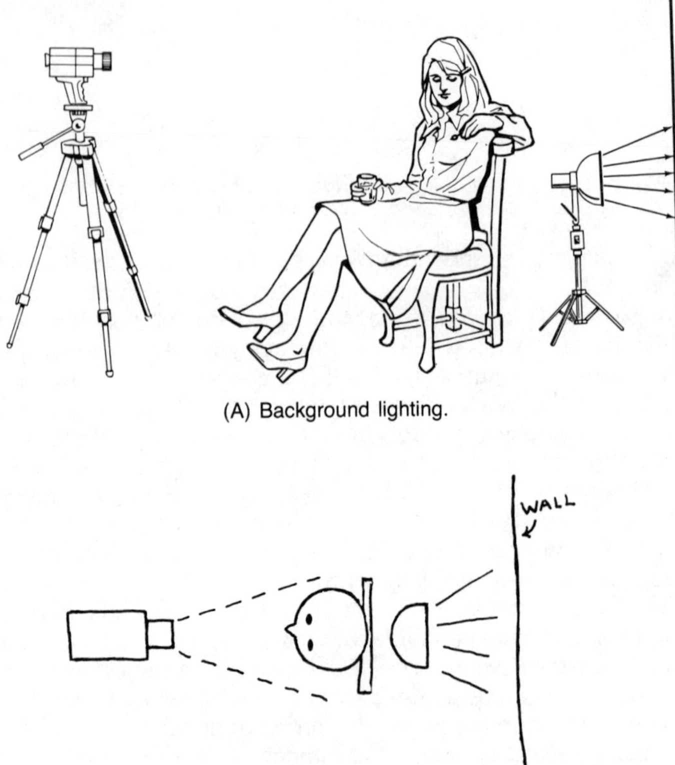

(A) Background lighting.

(B) Arrangement of light and subject.

Fig. 8-7. A background light will accomplish the same effect as a backlight.

If reducing the contrast ratio or filling in shadows is the main problem, the use of small-wattage direct floodlights is the best solution. Place them near the camera and about the same height as the lens, much like you would place fill lights. And, as with fill lights, they should be on the opposite side of the camera from the bright side of the subject.

Providing some separation of the subject from the background is best accomplished by use of the key-fill-backlight design. But, it is also possible to create some separation by lighting the background itself (Fig. 8-7). Place a light either to one side of the subject and out of camera range, or directly behind the subject. Mount it at the same level as the subject, or slightly lower, and aim it directly at the background. This light need not be of very high wattage—half the power of the fill light would be adequate. What this light does is brighten up the background so that the subject will appear to stand out from it. The background light is somewhat easier to use than traditional backlight as the placement of the background light is not nearly as critical.

The lighting of exteriors at night presents some additional problems that are not ordinarily encountered with interior setups. Our suggestions are either to augment the existing light with floods and pretend that the light you get is coming from the existing source, or use a bright off-screen light that is balanced on the opposite side by reflectors in order to provide some fill. There are more complex situations but most of them are beyond the range of ordinary amateur lighting equipment.

There are a great many other specialized lighting problems that we could consider and offer specific remedies for. But, the lighting designs we have discussed will work for most of the problems that you will run into. As a general rule, we suggest that you use the *least* amount of additional light that is necessary to fix the problem encountered in a lighting situation. This will give the double benefit of allowing the simplest and quickest setup possible and will, probably, keep the lighting situation looking as natural as possible. Start with simple solutions and go to more complex solutions only if you must. We have also found that nearly every lighting situation is different from the ones that we have encountered before. You should experiment with lighting every time you make a film, and you probably will. The best way to learn about lighting is to do more lighting.

SOUND RECORDING

In order to make good sound recordings, we must know something about the nature of sound. Sound is a form of energy that travels in waves in all directions from the source of the sound. Sound waves can be transmitted directly through the air to our ear or to a microphone. They can be transmitted by reflection, by reverberation (echo), and by vibration. Sound waves can also be absorbed. Most of the sound waves that we, or our microphone, hear will be either direct waves or reflected waves.

There are several general rules about the transmission of sound waves in the air that we should remember. Hard surfaces tend to reflect sound waves and soft surfaces tend to absorb them. The larger the enclosed space, the greater the chance for reverberation. Reverberation, or echo, is the result of the reflected sound reaching the listener at a different time than the direct sound. Our perceptions of sound are such that a difference of 35 to 40 milliseconds between the direct and reflected sound will cause us to hear an echo. Reverberation is also directly proportional to volume—as the volume increases so does the reverberation. Absorption of sound is usually accomplished by dampening or muffling the reflected waves so that only the direct waves are heard. As stated before, most sounds that are heard are a combination of direct and reflected sound waves. There are two notable exceptions. In gyms, auditoriums, and in theatres, we will often hear sound waves that are augmented by reverberation. In broadcasting and recording studios, most of the reflected sound is dampened or muffled so we only hear direct waves.

Will physical spaces affect our recording of sound? Although microphones are not exactly like our ears, they do tend to respond to sound waves in the same way. Microphones will hear echos in large rooms, and will record a lack of the same in small crowded spaces. Harsh surfaces will reflect more sound back to microphones just as they do to our ears. So we should be able to make some fairly accurate judgments with our own ears about how the sound will "sound" before we record it.

What kind of "sound" are we listening for? We want to get a natural sounding "sound," one that comes across to the listener as being the same way it would have sounded if he or she had been there on location. Every time you record sound, you also record the surrounding noise and the relationship between your sound and that noise. We call this *presence*. It is the same kind of noise you hear in the background during "live" recordings at concerts. It is the same mixture of noises and sound that anyone would hear if they were at the same location. Presence adds a dimension of reality to what is otherwise a mere mechanical reproduction of a familiar sound. Like the naturalness we espouse in lighting, presence in sound recordings adds depth and realism to the sound track. For this reason, we recommend recording the sound "live" on location, whenever possible.

Does this mean that we will have to accept all the imperfections of the sound as it occurs on location? Not anymore than we would accept the imperfections of light and shadow that restrict us from taking the perfect exposure. Through use of different kinds of microphones, through careful microphone placement, and through careful attention to the recording process, we can usually record better quality sound and still retain its natural quality.

Before examining the techniques of sound recording, we must make one additional note. Although there are slight differences between single-system sound and double-system sound, the recording techniques are quite alike. What works for one system will generally work for the other.

Microphones

Choosing the correct microphone for sound recording is a lot like choosing the correct focal-length lens in photography. With a wide-angle lens, you get a large field of view, while a telephoto lens will show you a much smaller field of view. Similarly, mikes are chosen for their "field of hearing" or pickup pattern. An omnidirectional mike will hear from all sides, a bidirectional will pick up only from its two faces, while the cardiod and shotgun mikes will only pick up sound from in front of themselves in a particular kind of pattern.

However, there is a second complicating factor here, one that is not present when choosing the correct lens. There are two kinds of microphone designs, the dynamic and the condensor. When we discussed the tools of the film maker, we mentioned that each kind of mike has certain advantages in specific recording situations. Ideally, you should have both kinds available. The following list gives some specific recommendations for given recording situations, using both kinds of mikes and all types of patterns.

Sound-Recording Situation	**Type of Mike and Pickup Pattern**
News interviews on location.	Dynamic, cardiod pattern.
Studio sound work.	Condensor, bidirectional or cardiod pattern.
Music.	Condensor, bidirectional or cardiod pattern.
Live locations with controlled-sound conditions.	Condensor, bidirectional or cardiod pattern.
Live locations.	Dynamic, omnidirectional or cardiod pattern.
Sports events.	Dynamic, shotgun or cardiod pattern.

As a general rule, if you can control the ambient sound at your location, use the condensor mike—it's more sensitive. If mike handling might prove to be a problem, use the dynamic mike—it's more rugged. The pattern choice is dictated by the amount of background noise that you can tolerate on the track. If you can control the noise, the omnidirectional pattern gives a much better presence than does the cardiod pattern. But, in large crowds or on live locations, you will be better off using the cardiod pattern microphone with its rejection of signals that are not located in its pickup pattern.

Microphone Placement

The ideal microphone placement is near the sound source and pointing directly at it. The mike should be as far from the camera as possible to avoid camera noise. This kind of mike placement, best exemplified by the hand-held microphone, works well for news interviews but, in sound recording on location, we rarely achieve this ideal. And, in dramatic films, the microphone should not be seen in the picture. This leaves us with two possible mike positions—the boom mount and the concealed mike. Both have their problems but both meet some of the requirements of the ideal location.

Boom mounting means the microphone is suspended in a shockproof cradle and is fastened to a long pole or boom. This boom is balanced on the shoulder of the sound person (or mounted on a stand) with the mike hung directly above the sound source but out of the picture frame. The omnidirectional mike is a good choice for

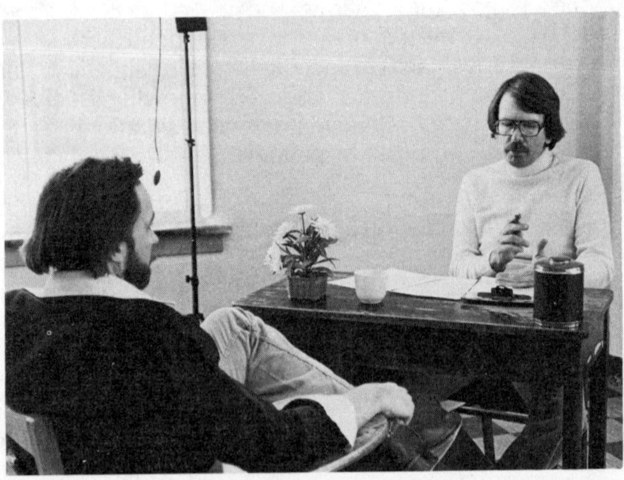

Fig. 8-8. Several objects on the desk can be used to hide the microphone.

boom mounting. Because of its pickup pattern, the omni mike will not have to be moved every time the sound source shifts or moves. Boom-mounted mikes have several problems, however. They can get in the way of lights and cause shadows. And, you must be careful to keep them away from buzzing light fixtures or noisy ventilation ducts, either of which can ruin a sound take.

The concealed microphone (Fig. 8-8) offers good sound-recording possibilities because it can be located directly at the sound source or close by on the set. This means you can use a more sensitive mike with a cardiod pattern to limit unwanted noise. *Lavalier and tie tack-style* microphones are small enough to be concealed on the person who is talking or on one of the people in the group. This allows the direct pickup of the sound. The problem is the cord. If the floor of the set will not be seen in the shot, the cord may be run there. Make sure no one trips over it. The cord will also limit the amount of movement that the "mike person" can make. A good compromise, in this case, is to conceal the mike somewhere on the set close enough to pick up the sound that you want but not so prominent as to be noticed. We have hidden mikes in book cases, on furniture, behind salt shakers, and in the shadows. Be sure that the location picked is not one that will pick up a lot of unwanted noise. Our salt shaker location was scratched when we discovered that any coffee cup being set down on the table produced a distinct thud on the sound track. We moved the mike to a boom position.

Miscellaneous

After you have positioned the microphone, you must run the cable. There are three things to watch out for here. Use the shortest run possible. We never exceed 50 feet and try to keep under 25 feet on any location. Make sure the cable connectors are firmly fastened and are taped together. We usually tape the cable to the boom and to the floor as well, so it will not move and generate additional "noise." Do not run cables parallel to ac power lines. Alternating current will produce a 60-cycle hum on your sound track. If you have to cross ac lines, do it at right angles to minimize any potential interference.

Setting the sound level is easy if you have manual control of the input volume. When running the sound test, before recording, increase the volume until distortion begins. Then, back off the volume slightly. This will give you the highest recording level, something that will be very important when transferring or dubbing the sound track.

Always listen to the sound, in a sound-level test, before recording. This is the time to make a judgment about the mike placement, the recording level, and the sound quality. Make any adjustments before shooting starts because a bad "sound take" will also render the corresponding picture take useless as well. If you are using double-system sound, do a test recording before doing a take.

With single-system sound (sound-on-film), extra care must be taken with the microphone placement and with the recording of the sound. Although it is relatively easy to dub over sound-on-film sound tracks, this kind of dubbing, in practice, tends to muddy the original track and cause some loss of signal. Unlike the double-system sound, where the separate tape track can be dubbed, mixed, etc., the single-system track is the *only* basis for all the sync recording in sound-on-film.

If camera noise is a problem, muffle the camera with a styrofoam cover or a heavy blanket. Most single-system sound cameras are quiet enough to be used without any additional sound dampening but some "silent" film cameras are almost too noisy to be used with double-system recording. Keep the mike as far away from the camera as possible and aim it toward the sound source. The problem of camera noise is more evident indoors than out of doors because of the sound reflection off the relatively hard surfaces indoors.

Tips for Good Sound Recording

1. Keep all microphones, recorders, cables, and connectors clean and in good repair.
2. The impedance of all mikes should match that of the sound camera or tape recorder. Check the camera or recorder instruction books for microphone impedance specifications.
3. Keep the mike close to the sound source.
4. Always test the sound level before recording.
5. Use the manual volume setting (if available) and set recording levels as high as possible without distorting the signal.
6. Wear *headphones* when monitoring or playing back sound. Earplugs may be more convenient but headphones are more accurate.
7. Use a windscreen on any microphone used out of doors.
8. Listen for unwanted noise, especially when using boom mikes or mikes with an omnidirectional pickup pattern.
9. Always monitor sound while it is being recorded (and play it back if using double-system recording).

CHAPTER 9

Producing Your Film

There are five steps in production that can be applied to all types of movies. These are *Setting Up the Shot, Directing the Action, Maintaining Continuity, Record Keeping,* and *Tearing Down.* These steps vary in complexity from Record Keeping, which is merely a matter of keeping the shooting log, to Setting Up the Shot, which involves placing the camera, blocking the action, setting lights, sound, etc. But each step is important and it should be done as if your film depended on it, for in fact, it does.

SETTING UP THE SHOT

The most important part of Setting Up the Shot is camera placement. When you wrote the script (or when you scouted this location), you had a fairly good idea of where you wanted the camera placed and how you wanted the action to be filmed. Check your shooting script and place the camera in the Master Shot camera position you have selected for this location.

Now select the field of view and compose the shot. You may have to move the camera closer to the subject, or farther away from it, before you get exactly the point of view that you want. (Or, you can zoom in or out to accomplish the same thing.) Keeping in mind the rules of composition, find the field of view that will best show what you want your audience to see in this shot.

After you have placed the camera, practice those camera movements that you will be making during the shot. Find the start and finish of any pan, dolly, or trucking shot. Mark the movement on the head of the tripod (for a pan), or on the ground or floor (for a dolly or truck shot). If you are planning to zoom, determine the field of view at either end of the zoom. Mark the start and finish of the zoom shot with a bit of masking tape taped onto the zoom ring so the camera operator can find them easily. The same thing should be done if a focus shift is planned. (Place the tape on the focus ring. See Fig. 9-1.)

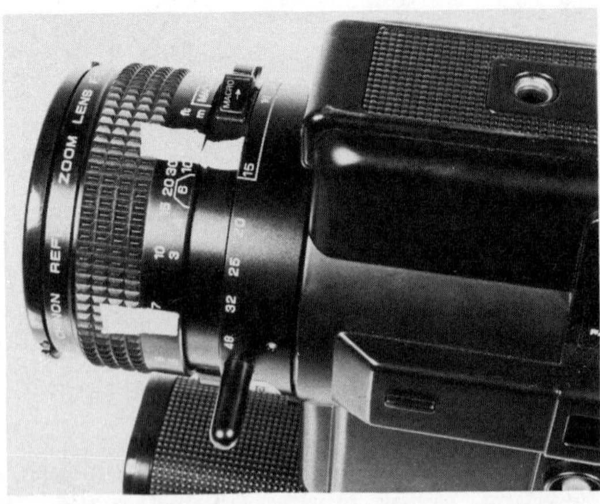

Fig. 9-1. For a focus shift, use tape to mark the start and stop points on the focus ring.

To get a smooth movement at the start of a pan (or tilt), have the pan and tilt controls loosened before moving the camera. This will ensure the smoothest camera movement. Always lock up the controls when the pan or tilt is finished. When dollying or trucking, make sure that the wheels of the dolly are pointed in the opposite direction from that which you intend to move. This will help assure a smooth launch without a lot of wavering. We usually assign one person to push or pull the dolly while another runs the camera. The camera operator may be able to do both but her attention would be split and, thus, both operations might suffer.

The same situation could apply when you are doing a focus shift or a complicated pan-tilt-zoom. One person runs and moves the camera while the second "pulls focus" or moves the zoom lens. For additional smoothness, we usually run all our camera setups with a remote run switch. Then, we do not have to touch the camera at all except to move it.

After rehearsing any camera movement, lock up the tripod head and set up the lights. (If outdoors, you may only need to place the reflectors.) When you blocked this set in the shooting script, you probably chose the lighting design to use. Set up the lighting instruments in this plan, run the cables, and test the lights. Look through the viewfinder to check the coverage. Adjust the lighting setup to get rid of hot spots and bad shadows.

Switch off the lights and load the camera with film. After making sure that the filter is in the correct position, switch on the camera, turn on the lights, and check the exposure. Is there a reasonable contrast range between the brightest and the darkest objects in the shot? (A range of two f/stops is okay.) If the camera is to move, is the exposure all right through the entire range of movement? If the camera is zooming, will the exposure vary as the size of the field changes? Adjust your lighting accordingly. This is also the time to lock in the correct exposure manually, if you are planning to do that. Shut off the camera. Turn off the lights.

Set up the sound-recording system. If it is single-system, place the microphone, run the cable, and plug it in. For double-system sound (Fig. 9-2), set up the recorder, connect the camera-recorder link, and then place the microphone. Make sure that the mike is away from noisy lights and loud footfalls. No mike lines should be run parallel to ac power lines, either. Run a test to be sure the sound system and microphones are working properly.

Bring in the actors. Explain what you want from them in this shot, and how this shot relates to the rest of the film. Since you are usually shooting out of sequence, it is often difficult for an actor to realize the total impact of his fragmented performance before he sees the completed film. Be sure the actors know what is required of them.

Now, block the scene and have the actors run through it once or twice. As they are rehearsing, put the camera through its paces and watch the entire affair through the viewfinder. Then, ask yourself the following questions. Is the important action still clearly visible in this shot? Is the composition okay? Do the actors look all right under this lighting arrangement? This is your chance to make those final corrections to the picture.

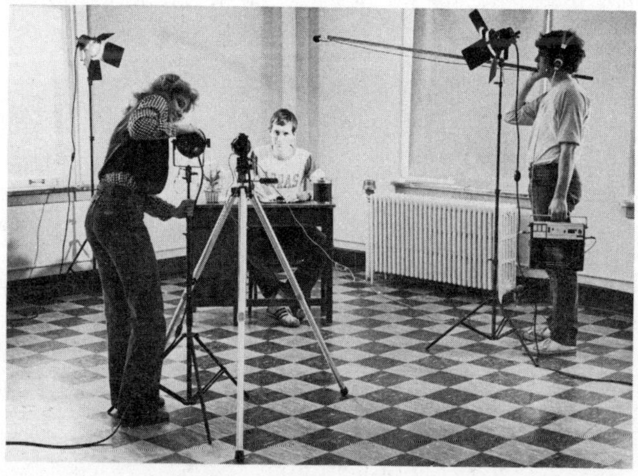

Fig. 9-2. Double-system sound on location. Note key-fill lighting and the boom microphone position.

Run a sound-level check. If you are using double-system sound, you will want to record the test and play it back. With single-system sound, you can only listen to the sound "live" and adjust the level. In either case, sound-recording levels should be set and noted at this time. Our method of setting sound levels is to turn the volume up until the sound just begins to distort and, then, back it off slightly.

Check the focus. Zoom all the way in. Turn the focus ring until the object is in good focus. Then, go slightly past that setting and return. This will ensure that you have gotten the best focus you can see. We usually focus on a person's eyes. If this isn't possible, have the actor hold his hand, palm out, next to his face. You can use the outline to focus on. If you have any doubts about the focus, measure it—from the subject to the film plane of the camera. After focusing, zoom back out to your chosen focal length. Since you now have all three elements needed to compute the depth of field, go to the tables and work it out. Will your subject move out of the limits during the shot? Will the camera movement or the zoom shot drastically alter the depth of field? Adjust focus as necessary.

Turn the camera back on and check all systems. Are the lens and the eyepiece clean? Batteries up? Be sure there is enough film for this shot. Are zoom and focus set correctly? Are they marked for any point-to-point changes during the shot?

Prepare the slate. (We slate every shot, and most takes, as it helps enormously in editing.) You can use bits of masking tape to write the numbers on, and stick them on the slate, instead of using chalk on the board itself.

Check the focus again. Get everyone in position. You are now ready to take the shot.

CHECKLIST FOR SETTING UP SHOT

1. Camera position (from shooting script).
2. Select field of view.
3. Rehearse camera movements.
4. Set up and test lights.
5. Load film, check filter position and exposure.
6. Set up and test sound (if double-system sound, record and play back the test).
7. Block and rehearse actors.
8. Set sound level.
9. Check focus.
10. Compute depth of field from charts.
11. Check all camera systems.
12. Prepare the slate.

13. Check focus AGAIN.
14. You are now ready to take the shot.

DIRECTING THE ACTION

Directing the action is the most complicated part of taking a shot. The rest is really routine. After all, this is the moment you have been working toward since you thought of this concept. Now that the moment is here, all you have to do is follow the procedure.

TAKING THE SHOT CHECKLIST

1. Turn on the lights.
2. Position the actors.
3. Call SOUND for double system. (Rolling)
   Call CAMERA. (Rolling)
   Run the SLATE. (With scene, shot and CLAP)

   Call ACTION. (Do the shot)
4. *CUT.* (Everything stops)
5. Check with camera.
6. Check with sound. (Play back if double-system sound.)
7. Check action, blocking, movement, and dialogue.
8. Do record keeping.

We always take the shot within the run of the camera. Start the camera before starting the action and do not cut until the action is completed. Always watch the action through the viewfinder or from the camera point of view. This will allow you to follow every portion of the action as it would appear on the screen.

There are three things to keep in mind about action. Action must be correct for the shot, action must be complete, and the action should seem like parts of a continuous performance. These are the actors' problems, of course. But, because you are the only one who can observe the action while it is going on, you must take the responsibility to note and correct any problems that arise. Correcting any mistakes or omissions in action is usually done by referring the actor to the script or by running through the blocking again. Making the action seem complete is no more difficult. When shooting *insert shots*, for example, your tendency may be to only take that portion of the shot that you know you are going to use. But this puts an additional burden on the actor. The best thing to do is to shoot the entire piece of action again and, later, edit out that portion that you do not want to use.

Making the bits of action in a shot look like related parts of a whole is a more complicated process. By telling the actor(s) what relation this shot bears to another, or to the whole film, you have laid the groundwork for consistency of action and character. But, even then, the actor may not know just where he should be in developing his character. This can lead to some very wooden acting or some embarrassing inconsistencies. The solution is twofold. Shoot the Master Shot first. This allows the actors to have consistent development within the scene, anyway. Check the script to see what has happened immediately before this scene or shot and what will happen immediately after. This will give *you* the mental picture needed to direct the shot appropriately and it can provide you with an explanation of the action and characters for the actors.

If it is necessary to retake a shot to correct a technical problem (lights, sound, camera, etc.), encourage the actor to repeat his or her excellent performance in just exactly the same way that it was just done. If the retake is due to his or her error (lines or blocking), be gentle in your corrections. But, make sure that the actor knows exactly what is required.

MAINTAINING CONTINUITY

A good film actor is the one who can perform the role in a consistent way from shot to shot and from scene to scene. You can help maintain this consistency by shooting with an overlapping action and by maintaining a visual continuity. Shooting with *overlapping action* means that in successive shots (and in related shots, too), part of the action of the previous shot is repeated. This is done so that the actor can go through more complete actions and, also, so you have more footage of each action. For example, in the film of *The Bandits*, Shots 3, 5, and 7 are to be filmed from the same camera position. (Refer to the scenario and the shooting script in Chapter 2 for details.) Since all these shots are of the Boss, by using the concept of overlapping action, we can shoot all three at the same time in one long take (Fig. 9-3). This will allow the actor playing the Boss to work out the action and speak the dialogue smoothly and naturally. In the finished film, these shots will be separated by Shots 4 and 6, which will be inserted during the editing process.

If these three shots were not to be shot from exactly the same camera angle or with the same field of view, the action could be shot in the following manner. For Shot 3, the Boss would begin the action by looking around, then he would flick the ash from his cigar, and speak his line. In Shot 5, the Boss would begin the action with the previous line (from Shot 3), then look at the sky and, then, give his next line. In Shot 7, the Boss would begin with a look at the sky, give his previous line, and, then, get out pencil and paper, and draw the map.

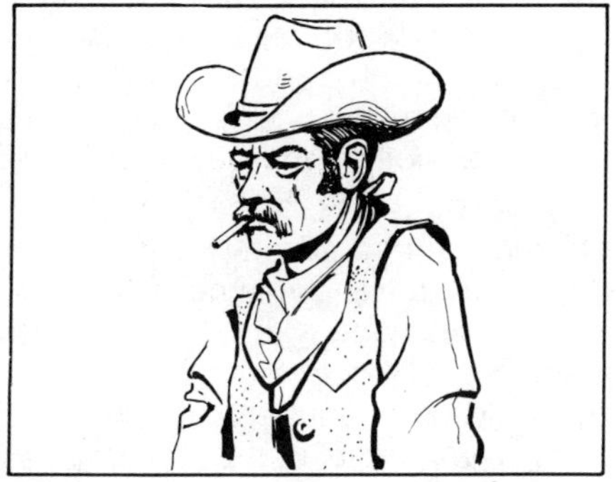

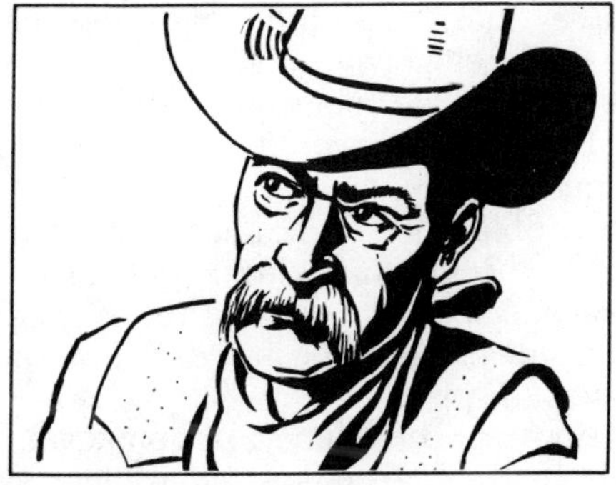

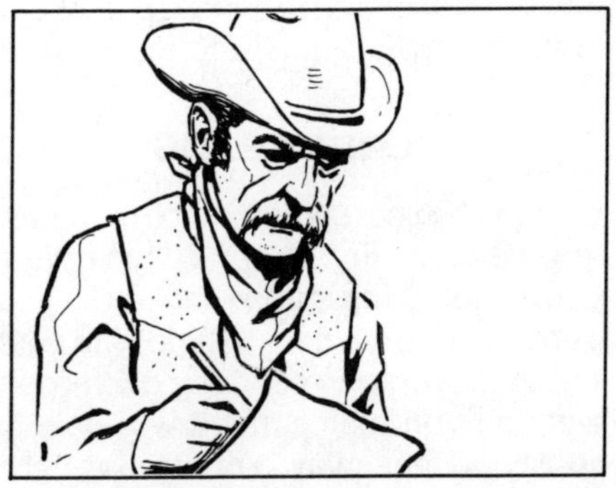

Fig. 9-3. Storyboards of Shots, 3, 5, and 7 of "The Bandits" film.

In both these cases, by shooting in overlapping action, we have given the actors a chance to work small character builds within the scene, and we have given ourselves more footage from which we can create the finished film. No matter which way you do it, shooting in this manner makes for smoother and better looking films.

The second way that you can assist the consistency of the actors' performances is to maintain an accurate visual continuity. Visual continuity refers to the position and attitude of persons and objects in the shot. Visual continuity (along with consistency of characterization) helps the audience to understand that the shots indicate a continuous flow of action even though the point of view changes.

When we blocked *The Bandits* in the shooting script, the exact positions of the actors and their movements were indicated. If the same action is filmed from two or more camera positions (as would be the case with overlapping action), the actors must start from, and end up in, those indicated positions during each shot. They must also do the same gestures, make the same facial expressions, etc., so that when one shot is cut together with another, the action will appear to be all of a piece. Remind the actors to remember their movements and gestures from take to take, and from shot to shot. Assign someone to watch this kind of continuity, also.

The placement of objects in a scene must also remain consistent. If the treasure map that the Boss makes in Shot 7 is placed faceup on the rock, it must be faceup on the rock in Shot 19. If the horses were tied to a tree on the far side of the ravine in Shot 1, they should be in the same place for Shot 17.

To help maintain visual continuity, take a photograph of the scene and of each of the actors with an "instant" camera. On the back of the photo, note the details of the set or the costume of the actor. If it is necessary to retake that shot or match it with another, days later, you will have a visual record. There can be no doubt about what the actor was wearing or how he parted his hair. These photos can also be used to note the position of props, actors, etc.

RECORD KEEPING

After you have taken the shot, you should do the record keeping. We use a Shooting Log (see Fig. 9-4) in which we record all the information about the shot. A log is important for several reasons. It is valuable to catch errors in production, to help with continuity, and to aid editing. For instance, you are recording the focusing distance of the shot in the log, and you notice that it was only 5 feet yet your subject was obviously 10 feet away. You have caught a production error. It is a much simpler matter to reshoot at this point than it is to try to correct it on the editing bench later. Knowing what film stock,

SHOOTING LOG

TITLE: __THE BANDITS__   DIRECTOR: __GLENN__   DATE: __10-24__

SCENE	SHOT	TAKE	FILM TYPE & ROLL	FILTER	LENS	FOCUS	F/STOP	FOOTAGE/TIME	SOUND	REEL NBR.	SPEED	COUNTER
1	2	3	K40 4	IN	12 MM	8 FT	F/5.6	5 FT/15 SEC	YES	2	7½	053 - 062
1	2	3	K40 4	IN	10 MM	8 FT	F/5.6	5 FT/15 SEC	YES	2	7½	062 - 072

Fig. 9-4. Example of a shooting log. Two takes of "The Bandits" are shown.

what focal length, f/stop, focusing distance, and sound level you are using can help you recreate or match an effect that was obtained earlier if you have to retake shots.

On the editing bench, much time can be saved by referring to the shooting log. It tells what shots are on what rolls, what special effects (like fades or dissolves) were used between shots, and where the sound is for each take. Finally, keeping track of the film-making process should be just as orderly as making the film is. The shooting log is one of the last steps in organizing the film-making process.

There is one more thing that should be recorded. If there were any changes made in the shooting script (camera position, blocking, dialogue, etc.), note these on the script itself.

TEARING DOWN

Tearing Down and Moving are among the easiest tasks you have. Here is a brief series of DON'T FORGETS for this operation.

1. Don't forget to switch off the camera. If this is the last shot of the day, you might want to unload the film. Don't forget to mark the amount of unexposed film on the side of the cartridge. Check the film gauge or footage counter before you take the film out of the camera.
2. Don't forget to let the lights cool before you take them down.

Wait at least 10 minutes. The filaments are very fragile when they are hot and you could lose a lot of lamps by rushing this job.
3. Don't forget to thank your cast and crew for their work, and don't forget to thank your hosts for their cooperation.

END OF PRODUCTION CHECKLIST

1. Send film in for processing, promptly.
2. Check and clean the camera.
3. Check and clean the sound equipment.
4. Pack up lights and stands.
5. Check and repair cables and cords.
6. Reward cast and crew.

If there is any film left on any cartridge, run it off in the camera with the lens cap left on. This will facilitate processing. Remember, the "EXPOSED" mark must appear at the end for the film to be completely run off. Do not let the film sit around, especially not in the hot glove box of your car. Send it in as soon as possible.

Remove the batteries from the camera and clean out the battery chamber. Clean the lens and eyepiece. Swab the film gate with a cotton swab and brush out the film chamber. After wiping off the outside of the camera with a soft cloth, place the camera in a plastic bag and store it in a cool dry place.

The tape recorder and microphone(s) should also be inspected and cleaned. Again, remove any batteries and clean the battery chambers. Clean the sound heads with denatured alcohol or head cleaner.

Put the lighting instruments and stands back in their carrying cases. We usually leave halogen lamps in their instruments since taking them out and putting them back in could cause them more harm. We usually remove incandescent lamps, however, as their larger size makes them more prone to breakage while in storage. Look over the cables and cords carefully for frayed spots or damaged connectors. After you have repaired them, coil them up and put them away.

Reward your cast and crew. Make arrangements for the next shooting day, the big party, or the premier showing of your masterpiece.

SOUND-ON-FILM PRODUCTION

All of the filming procedures mentioned previously apply to most kinds of sound- and silent-film making. But there is a special case that uses slightly different techniques. This is the sound-on-film interview shot in the tv news style (Fig. 9-5). The major difference between

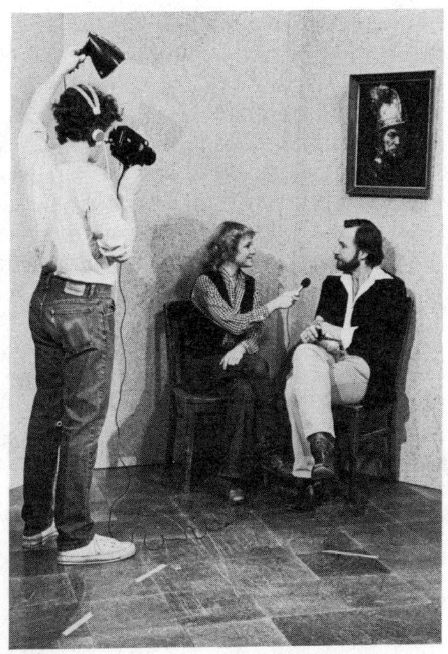

**Fig. 9-5. Sound-on-film news interview shootings commonly use
2-person crews.**

regular film production and sound-on-film news stories is the amount
of time that one has to set up, shoot, and tear down. The tv news
people have to shoot and run, while regular film makers have (or
take) much more time to get the same amount of footage.

Here are a few tips for effective filming when shooting
sound-on-film in the tv news style.

1. *Lighting*—Use bounce lighting for fill if possible. Bring along
   one quartz floodlight and stand, and set it halfway between the
   key and fill positions. If more direct light is needed, aim the
   flood at the subject. The last choice in lighting is the
   camera-mounted spot, although this is often necessary for
   quick takes. If it must be used, this light should be bounced to
   soften its glare.

2. *Sound*—Get the mike as close as possible. The hand-held
   position is best, but have the newsperson hold it. If this is a
   one-person operation, leave the microphone on the camera
   and be prepared to sacrifice considerable sound quality (and
   sometimes audibility).

3. *Filming Procedure*—Always allow the sound-on-film camera 3–5 seconds run-up before starting the sound recording. This period of time gives the machinery a chance to get up to running speed and the electronic circuits a chance to come up to full volume. Another reason for doing this is because of the relationship between the sound and the picture in sound-on-film filming. The sound is 18 frames ahead of the picture. If shots are taken without any interval between them, the beginning sound for one shot might be on the tail of the previous shot. This would cause some real problems during editing.

Shoot as much footage as possible from as many angles as you can. Take additional shots of the action, location, etc., for cutaway shots to be inserted and dubbed in the final story. Do not worry about having too much footage. It is the editor's job to cut the footage to fit the air time.

4. *Record Keeping*—Skip the slate, it takes too much time. Keep a log of the shots, however, so the editor will know what is where. The following is a sample log:

SHOT No.	SUBJECT	SOUND?	FOOTAGE
1	Mayor—Answer	Yes	0—30'

If you follow the other rules of good film making, your news-style sound-on-film footage will come out as good as your more carefully prepared dramatic and documentary films.

TITLING

We have already established the need for titles. Certainly you want to list all those people who helped to make your show the success it is going to be. And you may want to insert on title cards some of the information that is necessary to your audience's understanding of the film.

When planning titles, decide how many are needed and what should be said on each card. We usually use separate titles for the main title (the name of the movie), the cast, the crew, the director, and anyone who helped with the production ("Special thanks to . . ."). That means we will have a minimum of five titles in each of our films. Whatever you decide on will obviously be dictated, in part, by the complexity of your production and by the amount of time you want to spend on making and photographing titles.

Keep the message on each title as simple as possible so the audience can read it quickly and comprehend it fully. This is especially important if you are making dialogue titles (for insertion in the body of the film).

We often use rub-on or stick-on letters to make titles. Check your local art or school supply store for the types and sizes of lettering available. Put the letters on matte-finish cardboard or poster board. Make sure the contrast between the lettering and the mounting board is high (like black letters on a yellow background). Low-contrast titling makes your titles harder to read.

Composing

When laying out titles (Fig. 9-6), remember to balance the words on the card and keep in the same *safe area* (compose for the center of the card). Most titles that are longer than one word will fit better on two lines than on one long line. This is because the aspect ratio of the Super 8 frame, 3 units high and 4 units wide, fits rectangular-shaped messages more readily than it fits long lines of type. However, the 3:4 aspect places certain limits on the placement of lettering and the use of space. Balance your titles around the horizontal and vertical centerlines, keeping the mass slightly above the horizontal centerline. This will keep the title from looking like it is slipping off the card.

The *safe area* is that area within the title card that can be photographed without shooting the border of the card. Keep in mind that the viewfinder often does not give you the whole picture. What you see may be slightly less that what the camera is getting. To

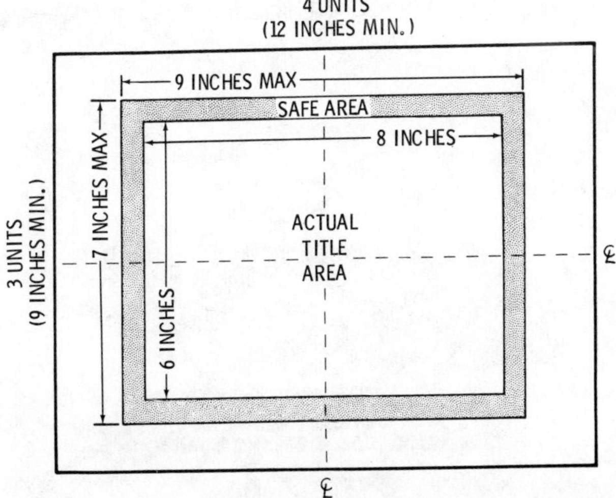

Fig. 9-6. A sample title card.

compensate for this misalignment, leave a border that is equal to one-quarter of the entire field around your titles on the card. If this area appears to be too large when framing, zoom in on the title and forget the borders. They will take care of themselves.

When applying letters, pictures, etc., to your title cards, make sure that all the lines are straight, the letters are evenly spaced, and all stick-on materials are wrinkle free. Even when properly photographed, with good lighting, little flaws on title cards will become apparent, because they are on the screen for a relatively long period of time.

Shooting

There are two ways of photographing titles, on the copy stand (Fig. 9-7) or on the easel (Fig. 9-8). For either way, the requirements for camera setting, lighting, exposure, and timing are the same. The only difference might be the focus setting (and whether or not to use macro-focus), and the size of the field of view. Set the camera perpendicular (in both the horizontal and vertical planes) to the title cards or the cards will look *keystoned*. Measure the distance from the card to the film plane and set the focus. Compose the field of view by zooming in or out. Make the titles as large as possible in the frame; then, back off slightly to get a small border.

Lighting should be done with two lights of equal wattage (one from each side), in the same plane as the camera, and at 45° angles to the work. The use of 500-watt lamps will give more than enough light for good exposures with slow film stocks like Kodachrome 40. Use slow film when shooting titles because it has a finer grain for better-quality pictures.

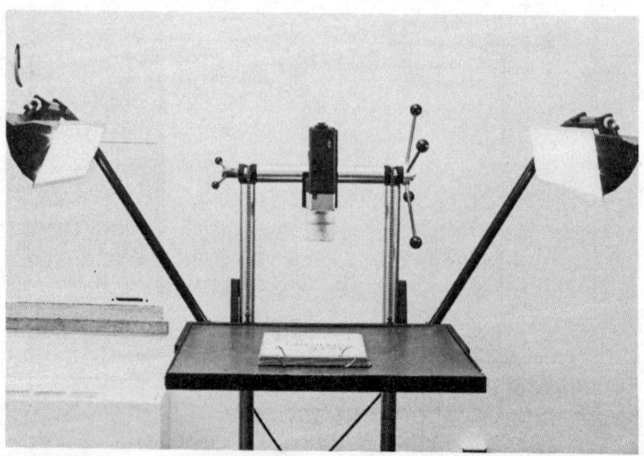

Fig. 9-7. A copy stand requires a close-focusing lens.

Take the exposure using the gray card method, and lock it into the camera. That way, you will avoid any exposure problems that could result from the difference in contrast between the lettering and the background.

How long should titles run? This is really an editing problem, but you should have some idea so that you will know how much film to take of each card. As we film titles, we usually read the title out loud, slowly, and then add two seconds extra. This allows even the slowest reader a good chance to get the intended message. Do not be afraid to shoot the title longer than that, however. If you find that the title runs too long when spliced into the finished film, trim it down.

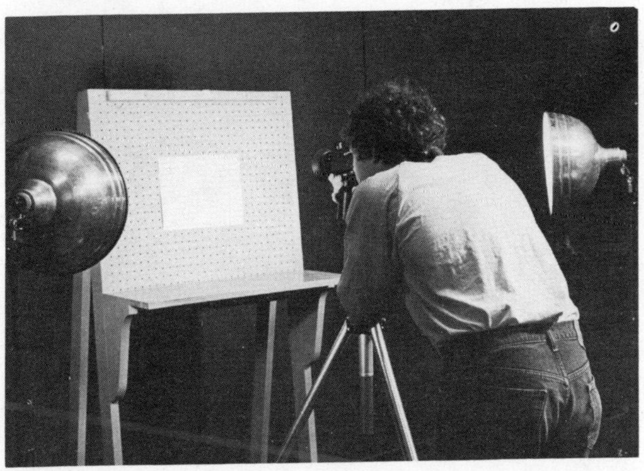

Fig. 9-8. The easel requires careful placement of the lighting.

Post Production

CHAPTER 10

Editing

Many film makers say that the really creative part of film making is in the editing. This is the time when all the pieces of processed film are brought together and arranged into a complete and coherent whole; it is the time when the sound track is mixed and dubbed, and the titles are added. The editing bench (and the editing process) is the place (and the time) where you can make some sense out of the series of pictures and sounds you have taken and recorded.

Editing consists of two processes, *splicing*, which is cutting apart and joining the pieces of film together physically, and *editing*, which involves choosing the shots to be included in the film, arranging them in order, and trimming them for time. (Don't be confused by the terminology here. Just as the all inclusive term *film making* also refers to the specific task of shooting film, so does the general term *editing* include all those parts of the post-production process that occur on the editing bench or in the editing room.)

Before we talk about the tools or the physical part of editing, let us take a brief look at the *concept of editing* and the *controlling philosophy* behind what the editor does. Editing is the creative manipulation of the raw footage of the film. We edit for continuity and sequence so as to bring order to the footage; we edit for time and pace to give the footage movement and speed; we edit for manipulation of content so that we can make the movie say what we want it to say. The editor is in charge of this stage of the film production just as the director was in charge during the shooting of the picture. The editor must make a conscious effort to control the film, otherwise, the editor is merely an assembler of parts.

To use an analogy, editing film is to the process of film making what delivery is to public speaking. You write and rehearse your speech like you write and shoot your script. Then, as you deliver it, you inflect it, emphasize it, and adapt it so that it best meets the needs of your audience and transmits the message you want them to hear.

That is what film editing is like. After you have created the pictures, you emphasize them, arrange them, and manipulate them in relation to one another to best say what you want to say to the audience. And you may even change or adapt them (the pictures) if you find that your intended message is not getting across to the audience. Professional directors still preview their films before ordinary audiences in order to test this very reaction. And, they often re-edit to make their message more clear.

Film is edited for three effects—*continuity, timing,* and *manipulation of content.* They are all parts of the whole, however, and it would be difficult to gauge their separate effects on the film. As you will discover, a change in the speed at which the action in a given scene takes place (a timing change) will effect the content of that scene as well as making a change between that scene and others (a continuity change). Nevertheless, for clarity, we will have to discuss these parts separately remembering that they are highly integrated.

CONTINUITY

Continuity is the arrangement of the scenes to create a certain reality or frame of reference upon which the audience can base its perception of the film. It is the arrangement of shots in a sequence to imply cause and affect, to indicate and emphasize certain actions, and to give reason and motivation to reactions. Continuity is accomplished by the arrangement of shots and scenes, by the juxtaposition of shots and scenes with one another, and by the insertion of one shot or scene within the "boundaries" of another.

We normally think of continuity in film as being chronological (arranging events by relating them to the time in which they took place). This is easy for the audience to understand and relatively easy to do. The simplest of these time-continuities is the chronological progression from first event to last event. Many films have been written and edited this way because it is the most comprehensible order, and one that best illustrates our story-telling conventions about events in real life. However, there are several switches on this standard chronological progression that are commonly used in motion pictures. These include the flashback (or return to a prior time), the flash forward (or look into the future), the time reverse (in which the last event happens first and we replay the past to find the first cause), and parallel or multiple lines of action where we see two or more events, that in real time would have happened at the same time, happening one after another.

But, continuity does not have to follow time progression at all. In a documentary film, for example, it may follow a progression of facts revealed, starting with the most important first and concluding with the least important, like the classic inverted pyramid structure of the newspaper story. Or, it may follow a continuity dictated by the form, shape, or colors of the images involved, like an abstract art film might do.

Continuity may arise from some internal order inherent in the footage or it may be imposed completely from the outside. The point is that the editor can create his own continuity by imposing his vision on the raw footage. He does not have to follow conventional types of continuity merely because other films have followed them in the past. He is free to create his own. However, any continuity established by the editor must be internally consistent. The sequence of shots must have been planned with some reason in mind. While any series of shots spliced together may assume a continuity to the audience, unless they were intended to be put together in that way, there is no true continuity.

TIMING

Timing is the second element of editing. It is, in the jargon of film editors, "What makes the movie move." The audience notices timing primarily as the pace of the picture. The editor thinks of timing as a way to speed up or slow down the pace of the picture, and a way to compress or stretch the screen time of real events.

Timing is imposed, established, and maintained by the speed at which action happens within the shot, by the length of the shots, and by the length of the combinations of shot (scenes). When the editor edits for continuity, he or she orders and rearranges scenes and shots. When the editor edits for time, he or she lengthens or shortens scenes and shots, or intercuts shots and scenes of various lengths to create a sense of pace.

Pace is the result of timing. It is the sum of the speed of the action plus the length of the shots themselves, plus the scenes and the interrelationship of the various shots and scenes. Timing is what the editor does, pace is the result.

There are three problems inherent in timing. How long should a shot be on the screen? How can action be speeded up or slowed down? What controls the pace of the picture? Although there are no absolute answers for any of these questions, we can establish some guidelines.

A shot should be on the screen long enough for the audience to get the information that you want them to get. A shot that contains a lot of information can be held on the screen longer than a closeup shot of the same scene which contains only part of that information (Figs. 10-1 and 10-2). If the shot is an establishing shot and you want the audience to see all the details of the location, then you will have to

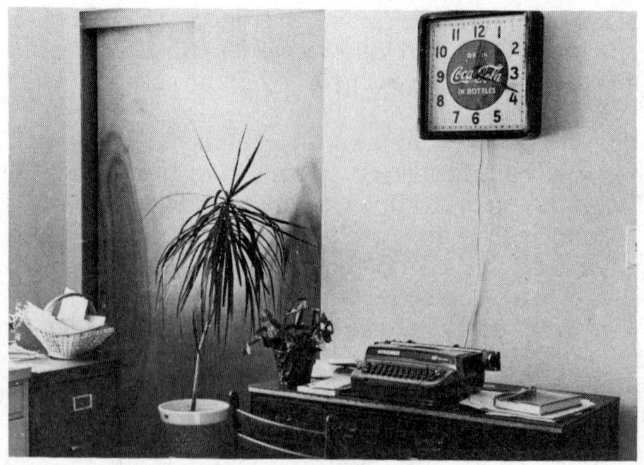

Fig. 10-1. Medium long shot of a detailed scene.

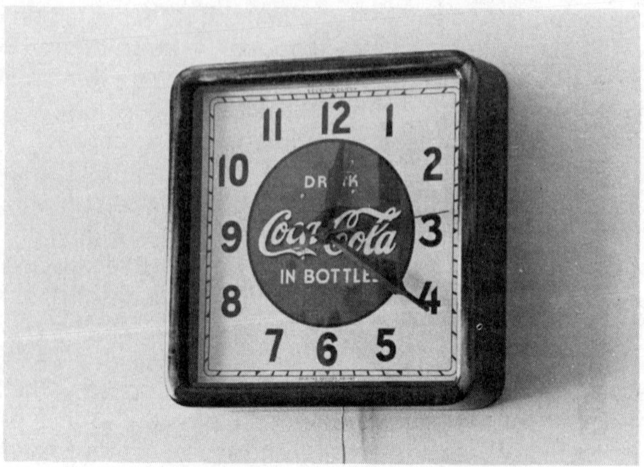

Fig. 10-2. Close up of the scene in Fig. 10-1.

leave it on the screen for a relatively long time. But if you only want them to see a brief glimpse and then take their attention to something else, you will need to cut it short. A good rule of thumb is: If the information in the shot is exhausted, then change it.

The other consideration for the duration of a shot on the screen is the action contained within that shot. We might think that we should keep shots on the screen from the beginning of the action to the end of it, because this seems realistic (it approximates the real time in which the action happened). But the convention(s) of time in film tell us that there is little relationship between real time and screen time. The determining factor for making cuts of action shots is what the audience will find believable. Our rule of thumb is: Edit the shot for the action. Cut into it when the action is underway and cut away as the action ends. If the shot needs to be shorter, then cut either end (or both), but preserve the essential action. Sometimes, actions may even be completely eliminated; the audience will fill in the gap in their minds.

This kind of cutting can also be used to solve the second time problem, that of making things seem to happen faster or slower than they did in real time. Shortening the shots will speed up the action, using the shots at their full length will slow it down. But the stretching or compression of action in time is best done by the cutting together or the intercutting of the shots of that scene. In this sense, the script dictates the basic timing that each scene will have.

Any scene is composed of action and reaction shots. In our Bandit film, for example, we have a shot of the Boss questioning the Henchman, a shot of the Henchman's reply. The Boss makes a statement, the Henchman responds. The Boss starts to draw a map, the map is finished. The speed of the action is controlled by the combination of action and reaction shots, and by what each shot shows us. The way the scene is written builds a sense of time that can only be traditionally altered by adding or eliminating shots.

The accumulation of these timing cuts and the internal speed of the scene results in "pace." Pace is the sum of the timing cuts. Pace is what the audience perceives as the "speed" of the picture. If the action seems to move rapidly, we say the picture is *fast paced*. If the action proceeds in a more leisurely fashion, we consider the picture *slow paced*. The actual length of the film has less to do with the pace than do the timing cuts, the speed of the action within the shots, and the length of the shots and scenes that are relative to one another. This principle is graphically illustrated on television if we compare the half-hour situation comedy with a news documentary feature. The comedy seems to have an almost frantic pace by comparison to the news show, even though the news show may only be one-half to two-thirds as long.

There are several ways to control pace. One is dependent upon the "speed" at which the action unfolds in the script, another is dependent upon the timing cuts of the shots. A third way results from the alternation of scenes of different pacings with one another. If all the scenes in a picture are of the same pace, the picture will seem rather dull. The sameness of the pace will bore the viewer. This is as true of a fast-paced picture as it is of a slow one. The best way to pace a film is to alternate scenes of different pacings with one another. This is partly a function of the script, of course. But, it is also a function of the editor. The editor's job, here, is to keep the entire film in mind, even when making a simple timing cut, to remember that any changes in timing will affect the pace, and to remember that the pace of the scene should match the meaning of the picture, according to the script.

MANIPULATION OF CONTENT

Everything that has been said up to this point, about continuity and timing, can also be applied to manipulation of content. Manipulation of content is changing the meaning, or changing the impact of what you have photographed, through the editing process. The need to manipulate content arises from the problem of translating the story from script to screen. Even if you are a skilled director, what you meant to show or say in a shot is not always what you did show or say. Furthermore, the impact or meaning of the shot could be blunted or changed by its placement relative to other shots in the scene, or by its internal or external timing.

The ways that can be used to change the meaning or impact of the content, in editing, vary with the kind of shots or scenes. The following gives some general principles.

Continuity

Movies are linearly additive. The first shot is followed by the second shot is followed by the third shot, etc. Anything that happens before a shot is its precedent, and anything that happens after that shot is a reaction to it. The whole structure of chronological time seems to be undermined by this film form. Things do not necessarily happen on the screen in the order in which they happen in real life.

Yet the audience still relates the information they receive sequentially. Things that happen in order are then related to each other in that order. In logic, this is called the *post hoc fallacy*. The original Latin phrase states "Post hoc, ergo propter hoc," which translates as "After this, therefore because of this." (A good example of the post-hoc fallacy is the belief on the part of the rooster that the sun will rise only if he crows.) Film makes its own sequence of action-reaction and relationships. This sequence is established by the order in which the shots are presented.

In this kind of sequential reasoning, it doesn't matter if the actual cause and effect are related, or if any cause and effect exists at all. Because one shot follows another, the relationship is established. If we show a shot of a bandit digging a hole and follow it with a shot of another bandit holding a rifle, the audience will assume that the first man is being forced to dig the hole by the second man, or that the second man is guarding the first. Some viewers will even read an emotional content into these shots, emotions that they perceive as being established by the sequence in which the shots were presented.

Timing

The timing of the duration of shots gives the following effects:

1. Holding a closeup heightens its impact.
2. Holding a long shot will eventually diminish its impact since the details visible in the shot are not great enough for the audience to continue to read it.

The timing of the frequency of shots has the following impact.

1. Repeating the same or similar action shots will give two impressions.
    (A) Initially it will slow the pace and increase the emphasis on that action.
    (B) Ultimately it will become so recognizable that only the "punch line" need be shown.
2. Double cutting of reaction shots (showing the same shots, action and reaction, twice in a row) makes them more obvious and softens their impact.

The cutting to and from shots will produce the following audience responses.

1. Cutting to a moving camera shot draws attention to the action.
2. Cutting into a zoom-in draws attention to the subject or object.
3. Cutting into a zoom-out gives a feeling of distance and alienation to the viewer.
4. Cutting from a moving camera shot to a static camera shot puts considerable emphasis on the static shot and makes it a reaction shot to the camera movement.
5. Cuts which eliminate or compress large parts of the action, or make large jumps in time or space, tend to draw us out of the previous scene with lingering memories of what we just saw. This kind of cutting, in action shots, allows the pace to be increased and deemphasizes the importance of that piece of action. When used in time or space situations, this kind of cutting allows large displacements of time without having to explain what happened in between. The viewer will tend to fill in his or her own explanation for the gap.

Initially, we control the meaning and impact of the film by scripting and shooting the story in a certain way. During editing, we adjust the meaning and impact to meet our expectations by manipulating content. This kind of fine tuning can best be done in the editing stage, when the picture is nearly completed, so we can judge the total impression that the film gives. Now that you have learned something about the theoretical aspect of film editing, let us take a look at the tools.

EDITING EQUIPMENT

The basic tools of editing are the splicing block (or splicer), the viewer (sometimes called the viewer-editor), and the projector. As with most film-making equipment, there are both simple and complex versions of these tools. In the following descriptions, we will explain what levels of complexity and accuracy you will need from your tools in order to do various kinds of editing.

The Splicer

The simplest tool of the editing group is the splicer (Fig. 10-3). The splicer is a machine used for cutting and joining film together. It holds the film in exact alignment so that accurate cuts and joins (or splices) can be made. There are two basic types of splicers—those which make tape splices and those which make cement splices. There are advantages to each type, depending on the kind of editing to be done.

Tape splicers—They cut the film at the frameline. Then, the ends of the film are joined together with short sections of transparent Mylar-based adhesive tape. The film is *butt-spliced*; the ends of the film are not overlapped. The tape is perforated to conform to the

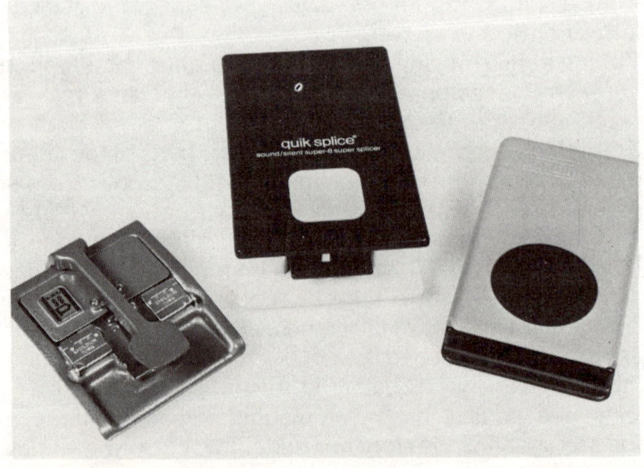

Courtesy Eumig

Fig. 10-3. Three common types of tape splicers.

sprocket holes in the film. The tape covers several frames on either side of the join and on both sides of the film (Fig. 10-4). We have used several different kinds of tape splicers and, for accuracy and ease of operation, prefer the splicers that utilize the one-piece wrap-around splices. Whatever brand of splicer you obtain, make sure it is a well-made one; this is the only way to ensure accuracy in cutting. It should cut the film easily, hold it firmly in place, and allow easy application of the splicing tape (Fig. 10-5). Our most recent

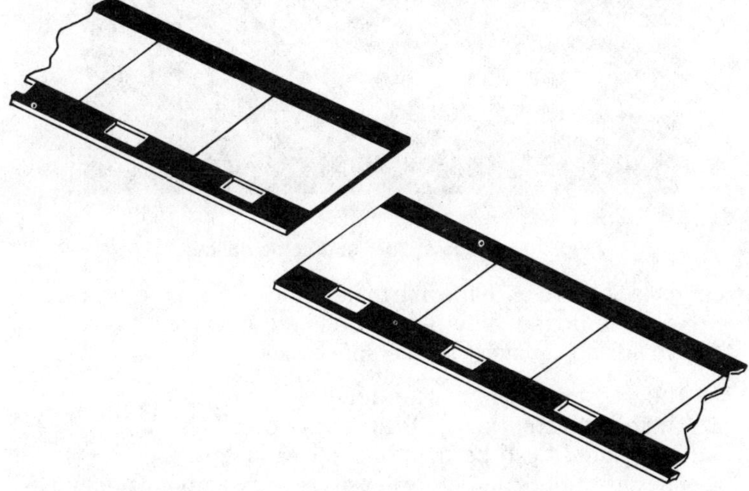

(A) The tape splicer cuts on the frame line.

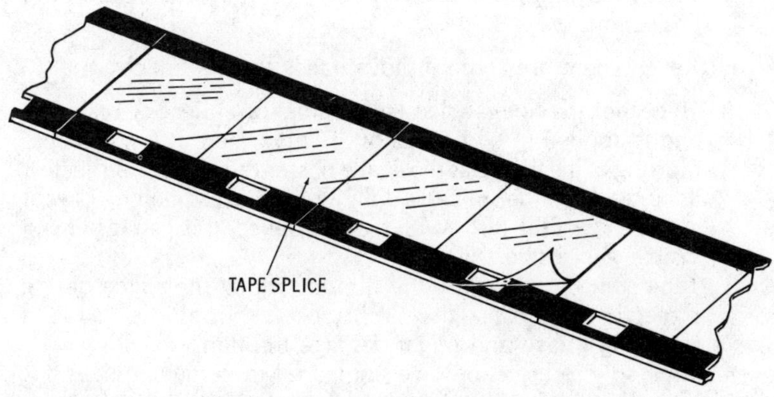

(B) The two pieces of film are joined together using a
wrap-around splice.

Fig. 10-4. A butt-type tape splicer.

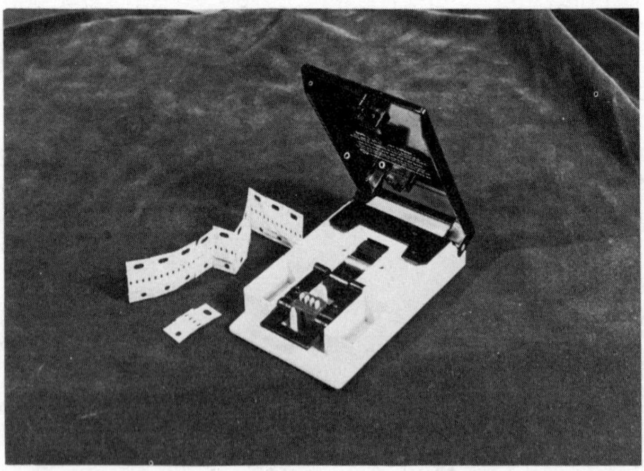

Courtesy H.P.I.

Fig. 10-5. Tape splicer and some splices.

experience showed us that while metal splicers are more rugged, for the price, the high-quality plastic units are all right.

The major advantages of tape splices are:

1. They do not break or tear apart in normal use.
2. Their popularity makes them easily obtainable.
3. Tape splices can be made quickly and easily.
4. They are more satisfactory to use when assembling preliminary versions of the film, like the *rough cut*.
5. They are excellent for quick repairs if a film should break during projection.

However, there are some disadvantages to tape splices.

1. Since the tape covers at least two frames on either side of the cut and is applied to both sides of the film, there is a noticeable blurring of the image as the splice passes through the projector.
2. If the blade on the splicer is dull, it may make a rather wide cut at the ends of the film. With the butt splice, this can result in a visible gap at the splice.
3. Tape splices may cause the film to kink at the splice during projection and cause the film to lose its loop. This causes a stuttering image and might damage the film.
4. Tape splices are expensive compared to cement splices.
5. If you have your film cleaned electrostatically, you must use cement splices, since the electrostatic cleaning process not only removes dirt, it also removes tape splices.

Cement splicers—They are made with an overlap splice rather than a butt splice. The film is placed in the splicer emulsion side up. After the film is cut, the emulsion is scraped away from a portion of the end frame of one piece of film, exposing the base. Film cement is brushed on and the second piece of film is laid on top so that the film is cemented together base-side to exposed-base (Fig. 10-6). This creates an overlap of approximately one-third of a frame. The film cement, usually an acetone compound, partially dissolves the base and, as it dries, creates a chemical weld of the two pieces of film.

Cement splicers (Fig. 10-7) are usually more complicated (and expensive) than tape splicers since they must scrape the film, as well as align it very precisely. For comparable quality in splicers, a cement splicer will cost about two to five times as much as a tape splicer. When purchasing a cement splicer, look for the same considerations as with a tape splicer—ease of cutting, accuracy of alignment, and easy application of the cement. Since cement splices need a drying time, the addition of a heating element is a good idea in any cement splicer.

The advantages of cement splices are:

1. Only one frame of film is affected by the splice, compared to three or four when using tape splices.
2. The splices are "cleaner" in projection.
3. Cement splices allow the use of professional cleaning methods and A & B roll editing.

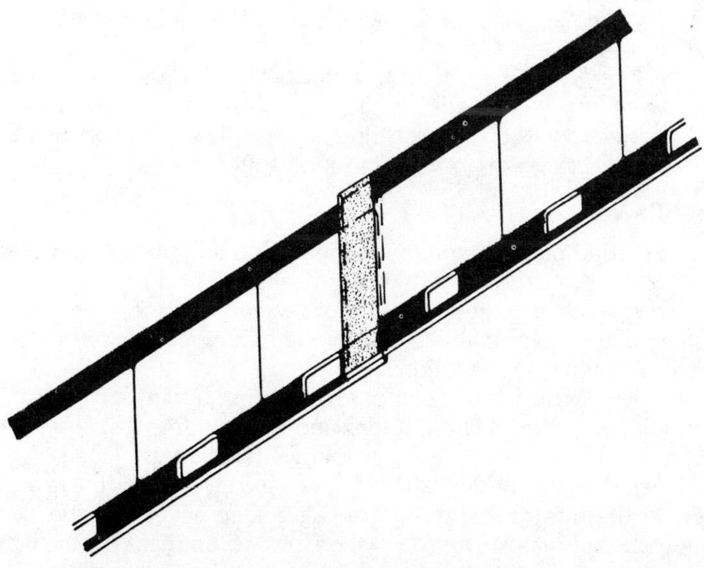

Fig. 10-6. An "overlap" cement splice.

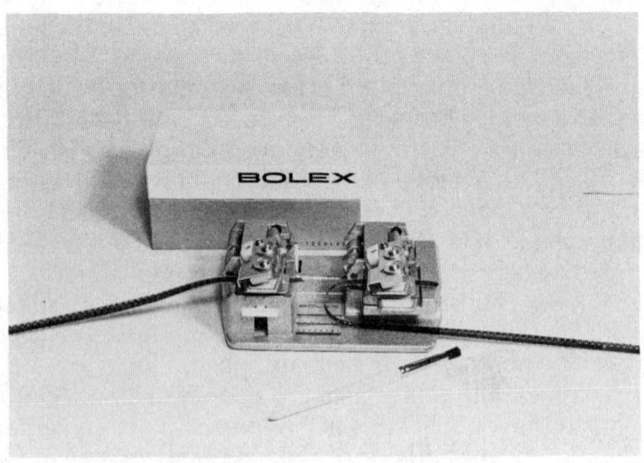

Fig. 10-7. A cement-type splicer.

The disadvantages of cement splices are:

1. A frame of film is lost in the overlap, and you lose a frame from each side of the splice every time you re-edit.
2. Making a good cement splice is more difficult and takes more time than a comparable tape splice.
3. Film cement deteriorates rapidly once a bottle is opened and it has to be replaced often.
4. All cement splices tend to deteriorate with age. Splices that were not well made in the first place can come apart in projection. We feel that the cement splice has more serious disadvantages than does the tape splice.

The Viewer

The second piece of equipment needed to edit film is the viewer (Fig. 10-8). It is called that because it is like a hand-cranked movie projector, with a built-in viewing screen instead of a projection system. The viewer enables you to examine your film, either one frame at a time or in motion.

The viewer consists of a pair of rewind arms, a transport system, a film gate, a shutter, a lamp, a lens and mirror transmission system, and a viewing screen. It works as follows. The film is placed on the feed reel, threaded through the film gate, and taken up by the take-up reel. In the film gate, the film engages a sprocket that turns the shutter, usually a prism mirror. The picture is illuminated by the lamp located above the film gate. The lamp shines down through the film onto one facet of the prism. This facet, in turn, reflects the image

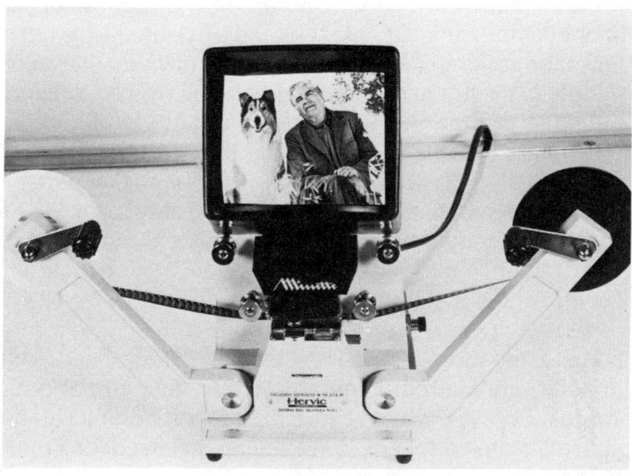

Fig. 10-8. A film viewer.

through a system of plane mirrors to the viewing screen. Every frame of the film is reflected through the system by one facet of the prism "shutter." When the frame is moved out of the film gate, that facet turns and the process is repeated with the next frame of film and the next facet. Cranked at a fast speed (anything over 12 frames per second), the rapidly changing images of the still frames give the illusion of motion just as they appear to do in projection. Because there is no "real" shutter, however, there is some flicker of the image on the screen during "normal" speed viewing. This is a minor problem which you will quickly become accustomed to.

As in the case with splicers, there is a wide range of Super 8 viewers on the market. Most are meant for occasional use and will not stand up to a lot of editing. The solution is to buy the most precise and rugged unit that you can afford, i.e., the best quality available. We prefer metal housings and rewind arms since they are more rugged than plastic. Other than that, a good viewer should have the following characteristics:

1. A large viewing screen (3 inch × 4 inch is a good minimum) with a bright lamp and sharp image resolution. There should be some focus adjustment to allow for the relative thickness of different film emulsions. The large bright screen is very important as it is difficult and tiring to try to edit film when viewing a small fuzzy image.
2. The lamp should be easily accessible and easily obtainable when replacements are necessary. Most viewer lamps have a life of about 20 hours, so you will be replacing them often.

3. A frame marker is a good feature. This device, usually located at or near the film gate, places a pin prick on the film to mark it for cutting. Some viewers have frame markers that punch the middle of the frame next to the one being viewed, others punch the edge of the film. We prefer the latter kind.

4. The film path must be designed to transport the film smoothly and cleanly. Look for well-polished sprocket wheels and transport deck. In addition, it should be easy to take the film in and out of the film path, since you will be doing this a lot, too.

5. The viewer should have geared rewinds to facilitate winding the film under load. The rewinds should have at least a 400-foot reel capacity.

6. Some of the more expensive viewers are motorized. This is an unnecessary feature unless, of course, they run at projection speeds. Even so, we have found that most editing can be done at hand-cranked speeds so we see no real need for a motorized transport.

The Projector

The third major tool you will need for film editing is a projector (Fig. 10-9). The projector is essential for showing the film, of course. But it is almost indispensable for getting a feel for the entire film after you have completed the rough cut, or when you are putting the final touches on timing. We use the projector, in editing, almost as much as we use the viewer.

The projector has a feed reel and a take-up reel, a transport system, a film gate, a shutter, and a lamp-lens system for displaying the film.

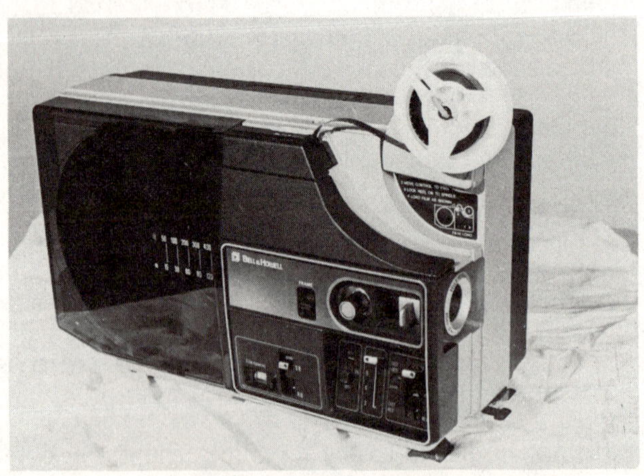

Courtesy Bell & Howell

Fig. 10-9. A film projector.

(Most silent-film projectors have multiple speed and allow still-frame and reverse projection.) They work as follows. The film is placed on the feed reel and threaded past the upper sprocket or roller and through the film gate. Here the claw takes hold of the film and pulls it into registration with the opening in the film gate. The pressure pad on the gate holds the film flat during this operation. The lamp shines through the film to the lens which magnifies the image and shows it on the screen. A frame of film is held in the film gate by the claw for three openings and closings of the shutter. This is to prevent flicker. When the shutter closes the third time, the frame is changed and the process is repeated with the next frame. From the film gate, the film passes the lower sprocket or roller, and on to the take-up reel.

Because the film is actually stopped in the gate (for a fraction of a second), instead of being run past it at a continuous speed, there is a need to cushion the film from the shocks of this intermittent motion. To do this, "loops" are placed in the film path just before and just after the film gate. These loops absorb the shock of the stopping and starting and allow the image to appear steady during projection. If the loop is "lost," either by passing a bad splice or through projector malfunction, the image appears to blur or chatter on the screen. This can be corrected by stopping the projector and reforming the film loop.

Although all projectors work on these principles, there are some differences between sprocketed projectors and roller-drive projectors. The sprockets and rollers perform the same function in the transport system but they do so in a different manner. The sprockets, like the claw, engage the sprocket holes or perforations in the film, and transport it positively through the system. Sprocketed projectors generally provide more stable images in projection. They need more carefully formed loops, however, and sometimes will not pass badly made splices without damaging the film. Roller-drive (or sprocketless) projectors use friction rollers to grip the film and pass it through. These projectors rely on the claw for accurate picture alignment and, consequently, do not have the precision that the sprocketed projectors display. But they are not fussy about loop forming and will pass virtually any kind of splice, albeit with some chattering and a little more noise than their sprocketed counterparts. We use both kinds in our workshop, preferring the sprocketless model for viewing during editing and the sprocketed model for final projection.

Initially, choosing a projector can seem as complicated as picking a camera, particularly when you begin comparing the features of the various models on the market. Regardless of price or number of features, any projector you choose should project a bright, sharp, steady image; the film gate should be accessible and easy to clean; the film should be self-threading (at least through the film gate); and the film path should permit *easy* removal and replacement of the film in mid-run. In addition, the transport mechanism should accept splices without causing the film to chatter or lose its loop, all controls should be positive in operation, and the machine should be quiet.

Before you buy a projector, run at least one roll of spliced film through the model whose features you like. Watch for smooth transport and a steady image. Make sure that the focus and framing controls operate smoothly and accurately. If the projector is equipped with a zoom lens, zoom out to the greatest enlargement and, again, check for sharpness. The image should remain crisp throughout the zoom range. To check image brightness, use this simple test from *Popular Photography:*

> Set projection speed at normal—18 fps. Place the projector (without film in it) about 10 feet from a screen, and switch on the lamp. Using an exposure meter, make five measurements—the center of the screen and the four corners. The falling off at the corners should not exceed one f/stop.[1]

We recommend that you obtain a projector with at least the following characteristics—a minimum of an f/1.5 lens (either fixed focal length or zoom), 25-foot throw, 18 fps and "still" speed controls, 400-foot film-reel capacity, reverse projection, rugged construction, and a sprocketless film drive. A better projector should give you at least an f/1.2 lens, a preheated 100–150-watt quartz lamp with a 35–40-foot throw, 18 and 24 fps plus fast motion, "step motion," and still frameability, 600-foot reel capacity, and a sprocket-drive transport mechanism.

Additional Editing Supplies

In addition to the machines that are used in editing, you will need several small items that will make the editing process faster, easier, and more accurate. Here is a list:

1. White cotton editing gloves.
2. Scissors.
3. White Leader and Black Leader.
4. Splices.
5. A supply of 50-foot film reels and at least two 400-foot reels.
6. Regular size envelopes.
7. Grease pencil or "China marker."
8. Masking tape and markers.
9. Stopwatch and film-timing scale.

---

[1] *Popular Photography*, Eds., "1973 Directory and Buying Guide," *Popular Photography*, 1973, p. 137.

10. Cleaning supplies, including blower brush, lens cleaner and tissue, dust rag, and dust-absorbing spray.
11. The Shooting Log of the film.
12. The Scenario of the film.
13. Note pad.

We have always used white gloves when we edit film. We find it keeps our greasy fingerprints off the film and helps to avoid scratches during the handling process. We buy them in packages of ten pairs and discard them when they get dirty. They can be washed, of course, in which case, they could be used as film-cleaning cloths or small polishing rags.

When doing the rough cut, scissors are the fastest way to separate individual takes. The end of the shots can be trimmed properly when they are spliced together.

White leader is essential for leadering your film. We buy it in 50-foot rolls and use 4 feet at the head and 1 foot at the tail of every film. The leader that comes with your processed film is all right to use as a tail but it is too short for a good head leader. And, we do not recommend splicing movie leader! Black leader is useful for special kinds of editing (A&B Roll), and for use in a film to indicate the passage of time, etc. You can purchase Black Leader in similar 50-foot rolls or you can use the end-of-the-roll camera run-off. We do both.

You will need splices that match the type of splicer you are using, of course. We buy four times as many splices as there are shots in our film. That way, we can edit every shot at least three times and still have some spares for last minute polishing cuts.

The more film you shoot and edit, the more spare film reels you will end up with. Do not throw them away. They are perfect for spooling off long takes and for storing shots not being incorporated in the finished film. We use open reels for editing storage and the reels with covers for long-term storage. Small pieces of film, like the trimmed ends of shots, or very short takes, can be stored flat in ordinary letter envelopes.

The two large reels (400 foot) will be used to assemble your rough cut, and wind it back and forth on the editor. Buy separate reels for this purpose, do not steal the projector takeup reel.

Grease pencils (or China markers) are quite handy for writing instructions on the film for editing purposes or what-have-you. Remember, though, that while a grease pencil will rub off, China marker is forever.

Masking tape and dri-markers are good for labeling reels and envelopes so that you will not have to view the shot to know what is on it.

We use a stopwatch during the final stages of editing so that we can time scenes and check the overall running time during projection. On the editing bench, however, we use a film-timing scale (Fig. 10-10) to measure the length of scenes, to time titles, and to keep track of how many seconds we have removed (or added to) a given shot. You can buy timing scales for Super 8 film; we made our own from strips of masking tape.

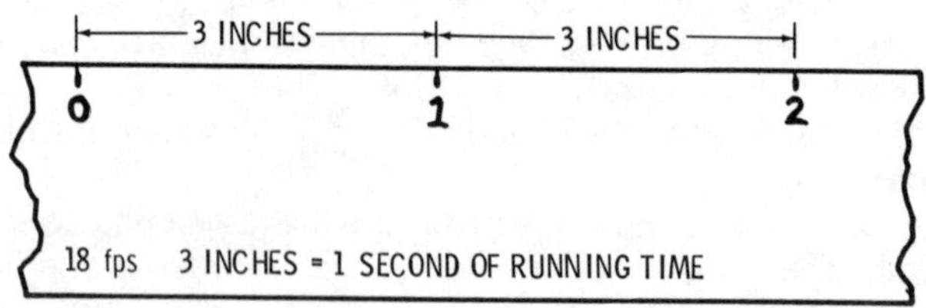

Fig. 10-10. A timing scale.

To make yourself a timing scale, measure out 3 or 4 feet of tape and stick it down on the front edge of the editing bench. At the left-hand end make a ZERO mark. From the ZERO, mark off intervals of 3 inches (for 18-fps running speed) or 4 inches (for 24 fps). Now, label these marks, from left to right, 1 second, 2 seconds, 3 seconds, etc. When you want to time a piece of film, merely place it at the ZERO mark, extend the piece to the right, and count the number of seconds that it covers. This method is especially good for timing titles.

In addition to the obvious cleaning supplies, for the care of the projector and viewer, we usually stock a dust-absorbing spray and some rags. Before we start to edit on a given day, we wipe down the area, especially the bench top, to make sure we have the cleanest and most dust-free working conditions. Dust is the greatest enemy of the photographic process and it should be controlled as much as possible.

Always have the Shooting Log and the Scenario with you when editing. That way, you will know what shots are on what roll of film, and in what order they should be arranged for the Rough Cut. We find that a note pad is indispensable for a variety of writing purposes.

Now you need a place to edit—a clean dry place, fairly dust-free, with a large flat surface. The surface should be hard and smooth so that it is easy to keep clean. Put a storage bin or reel rack at the back corner and have some convenient electrical outlets for the viewer and splicer. The work area should have its own light control (we have a large fluorescent overhead fixture that is turned on and off with a string pull), so you can work with the lights on or off as you need to.

Obtain a good chair if you can. We use an adjustable "secretary-type" chair that swivels and rolls. This editing area need not be fancy, but it must be fairly private so that you can concentrate on what you are doing and so that others will not be tempted to mess with your stuff.

CARE AND CLEANING OF EQUIPMENT

Editing equipment, like other pieces of film-production equipment, needs to be cleaned and maintained on a regular basis to ensure its continuing performance. The viewer, the splicer, and the projector get a lot of use during editing of even a simple film. While you may not be able to repair these items if they break down, you can do normal maintenance.

Viewer

The screen and mirror system of the viewer, the lamp, and the transport system all need regular care. Clean the viewing screen and mirrors with lens cleaner and tissue just as you would clean any optical-glass surface. If you must remove the mirrors or lens(es) during cleaning, replace them exactly as they were, to ensure correct picture alignment and maximum screen brightness.

Most editing lamps will last a long time if they are cared for properly. Follow the same rules for this lamp as you would for any film lamp. Handle the lamp as little as possible and always polish the envelope with a soft cloth, after you have handled it, to remove any oil left by fingerprints.

Always switch off the lamp when not using the viewer, and unplug the viewer when you are through editing. This will prolong lamp life. Some viewers have adjustable lamp bases; they can be turned to better align the filament of the lamp with the optical system. If you have one of these viewers, you will have to adjust the lamp every time it is replaced. Check the equipment manual for proper procedure.

The transport system should be kept CLEAN. Take a blower brush and blow out any particles of dust, dirt, or film that have lodged under the film gate. Run a clean soft cloth through the film path to remove any emulsion buildup. Dust the transport rollers, too. Once a year, open up the bottom of the viewer and blow out the accumulation of foreign matter. At the same time, check the lubrication of the sprocket wheel and rewind arms. If they are sticking, spray them lightly with a silicon-spray lubricant. If some parts of your viewer are excessively worn or not performing up to par, take it to your photo dealer for a checkup.

Splicer

There are three things that can be done to maintain the splicer. Keep it clean, keep it sharp, and keep it aligned. After every use, brush it clean of film bits and dirt. Peel off any stray splicing tapes that may have stuck to it and dust the deck. If the blade has dulled, replace it. Dull blades make for large gaps between pieces of film. Check the alignment of the locating pins, too. If the pins are adjustable, align them carefully so they will hold the film in place, accurately and firmly.

Projector

The projector is one of those complex pieces of film equipment that should be given regular checkups. But you can do several maintenance operations on the lens, lamp, and film path.

The lens should be removed from the projector occasionally and blown clean of dust and emulsion. Clean the lens surfaces with cleaner and tissue in the regular manner. After replacing the lens in the projector, make sure it moves freely in both the focus and zoom modes. If it is jamming, you may have installed it incorrectly.

Let lamps warm up before use, and cool down after use, for longer lamp life. Do not pack the projector away while the lamp is still hot; the filaments are very fragile at this time and could easily break. When you replace a burned-out lamp, wear gloves. This will prevent burned fingers (if the lamp is still hot), and will keep fingerprints off the envelope of the new lamp.

The film path in the projector needs regular maintenance. Every time a film is run through the projector some emulsion and dirt is deposited in the path. Once a week, open up the path and blow out the dust and emulsion particles. Then, run a cotton swab through the path to further clean it. Clean the film-gate area very carefully. After cleaning the inside of the projector, wipe down the housing and base with a soft cloth impregnated with dusting spray.

The greatest enemy of film editing is dust. If you can keep the tools relatively clean and dust free, you stand a good chance of having your film look the same way. In addition to cleaning our equipment, we always clean our editing bench (Fig. 10-11) before we start working. And, we cover the viewer, splicer, and projector with plastic bags or equipment covers when they are idle for a long period of time.

GENERAL EDITING PROCEDURES

Now you are ready to edit. Gather all the rolls of processed film, set them by the projector, get your log and note-pad, thread up the first roll, and begin viewing.

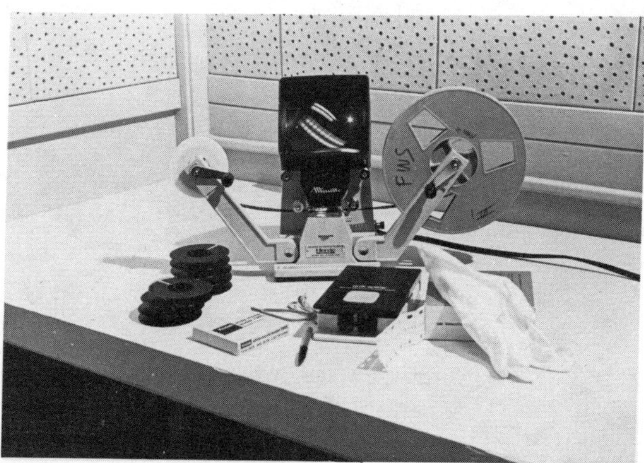

**Fig. 10-11. An editing bench. All the needed materials are present
and ready to go.**

Editing Stages

There are three stages to editing; the *Rough Cut*, the *Middle Cut*,
and the *Final Cut*. Each stage follows the same four steps; viewing,
cutting, arranging, and splicing.

Rough Cut—The Rough Cut is the assembly, in the sequence
described by the scenario, of all the usable takes that you
photographed. Here is how to put it together.

View all of the footage and note in the shooting log those shots
which came out all right. Make notes on your pad as to which shots
should not be included in the Rough Cut. Do not attempt to choose
the best take, leave all of them in. You can choose the best take later.
At this point, you want to eliminate bad footage, such as black film,
end-of-roll runoff, out-of-focus shots, and incomplete takes. When
you are finished viewing, take all the rolls, log, and notes to the
editing bench and begin cutting.

Run the first shot from the first roll through the viewer (Fig. 10-12).
Find the end of the shot, mark it, and cut it. Leaving the shot "tail" out
on the takeup reel, remove this reel from the viewer, label it with the
scene and shot number, and set it aside. Do the same for the second
shot on this roll, and for the third.

While unspooling the shots you want to save, cut out and set aside
all bad footage. Do not throw it away. As a matter of fact, do not
throw away any piece of your film until after the Final Cut has been
made. Even then, we recommend that you only discard that footage
which, in your opinion, is absolutely unusable. We tend to save
every scrap of good film. There have been several occasions where
this policy has saved our film project.

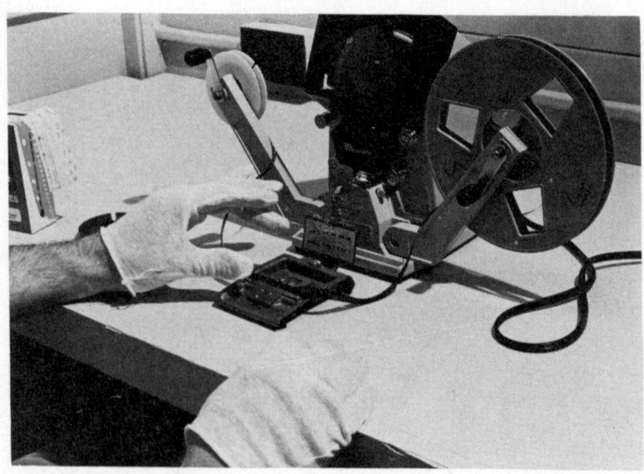

Fig. 10-12. An editor working at a clean and neat workbench.

After you have cut apart the entire film, you will have a stack of labeled reels (or a pile of envelopes) containing the whole film. Arrange these in order according to the scenario and begin to assemble the Rough Cut in the following manner.

Mount a large (400 foot) film reel on the feed arm of the viewer. Thread a piece of white leader (1 foot in length), called the tail leader, into the feed reel. Take the last take of the last shot in your show (from the orderly pile of reels on the bench), and attach the tail of this shot to the head of the tail leader. Wind it onto the feed reel. Attach the tail of the next take (or shot) to the head of the one you just spliced in. Wind this shot onto the feed reel also. Repeat this process for the remainder of the takes and shots. What you are doing is assembling this film in reverse order. Since all the shots were wound "tail out" and then cut, this order of assembly is the easiest to do.

When all of the film is wound onto the feed reel, attach four feet of White Leader to the head end of the film. Now you are ready to project the Rough Cut. This cut should contain all the usable footage that you have shot for this film. All the slates and all the takes should be here, and there should not have been any intercutting of Master Shots with insert shots. Back to the projector. Look at the Rough Cut and make notes of changes you will make in the Middle Cut.

Middle Cut—The purpose of the Middle Cut is to finalize the continuity and sequence. At this point, you can choose the best take, intercut those reaction and detail shots with the Master Shot, and start to get some sense of the overall pace of the film.

When trying to choose the best take, look for the one that shows all the action from the proper angle in the best possible field of view.

Secondly, consider exposure and good lighting. If none of the takes meets all the criteria, choose the one that satisfies most of the requirements, in the order in which they have been listed. Look for action first, then angle, then field of view, and, finally, exposure and lighting. It is essential that the audience be able to see the action of your film and it is only incidental at this point that the scene is correctly lit.

After you have chosen the best takes, make notes about those shots that are to be intercut with the Master Shot(s), like cutaways, reactions, and details. Look for any continuity problems that could be corrected by rearranging the sequence of the shots or scenes. Next, make notes about the points at which you will want to cut those takes for timing. Do not concern yourself with fine tuning at this point. Merely jot down a few words like "cut Shot 3 at the end of the Boss' speech," or "cut into Shot 9 as Henchman pulls self out of hole." When you get back to the editing bench, you will be able to find those spots and cut accordingly.

The purpose of making all these notes is to aid your memory while working between the projector and the editing bench. We make notes about every change we intend to make, even when editing our simplest films. That way, if we are interrupted in the middle of some editing operation, we can always go back to the right point and finish what we intended to do. Since editing is a complex process involving the juggling of a lot of details, it is easier to let your notes remember for you.

After you have finished viewing the Rough Cut and making notes about the Middle Cut, take the film back to the editing bench. Do not rewind it at this point. Start with the tail end and remove all but the best take from the last shot. (Use your splicer this time for accurate cuts.) Put the out-takes back on their respective reels and save them. Wind the best take of the last shot back onto the feed reel of the editor (don't forget the tail leader), and proceed to make the same kind of cuts with the next-to-the-last shot. When you have gone through the entire film this way, the feed reel will contain only the best takes, in correct order. Now, working forward, start your continuity and timing cuts.

Put the Master Shot from Scene 1 in the viewer. Mark and remove the slate (unless this is double-system sound film), and cut out any footage at the head or tail that is not part of the shot. Now find the other shots from this scene and get out your notes on intercutting these shots. Put the cutaways, reaction shots, and other inserts in correct order according to the script, and cut them into the Master Shot one by one. As you put them in, trim them as you did the Master Shot. But do not cut them too short at this point. This stage of cutting is more concerned with continuity than it is with timing.

Our basic rule for cutting in and out of a shot is: Always Cut On The Action (Fig. 10-13). Nothing looks more blank on the screen than a shot in which the action is waiting to happen. The action should begin in the first few frames of the shot. The way to achieve this is to advance the shot slowly in the viewer until the action starts to happen. Then back up several frames and make the cut at the head of the shot. At the tail of the shot run it until the action ceases, go a few more frames, and cut it. When you put these cut-on-action shots together with other shots, that have been edited the same way, it will make the scene, and the movie, move. (We leave the extra frames in at this point so we can make more subtle timing changes later on.)

When we are cutting related shots together, we also try to *match action*. Matching action is what you do to give the impression of a continuous flow of action, when intercutting two shots of the same action that are shown from different angles or with different fields of view (Fig. 10-14). For example, if we are filming a runner, and we start with a high-angle MLS and then cut to an eye-level MS, we must match the stride and the legs of the runner from shot to shot. If his right foot was on the ground in the end of Shot 1, it should be lifting up in the beginning of Shot 2. If the match is well done, it will make the transition from shot to shot much smoother.

While cutting on the action is essential for good pace (and to maintain an accurate impression of the real action), matching action is only important if you want to create the impression of a single piece of action continuing though several shots. Changing angles and fields of view is a legitimate way to compress the action and eliminate some of what actually happened. In such a case, matching the action would not be as important.

But, you must pay close attention to matching action when cutting between shots with similar angles and/or fields of view. Otherwise, you will create *jump cuts*. A jump cut is an omission of a portion of the action. It is often created by the intercutting of two shots that have very similar angles or fields of view. In appearance, it looks like the camera stopped, the action continued, and the camera started again to finish taking the shot. (Some beginning film makers do exactly that, by not depressing the camera trigger fully during the run of the shot.) One reason we suggest the use of the Master Shot concept is that it allows an easy way to avoid jump cuts.

If two succeeding insert shots are too much alike to allow good cutting, you can cut from the first shot to the Master Shot and then come back to the second shot. The interposing of the Master Shot between the two similar shots will break up the jump cut. Another way to minimize the effect of jump cuts is, of course, to carefully match action between the two cuts and hope that the audience will not notice that the camera angle, etc., has changed.

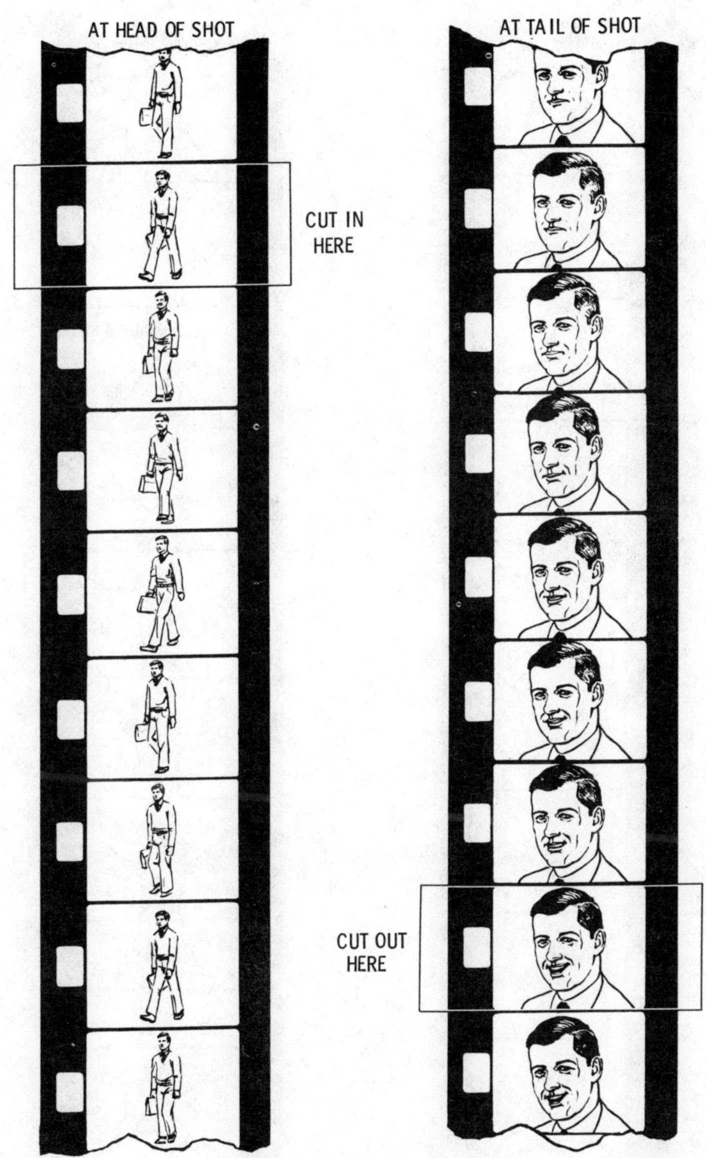

Fig. 10-13. To make your movie "move," begin and end the shots with the subject in action.

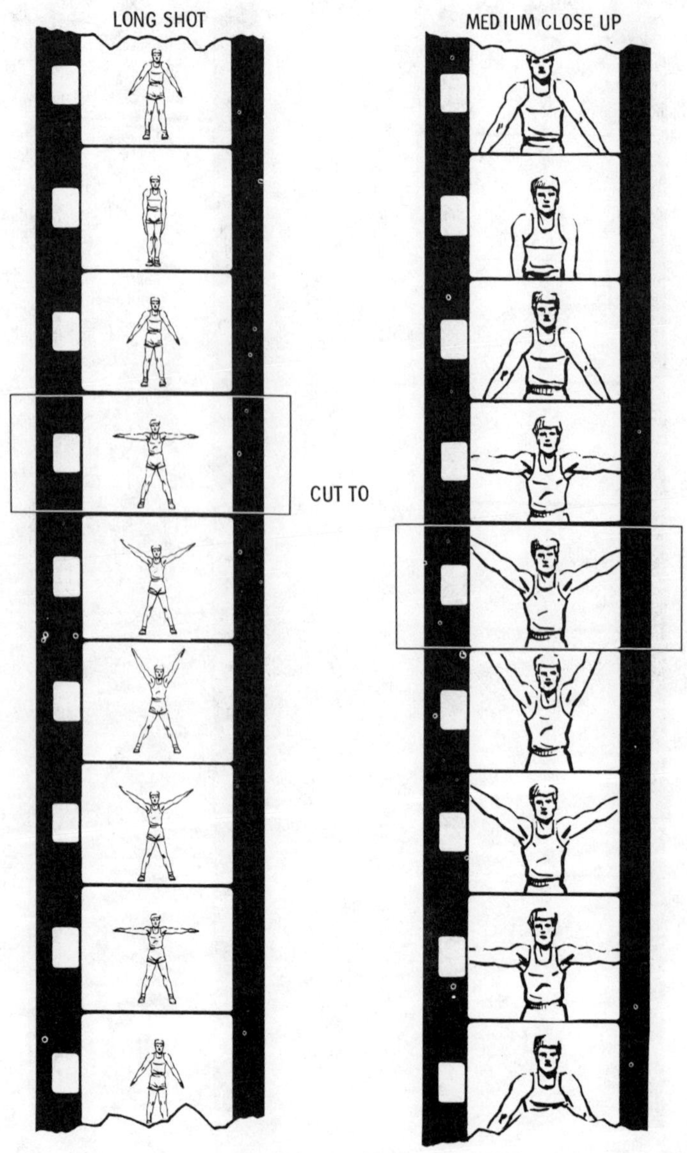

Fig. 10-14. To give the appearance of a flow of action, match the movement from one shot to the next.

To further illustrate these principles, let us look at the last sequence of "The Bandits," and see how we might edit it given the choice of shots listed above. Since the Master Shot covers the entire action of the sequence, it obviously will not be used in its entirety, although we can cut back to it at any time during the sequence. Let's begin with shot number 10, and cut it at the point where the two robbers have taken two or three steps toward "screen right." We will cut shot number 11 in on the action; the two men are still walking, but halt after a step or two as the Boss begins to search his pockets. We will also match action on this cut. If the two men (or the predominant figure) are striding forward with their right feet at the end of Shot 10, they should be continuing that stride as Shot 11 cuts in.

We can end this shot with the Boss' question and cut in Shot 12, the brief insert shot of the map left on the rock. We can follow this with Shot 13, the Boss' gesture, and then cut to the Henchman walking toward the rock (Shot 14). We cut Shot 14 just before the Henchman reaches the rock, and cut to Shot 15 of the Boss who is looking after him and beginning to draw his pistol. We cut Shot 15 just as the Boss begins to draw (but not so soon that we miss what he's doing), and cut in that portion of the Master Shot that shows the Henchman bending down for the map with the Boss in the foreground. We must remember to match the action of the Henchman bending down and the Boss in the background, still drawing his pistol. Now we cut to Shot 15—the Boss cocking his pistol. Cut to Shot 14, the Henchman whirling around at the sound. Cut to Shot 15, continuing the shot through the action of the pistol being fired, but cutting away before the smoke from the pistol shot has cleared away. Then, we can cut to that part of the Master Shot where the Henchman crumples and falls, matching the action of the smoke drifting away from the pistol muzzle. Continue the Master Shot until the Boss has taken a step or two toward the body, and then cut to Shot 17, matching the action of the Boss walking over to the body. Cut to Shot 16 showing the murdered Henchman from the Boss' point of view. Cut back to the rest of Shot 17, showing the Boss bending down and picking up the map. Then, cut to Shot 18; the Boss walks toward the horses, and rides off leaving the deserted scene.

Remember that shots can also be related in a sequence through the use of color, theme, patterns of movement, and directions of movement (of both camera and subject). Whatever the relationship(s), it will be discovered that cutting with an intent to relate the shots makes for a better looking film.

As you complete this stage of the Middle Cut, project the film and check the continuity. Does the sequence in which you have arranged the shots in each scene make sense? Is continuity maintained from scene to scene? Now is the time to correct those flaws. This is also the time to cut in the titles. Put them in the right place(s) and time them (with the timing scale) for approximate length.

We now have the shots placed in the order we want them, but we have not yet considered the duration of the shots—how long each should last before being replaced by the next shot. This is dependent on how much film is available but, more importantly, it is dependent on how the editor perceives the proper rate of progression or the pace of the film. For instance, we could edit "The Bandits" for a sense of slowly building tension or for a feeling of rapid-paced excitement. Examine that portion of our last sequence where the Boss draws and fires his pistol. If we are trying for a feeling of suspense, some of these shots might be delayed, by lingering on the deliberateness with which the Boss draws his pistol, his care in taking aim, and the long look of growing comprehension on the stupid face of the Henchman, culminating in a look of pure horror as he realizes, too late, that he is going to die. One of the takes of Shot 15—the Henchman falling—might have been shot in slow motion, and that take could be used to add to the visual irony of the scene.

On the other hand, if we decide that the scene should move along, the Boss will draw and fire his pistol without delay. A quick cut to a brief view of the Henchman's terror-stricken face will be followed immediately with the shots of the pistol firing and a normal-motion take of the Henchman falling. The same action of the same sequence happens in either version, but the emotional impact is entirely different.

We have used a stopwatch to time particular parts of the film, like establishing shots, reactions, and titles. While some of these may have been timed prior to their insertion, it is better to gauge their final timing when they are seen as part of the film. Until the picture is in its final form, as far as continuity goes, one cannot really determine overall pace or make any final decisions about timing. We do most of our scene and shot timing by instinct and reaction. If a particular part of the film seems to limp along, we will probably reedit it so that the pace improves. If the film seems to whiz by some important point, we will look for ways of emphasizing that point with the addition of shots—either by replacing footage that had been previously cut or by the rearrangement of shots.

Once you have gone through the entire film in this manner, rewind it and take it back to the projector. View it from beginning to end. If your editing has been thorough, the film will look a lot like the form in which you would like it to be shown. Don't be fooled by this. Since the Middle Cut has been the most complicated piece of editing so far, your tendency might be to say, "Hey, that looks okay. Let's leave it that way." This is the moment to stop looking at the film and take some time off.

Final Cut—The problem here is that "you cannot see the forest for the trees." You lack *aesthetic distance* from the film—that is, you are so personally involved with the film that you are unable to see its flaws. The solution is to get away from the film for a while. After you have finished looking at the Middle Cut, let the film sit in the can for a period of time (at least overnight). This break will allow you to regain some of the perspective you might have lost while you were editing the film and this, in turn, will help your critical judgement.

After you are rested, go back to the projector and look at the film again. Put yourself in the place of a member of the audience, looking at this work for the first (and probably the only) time. What do you see? What is the message of this film? How well does it come across? Does the continuity confuse you? How is the pace? Are the reaction shots long enough? Too long? Does this movie move or does it drag? Take notes on your observations.

What you are looking for at this stage in the editing are ways to bring the picture into its final form; ways to emphasize and underline those points that you wished to make when you first thought of the film concept. The ways that you can change the film, at this point, are the same ones that you have used throughout the other two stages of the editing process—continuity, timing, and manipulation of content. The degree to which you will make these changes is rather small now for this is the fine-tuning stage. Your film should be close to the way you want it to be. (There are exceptions, of course. During the Final Editing of one of our silent films, we discovered that a particular scene was not really necessary to advance the story line at all. We cut the scene and bridged the gap with a simple title card. This drastic cut changed the entire pace of the film, for the better. And it's likely that the audience never missed that scene.)

After you have looked at the film and made your notes, rewind the film and return to the editing bench. Go through the film and make the continuity adjustments first. Review every scene to make sure that you are cutting on the action and that each shot leads into the one that follows. Put the film back on the projector, observe and make notes on any additional continuity changes you should make. After this process is finished, start working on the timing adjustments. Trim out any frames that do not add anything to the shot or to the story. Make the movie move. The question will arise, "How do I know when the editing is finished?" The editing is finished when you decide that there is no more that you can do with it, or when you become tired of the film and are anxious to move on to a new project. Each time we screen one of our old films, we discover places where a transition could be smoothed out, where a cut could be tightened, where we should go back and reshoot. But it is necessary to call a halt sometime, decide that the film is finished, and move on to the next film, incorporating in that one all that you have learned about film making from this one.

Summary—The editing principles that we have just discussed are the basics, and they are common to any type of film, whether silent or sound. There are further possibilities, however, which are available to the amateur film maker, and which will also be applicable to either silent or sound film. (We will discuss the special problems inherent in editing sound film in a later section.) For example, sooner or later, you will become dissatisfied with the limitations imposed on you by always having to work with original camera film. Inevitably, it becomes damaged during the editing process regardless of how careful you are. In addition, working with the camera original does not allow you to employ the "professional" editing techniques that you see displayed in professional films. There is a tremendous attraction to the thought of being able to use fades and dissolves, in having "invisible" splices, in employing superimposed titles, etc. Although these sophistications were once available only to the 16-mm film maker, they are now available to the Super 8 film maker, too.

Work Prints

The first step toward a greater degree of professionalism in your film work is to edit a *work print* rather than the original camera film. A work print is nothing more than an inexpensive copy of your original footage—all of it. This means that you will increase the amount of money you spend on your film, but the benefits you will gain are worth the additional expense. There are two types of work prints available to you—a *one-light* print and a *timed* print. A one-light print is a copy that is struck rapidly, with no attention paid to balancing the exposures or correcting the color values—and, you can even get cheaper black-and-white one-light prints made from your color original. The disadvantage of working with a one-light print is that it can be difficult to determine the quality, or even the potential quality, of the original. (You will never project your original film if you go the work-print route.(A timed print, on the other hand, although it is more expensive, is exposure balanced and color corrected. Most film makers think that the additional expense of a timed work print is not worth it, and use one-light prints to reduce cost.

The major advantage of working with a work print, as hinted above, is that the only time the original film is handled is when you *conform* it to your completely edited work print. Your original footage thus remains blemish-free when it is finally edited, and it can then either be projected or used only for making *release prints* (copies) of your finished film. Even though you use all the available laboratory services, you will still bring in a Super 8 film for about two-thirds less expense than you would using a comparable 16-mm film.

If you do decide to make prints from your original film, this decision will determine in part what film stock you will use to shoot the movie. Some film laboratories recommend that Kodachrome II be used to shoot the original, since they print on a low-contrast Ektachrome stock. Others prefer that you shoot on an Ektachrome stock, since they print on a Kodachrome print stock. It is probably best to pick the lab that you will be using before you begin shooting, and follow their recommendations as far as possible.

When working with a work print, some method is needed to assist in the *conforming* or matching of the unedited original footage with the edited work print. This is done by *edge numbering* both the original film and the work print (Fig. 10-15). When you send your original camera film to the lab for work printing, the lab will print a series of numbers along the edge of the film at short intervals. These numbers will be identical at a given location on both the original and the print. When you conform the two, the edge numbers on the edited work print are matched to the edge numbers on the original—the original can then be easily cut to match the work print.

Editing a work print, with the goal of conforming your camera original to it, gives you the opportunity of utilizing a more advanced system of conforming—the so-called "checkerboard" or "A & B roll" editing. This is a process that allows you to employ all of the optical effects of professional films—fades, lap dissolves, superimpositions, etc., as well as invisible splices. It is this last aspect of A & B roll editing which really makes it valuable. Even if you plan to have only straight cuts in your finished film, with this system your splices will be absolutely unnoticeable in the final print.

The process of preparing a film for A & B roll editing differs from laboratory to laboratory. Before deciding to edit your film in this

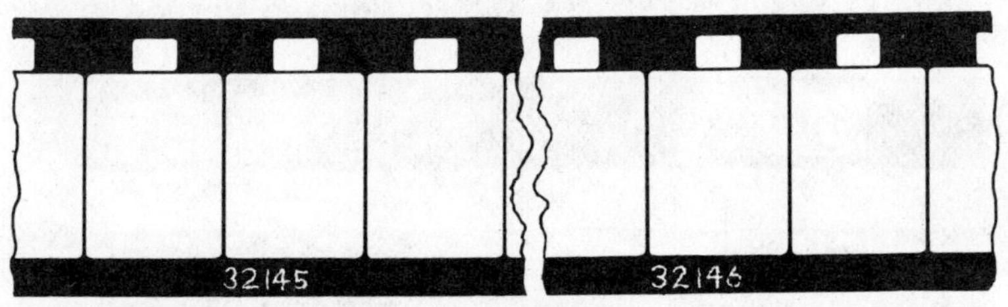

Fig. 10-15. To save time in "conforming" the films, "edge number" both the work print and the original film.

manner, check with the lab you intend to use for printing and get their instructions. Basically, the A & B rolls consist of two rolls of equal length made from your conformed original film. The A roll contains Shots 1, 3, 5, etc., with Black Leader that is equal in length to Shots 2, 4, 6, etc., placed in between. The B roll contains these even-numbered shots with equal lengths of Black Leader for the odd shots. These rolls are run through the film printer one at a time, with the same piece of print film being exposed to both rolls. The result is a composite print containing all the shots of the film, in order, with all the effects between shots that were programmed. Again, check with your lab before attempting this process. Their procedures must be followed to the letter if good results are to be obtained.

SOUND EDITING TOOLS

When you begin to edit sound movies, either single-system or double-system sound, you will need a few additional editing tools. The main ones are a sound projector and a sound sync viewer/editor.

The guidelines laid down earlier, for projectors, apply here too. But, in addition to those guidelines, a sound projector should include the following things:

1. A sound recording system (as well as playback), with manual volume control and a VU meter.
2. A positive lockout of the record mode while playing back.
3. Sound-on-sound recording capability.
4. A film-footage or frame counter.
5. Pulse sync for use with double-system sound recorders.
6. Provision for input of external sound sources and output to external speakers.

There is no sense buying a Super 8 sound movie projector that cannot be used as a sound-recording projector as well. By the same token, you should have some form of manual control over the sound

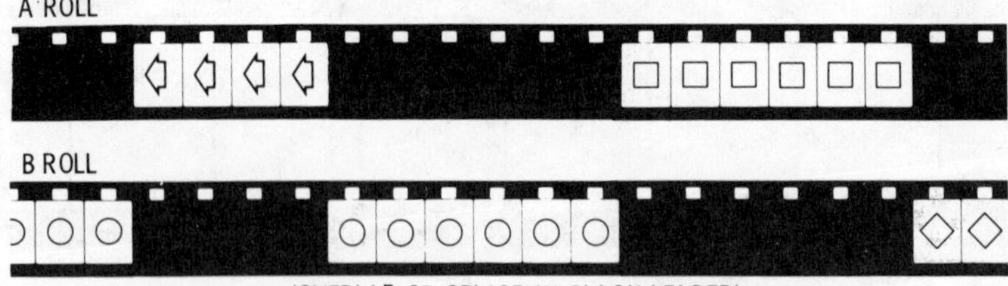

Fig. 10-16. Checkerboard pattern of preparing A and B rolls.

recording on the projector as it is difficult to get a high-quality recording on the sound stripe using automatic level control. Most good machines have both features.

It should also be necessary that some definite action has to be taken on your part in order to put the machine in the record mode. Otherwise, you might erase your precious sound track when you only intended to play it back.

The ability to record over an existing sound track *without* erasing it (sound-on-sound) is necessary for most kinds of sound-film production. All sound-recording projectors will erase the previously recorded track when playing in the record mode, but the sound-on-sound capability is not universally used yet. With sound-on-sound ability, a frame or footage counter is a must for accurate work in dubbing, mixing, and sync work.

The sound projector we use in our Film Workshop has provisions for monitoring, external speaker(s), microphone input, high-level input (tape recorder or phonograph), and sync pulse. It has been adequate for all of our sound film making to date. We recommend the use of an external speaker with the sound projector, as the quality of the sound is really enhanced (Fig. 10-17). We also use a low-priced pair of monophonic headphones for monitoring. These phones are much easier to listen to than the earplug that came with our projector.

On the editing bench, you will need a few additional pieces, also. For single-system editing, a viewer with an attached sound head will be sufficient (Fig. 10-18). Most viewers come with attachable sound heads that fit into the film path, 18 frames after the film gate. The ones we use are bolted onto the face of the viewer and are powered by a 9-volt battery that fits in the back of the amplifier case.

For double-system editing, you need a sound reader (a separate and moveable sound head in the sound-track path), a synchronizer block with two *gangs* (one for sound, one for picture), a pair of rewinds, and a standard viewer. Either headphones or a small speaker (called a squawk box) can be use to monitor the sound.

For single-system sound-film splicing, use a splice that keeps the sound track clear. Most tape splices have a long and a short side. The short side should be applied to the base of the film so that it covers the sprockets but not the sound stripe. For double-system sound, the picture film can be spliced with any type of tape splice. The sound track (mag film) has to be spliced with cement splices.

Editing Sound-On-Film

The procedures for editing sound-on-film are the same as those for editing silent film in regard to the kind of cuts to make (i.e., Rough Cut, Middle Cut, etc.). But the method for editing the film itself is

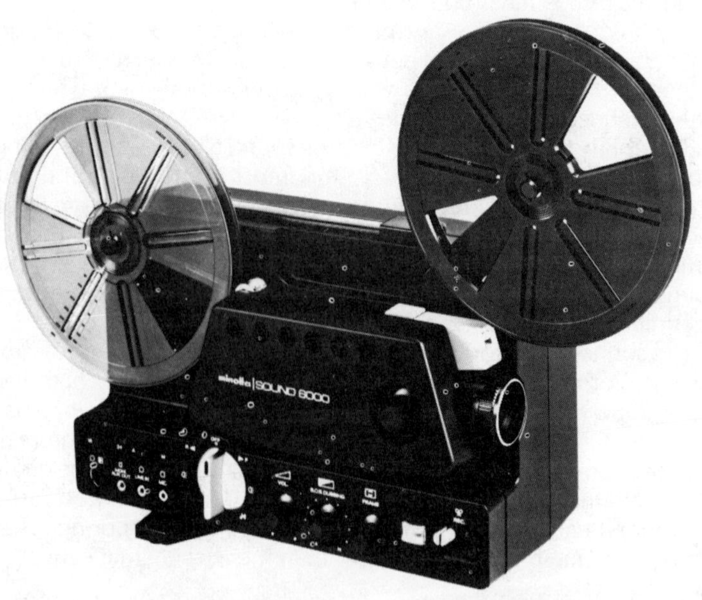

Fig. 10-17. Contemporary sound projectors offer sound recording, mixing, and sound-on-sound recording.

governed by one immutable rule: "When editing sound-on-film, cut *on the sound* at the head of the shot and *on the picture* at the tail of the shot."

It is done like this. Thread up the film through a viewer with a sound head. Turn on the viewer and the sound system, and put on the headphones. Crank the film forward until the first shot is visible in the viewer. Now, inch the takeup reel forward slowly while listening for the first sound. Just 18 frames after you see the first picture, you will hear the first sound on the track. (You may have to run the film back and forth over the sound head in order to find the exact start of the first sound. Watch the mouth of the speaker while you are listening to the sound track.) This sound corresponds with the picture that is on the screen of the viewer at the moment that you hear it. Mark this sound point on the film just above the sound head with a China marker or a grease pencil (Fig. 10-19). Continue to wind the film forward until the end of the shot is reached. At this point, you will be listening for the final words and looking at the last picture. As the final word passes the sound head, mark the corresponding picture in the film gate of the

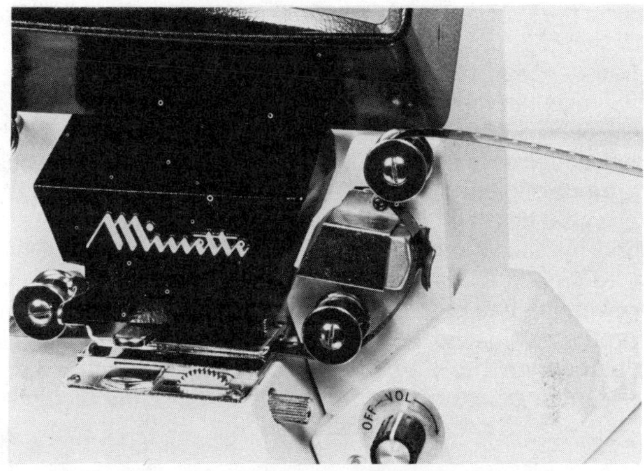

Fig. 10-18. Most silent-film viewers can be adapted to sound-on-film work with the addition of a sound head in the film path.

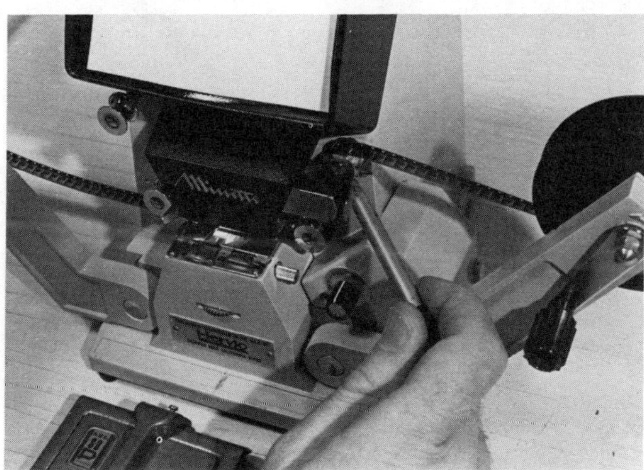

Courtesy Minolta Corp.

Fig. 10-19. Use a grease pencil to note the start of the sound.

viewer. Wind the film back to the beginning of the shot (the mark at the start of the sound), and remove it from the viewer. Put it on the splicing block and cut it to the right of this mark. This is the head of the shot. Unspool the shot from the feed reel until the end-of-the-shot mark appears (opposite the last picture in the shot). Cut to the left of this mark. This is the tail of the shot. The film clip that results from this editing is one complete shot with complete sound.

Why cut the sound at the head and the picture at the tail? Because of the design of sound-on-film movies. The sound head in the camera is 18 frames ahead of the film gate. When sound and picture are recorded together, there is an 18-frame separation between the two, with the sound always being ahead of the picture (Fig. 10-20). If the shot were edited as in normal silent-film practice, cutting the head at the first frame of picture, the first second of sound (the sound for that picture) would be cut off. If the shot were edited at the tail, by cutting on sound instead of cutting on picture, the last second of picture would be cut off.

However, this type of sound-on-film editing does leave us with one small problem. What do we do about that one second of picture that precedes the shot? Those are the 18 frames that carry the first sounds so they cannot be removed. On the other hand, the pictures they

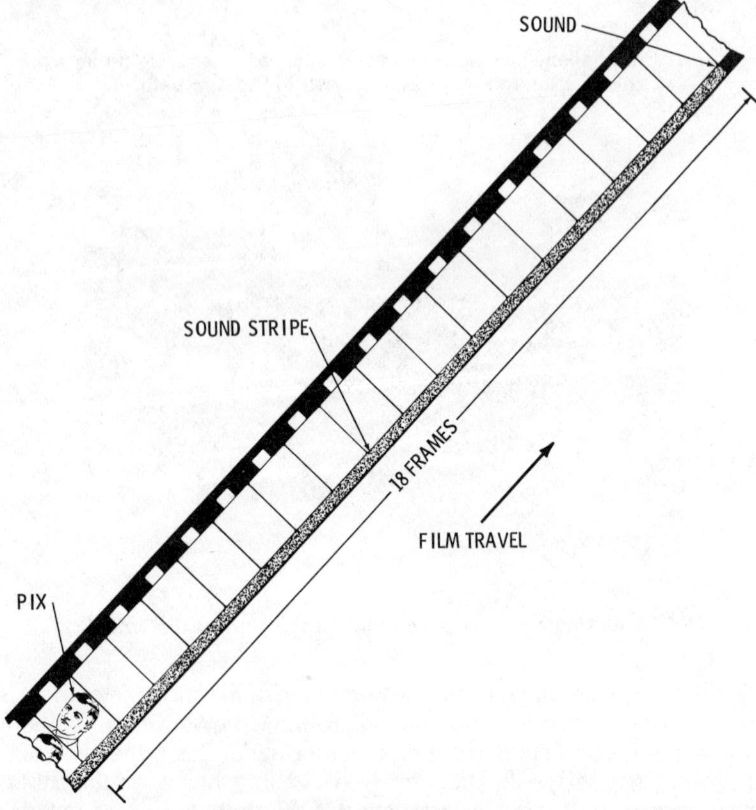

**Fig. 10-20. The sound is always 18 frames ahead of the picture
in sound-on-film movies.**

show are not necessarily the ones we want. We can do several things about this situation; we can ignore it, we can cut around it, or we can dub sound in to cover it.

Ignoring the problem is not as bad as it sounds. For most purposes, editing of sound film does not have to be so tight as to have to account for that second. And, most audience members will not notice one second of "dead" air on the sound track. In news film editing, which we will explain later, these gaps are routinely ignored.

Cutting around this gap is slightly more difficult but it does give a continuous sound track without any noticeable break. The way to do it is as follows. When editing the tail of the shot, mark the film at the last sound, when the last picture is on the viewing screen. Cut the film at the sound instead of the picture and set it aside. When joining this piece of film to the next shot, the one that will follow it, splice them together in the regular manner. When viewing the shots together, you will hear the sound of the previous shot under the picture of the current shot. It will appear as though the person in the previous shot is continuing to talk even though the film has cut to the other person. The effect this gives is one of speeding up the conversation. Cutting to the second person before the first is finished speaking seems to indicate that the second person is giving some thought to the previous question (or answer) and responds directly. This kind of editing is effective for closing that gap but it may give impressions about the speakers that you do not really want to give.

The third solution is to *dub* in some background sound or some other related noise to cover up the blank spot. This is more difficult to do as it involves some very careful timing on the part of the person who is doing the dubbing.

Since we made shooting sound-on-film, in a tv news style, a separate case in the section on production, we will treat it in the same way in editing. The process goes like this:

1. The film is not screened first. With the Shooting Log beside you on the editing bench, run through the roll of film looking for shots that you think will best tell the story. Mark these at the head on the sound and at the tail of the shot on the picture. Cut them out and run them through the footage counter or timer. Hang them on the board with a piece of masking tape and mark them as to their shot number and their timing.
2. When all the shots are pulled, splice them together—in the sequence in which you want them to appear on the air. Check continuity at this point. Does this story say what you intended it to say? Are there any other shots which would be more meaningful than the ones spliced in? Make any additions or changes at this point.

3. Begin to cut for time. Cut all questions to the bare minimum, cut all answers to their essential points. Do not be afraid to cut answers short or use jump cuts. The cutaways you shot can be used here to break up long answers and to make the piece more interesting visually.
4. View the story again for continuity and check it for timing. If you have to write a script to go along with this footage, now is the time to get out your notes and type it up.

News footage is not the neatest or most complete form of film making. The deadlines put on tv news gathering prevent it from being anything more than a quick look at what is happening. However, this "time bind" should not keep you from doing the best job of editing that you can do, even on a simple news story. The key to doing good work here is practice. The more time you put in here, the more that you will be able to do with your footage.

Editing Double-System Sound Movies

The makeup of the Rough Cut, Middle Cut, and Final Cut is done in the same similar ways, in double-system sound film editing, that it was done in silent-film editing. The major difference is that in double-system film editing, you have to cut sound when you cut a picture. This part of the editing process is simplified when you use a sound-editing bench. Here, the picture and the sound track (recorded on *full-coat*) are threaded up and locked together in a sync block. (This is the only method of maintaining sync in a double-system sound film.) Once the sync marks are located and the film and full-coat are locked in sync, both film and sound track can be edited together (Fig. 10-21). In professional parlance, having the sound exactly opposite its corresponding picture is called being in *edit-sync*.

The procedures for establishing edit-sync are as follows:

1. Thread the film through the viewer and run it forward to find the slate on the first shot. Locate the frame with the clapstick hitting the slate. After centering the sync block and zeroing the footage counter, move this frame to the center of the sync block and lock it in place on the ZERO mark.
2. Thread up the sound track for the same shot through the sound head. With your headphones on, run the sound track past the sound head until you hear the sound of the clapstick hitting the slate. (If you are not used to hearing the sound at less than normal sound speed, whipsaw the tape back and forth across the head until you are sure that you have found the first clap sound.) Mark this point on the full-coat with an X and run it up to the sync block. Lock it in place opposite the picture track.

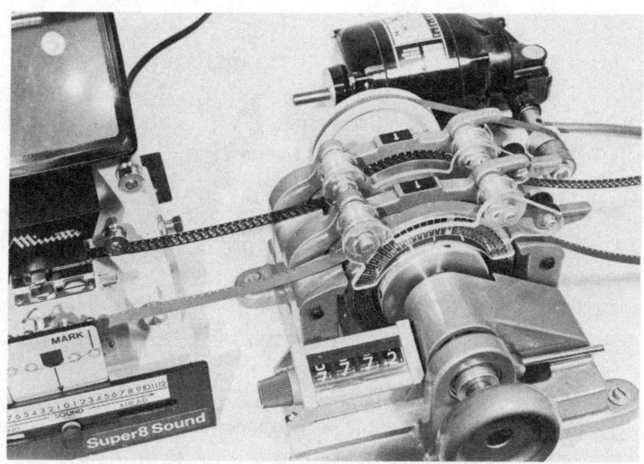

Fig. 10-21. A full-coat and picture-track gang sync block.

3. Connect the picture and sound tracks to their respective takeup reels and run the sync block backwards about two feet. Put on the headphones, turn on the viewer, and start the editing-bench drive motor. Watch and listen for the clap. If the two do not seem to be precisely lined up, rewind and check again. Adjust the picture to match the sound track. After both are in sync, mark the clap frame on the picture track with a punch hole placed right through the center of the frame. This should correspond with the X on the sound track.

4. Rewind to the start marks again and run the shot all the way through. Watch and listen for apparent slippage between sound and picture. Some double-system units will allow the sound to "drift" relative to the picture during sound recording. Although there is little you can do to correct it at this point, make note of the "drift" so it can be corrected when sound and picture are cut.

5. Repeat this procedure until sync has been established for each shot.

Assembling the Rough Cut with double-system sound can proceed in the standard way after establishing the edit-sync. All picture takes and sound takes should be joined together in order. When the entire Rough Cut is assembled, run the sound and picture to judge the quality of the takes and to decide what to remove (or leave in) for the Middle Cut.

Since the picture and sound are not joined to each other at this point, there might be some problem in running them together in sync. It is possible to do this on the editing bench, of course, but the sound quality of the head on the bench does not always lend itself to good reproduction. You can look at the picture takes separately on the projector and play the sound back on the tape recorder. Since edit-sync has already been established, it is merely a matter of choosing the best takes and marking them for inclusion in the Middle Cut. This kind of selection can cause some confusion for you as you might choose the sound take from one shot and the picture take from another shot. Our first solution is to use the Master Shot sound track as the basis for all editing of the sound. Just as the Master Shot is a good place to start the editing of the picture in a scene, so the Master Shot sound track is also a good place to start the editing of the sound. If the sound take lacks some bits of dialogue or some background noise, they can always be dubbed in. But the rhythm of the picture and the sound that is established by the Master Shot gives one a good starting point for editing for timing and continuity.

Our second solution, to the potential problem of mismatched sound and picture takes, is to judge all takes by the same standards. Our philosophy here is that most sound can be dubbed or corrected in the editing process. You cannot correct many picture mistakes without reshooting (in which case, you could rerecord the sound track, too). And, though audiences will notice visible lip-sync mismatches, most of the audience cannot tell the difference between a live location sound and a dubbed studio sound. Our rules for choosing double-system takes are:

1. Master Shots should go with the best picture take.
2. If the cadences of the dialogue affect the rhythm of the shot, go with the best sound take.
3. If the lip sync is highly visible, go with the best sound take. (Obvious lip sync is the easiest to dub, though.)
4. If the sound source is off screen, go with the best picture take.

After you have finished the Middle Cut, you will want to screen your almost completed picture. Get a projector that uses a pulse-sync system compatible with the double-system sound recorder that was used on the film. Connect these two machines up, thread up picture and sound, and run them off together. You will not have any trouble maintaining sync, but starting in sync can be a big problem. While it is possible to turn both machines on at the same time, their run-up-to-speed times are usually different and this can cause some loss of sync.

Super 8 Sound has come up with a solution to this loss of sync in the form of their Photo Start Unit. This is a photo-electric switch that is wired into the remote-run socket of the tape recorder. It works like this. A flash frame (Fig. 10-22) is created by punching a hole in the Black Leader that will be used to trigger the Photo Start Unit and, thus, start the mag film recorder in sync. The tape is cued up to the clap mark and the tape recorder is put in PLAY mode. The film is threaded through the projector film gate until the punched frame is in the gate. Then the projector is reversed and the film is run backwards for about 5 seconds. This is so that it will be running at speed when the flash frame goes through the gate. The projector is started, forward this time, and the Photo Start Unit is held in front of the lens. As the flash frame passes the film gate, it activates the photo-electric cell in the Photo Start Unit, which triggers the cued-up mag film tape recorder, which starts in sync with the film (Fig. 10-23).

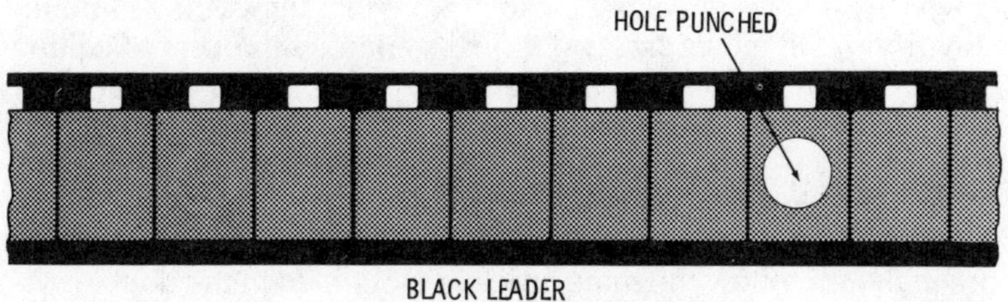

Fig. 10-22. Illustration of a picture track that has a hole punched in it to create a flash frame.

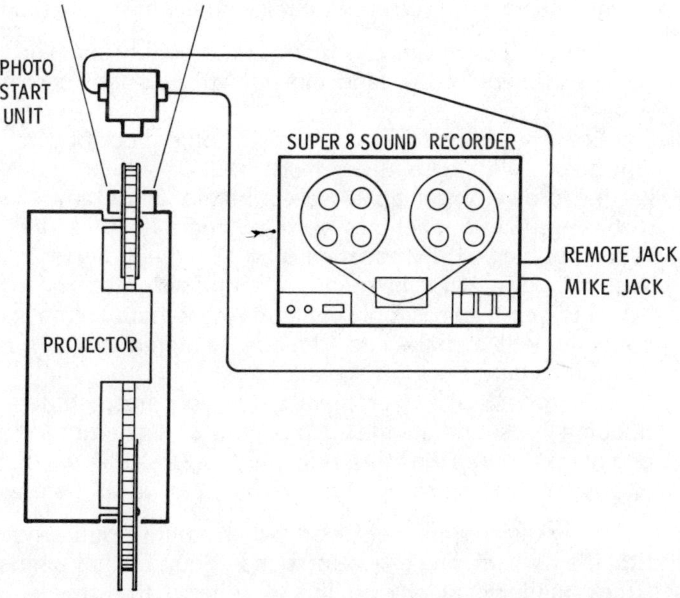

Fig. 10-23. Diagram of the operation of a Photo Start Unit.

Other than that, the procedure for editing from Rough Cut to Final Cut is performed as it would be for a silent film, except that when you cut picture, you also cut sound. When you splice picture, you splice sound. Every time you cut a frame of the work print, you cut a corresponding frame of sound. The advantage of working with Super 8 full-coat is that you can physically count the number of frames of sound to be cut or added, since picture and sound are literally in frame-to-frame sync.

If you are editing a work print, you will, of course, conform your original camera film to it when you have reached your final cut. However, if you are editing a camera-original film, you will do no conforming. In either case, your final step in the process of editing double-system sound is to have a sound stripe added to your Final Cut original and, then, transfer your edited sound to it.

Dubbing and Transferring Sound

When you are ready to dub your own sound track to your striped original film, follow the same procedure outlined in the double-system editing section. Use the Photo Start Unit, or some other foolproof method of starting in sync, and transfer the sound track to the sound stripe.

There are several tips you should know about this process. Some are especially important if you are working with single-system sound.

1. Read the projector instruction manual thoroughly until you are certain that you understand the operation of the recording system.
2. Practice recording, dubbing, or mixing on a piece of practice film before working with your original.
3. Let the projector get up to speed before doing any sound recording. (Some machines need as much as 10 seconds.)
4. When dubbing or mixing sound, start with the projector in the Record mode and use the sound-on-sound system to fade in the new track, instead of simply punching the Record button at the correct time. When the Record mode is entered into abruptly, there is usually a loss of signal.
5. If projector noise is a problem when you are recording or dubbing live sound, muffle the projector with a cardboard box or a blanket. Keep the mike as far away as possible, of course, and have it facing away from the projector at all times.

It is infinitely easier to augment sound when editing double-system sound than it is with single-system sound. You can have several sound tracks made up, all on mag film, all edited to the same length. One track will be your original recorded-in-sync sound (usually dialogue), another might be an edited music track, while still another can be sound effects or a voice-over narration. Using a sound mixer, these separate tracks can be rerecorded and blended together to form a single master sound track that is synchronized with your film. Since you are working with separate units, you never run the danger of destroying the original sound (by making a mistake in recording sound over it) as you do when working with sound-on-film. If you make a mistake in building up your master track, you need only go back and rerecord—you have not damaged your original sound in any way.

Once you have built your master sound track, you can utilize the same sync sound-projector recording techniques to transfer it to your original film or to a release print. If you mark your master tape with the same sync marks as your conformed original film, your lab can make the transfer in sync for you at the same time that they make your answer and release prints.

SUMMARY

The editing process, whether it's as simple as refining an "edited-in-camera" single roll of film, or as complicated as A & B editing a double-system sound film, is the final creative process in making your film. Everything you have done in the preplanning and shooting processes has been done with the editing process in mind. To some extent, how carefully you planned and shot your film will determine how easily your editing goes, but it is still the editing that is your final creative effort.

There are many other things that could be said about editing. But, as with any of the other parts of the film-making process, it must be experienced to be understood. The more you do with it, the more you will be able to do.

CHAPTER 11

Presentation

Your film is finally finished and you're ready to show it. This is the moment that you and your audience have been waiting for. You shut off the lights, grope your way to the projector, turn it on, and the leader refuses to thread. Whoops! Have you forgotten something? Yes. You have forgotten that presenting your film is just as important as making it.

There is a tendency among amateur film makers to think that their work is done when they have finished editing their film. That's just not true. The members of the audience, regardless of who they may be, are familiar with a professional presentation. They may never notice sloppy camera work or be aware of the hastily done editing of an action sequence. But they *will notice* if the sound is too loud or if the picture is out of focus. All of them have been to commercial theatres (some of them, thousands of times) to see movies that were professionally presented. They expect a similar performance from you.

The other reason for a careful presentation is equally obvious; it will make your film look and sound even better than it is. Ideally, you want the audience to file in, you will cut the lights, start the projector, and transport everyone to the dream world of your film.

PREPARING THE FILM FOR SHOWING

But first, the film must be ready for presentation. It must be clean, carefully spliced, properly leadered, and correctly wound on a projection reel. You know your film has collected a lot of dust and dirt during the editing process. This is inevitable, no matter how careful you have been. So, you will certainly want to clean it before showing it. But first, let us put the film in shape.

Leader the head and the tail with the proper amount of new white leader (a 4-foot length at the head and a 1-foot length at the tail).

Next, check all splices to make sure they are cleanly made (so they will pass through the film gate during projection) and strong (so they will not come apart). We inspect the film by putting it on the rewinds and looking at every foot of it. You can do it on the viewer but, there, the picture becomes a distraction that may keep you from seeing the splices. When we are satisfied that all is well, we start to clean the film.

Clean the rewind area with a dust cloth. Wipe down the rewinds and the takeup reels. Put the film on the feed reel but do not thread it into the takeup reel. With a small amount of film cleaner on a cloth, wipe the head leader—away from the film. Now, thread up the film and crank it to the first picture frame. Put a small amount of fluid on the cloth, wrap it around both sides of the film (the emulsion and base), and squeeze gently. Winding the takeup reel slowly, draw the film slowly through the cloth (Fig. 11-1). Every 15 feet or so stop to remoisten the cloth with film cleaner and also to change its position on the film. Shifting the position on the cloth will prevent the old dirt from being ground into the remainder of the film. Cranking slowly will allow the cleaner to dry on the film before it reaches the takeup reel. This prevents streaking. You will notice that the film cleaning rag is turning green. This is because some emulsion is coming off during the cleaning. Do not be alarmed for the small amount removed will not affect your picture (and it would have come off anyway, probably during projection).

We use a film cleaner that also contains a lubricant. That way, it will help the film transport during projection. For cleaning rags, we

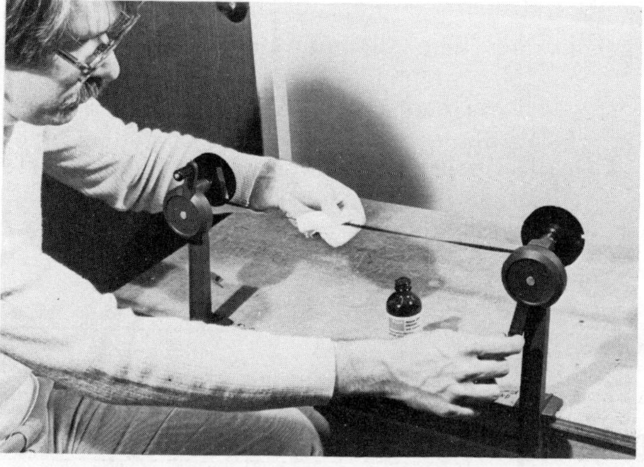

Fig. 11-1. To clean the film, wipe the film lightly with a soft cloth dampened with film cleaner while cranking the film between rewinds.

usually use recently washed old editing gloves. They are ideal for cleaning and polishing. Be sure to do your cleaning in a well-ventilated area. The fumes from most film cleaners are toxic so do not clean film in any tightly enclosed place. Our film workshop has a large ceiling fan/ventilator. You might want to work in the garage if you can keep the dust down.

If you are planning to have your film printed or sound striped, then your laboratory will probably professionally clean your film. All you need to do is make sure that you have made good cement splices. However, the cleaning procedure just described applies to prints as well as to original films. You should clean your film before every public showing.

After you have cleaned your film, dust off the projection reel, and rewind the film on to it. Do this very slowly and carefully so that you will pick up a minimum of dust during the rewinding procedure. Also, after the cleaning, label the film leader with the following information: Title, Running Speed, Silent (or Sound), and either Running Time or Length in Feet (Fig. 11-2). This information ensures that you will always be able to tell what film you are handling without projecting it, even if the reel or film can is not labeled. However, label the reel and film can as to their contents anyway, so that there can be no mixup during projection.

PREPARING THE PROJECTION EQUIPMENT

Now that your film is ready, you can get the tools of presentation set up. You will need a projector, a screen, a projection stand, and a speaker. We have already discussed projector specifications so we will just review them here. Minimum lamp capacity should be about 100 watts with 150 watts preferred. A zoom lens is a must so that the picture image can be made to fill the screen regardless of the throw distance. A 600-foot reel capacity and ease of cleaning are also high priorities. Finally, a sound projector should have an external speaker jack so that you can use an extension speaker.

There are two kinds of movie screens that are widely available—the flat or matte-finish screen and the lenticular or beaded-finish

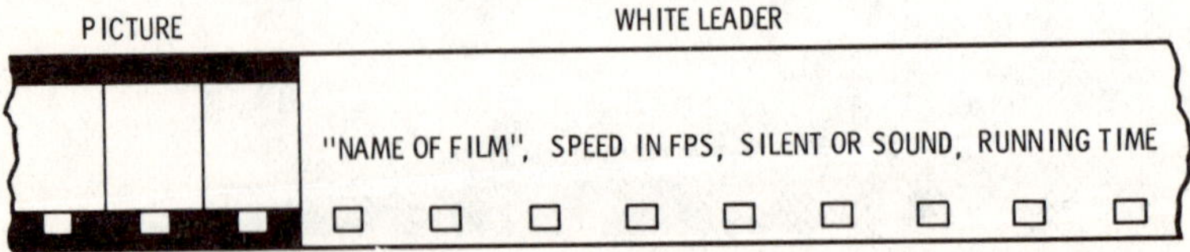

Fig. 11-2. Putting instructions and information on the leader saves time and prevents mistakes.

screen. The matte-finish screen has a dull reflecting surface much like the reflectors in lighting instruments. It is fine for rigidly mounted screens like those used in professional movie theatres. The matte finish shows off the film sharply and with good resolution because it reflects the light back evenly. Its weakness is that if it is not mounted perfectly flat, it will look wrinkled and show the film off in the same way. The lenticular screen has a beaded finish that tends to disperse some of the light instead of reflecting it all back. Its reflectance is acceptable, though not as high as the matte screen. It need not be perfectly flat nor perfectly parallel to the projected image in order to return an acceptable picture. For other than wall-mounted screens, we prefer the lenticular-finish screen.

If we had a choice, all projection screens would be rigidly mounted and easily accessible. But, because we often have to show films in places where we have no choice, we have to put up with other types of mountings. The ceiling-mounted roll-down screen is a good type if the bottom edge can be fastened securely. Otherwise, the tripod-base freestanding folding screen is the only solution. Try to get one that is adjustable for several heights so that different size rooms and crowds can be accommodated.

For sound-film presentation, you will need an extension speaker for your projector in order to get the best sound playback. Get the model made for your sound projector, if possible. We have found that factory speakers are usually well made and are always compatible. (They might be a bit expensive, however.) You can get a speaker from your local audio store. Remember to match the impedance of the speaker with that of your projector and have it fitted with a plug that will fit the external speaker jack of the projector. It's also a good idea to have an extension cable that is at least 15 feet long.

A steady projection table or stand, with an ac outlet and a generous length of extension cord is the last "tool" that you will need for your presentation. The table top should be waist high since it seems to be easier to thread and adjust a projector while standing. And, a high table makes it easier to project over the heads of the audience. A number of excellent projection tables (and carts) are available. Make sure that yours is at least 2 feet square and sits solidly on the floor.

THE PHYSICAL SETUP

For suitable projection of your film, you will need a dark room, a bright screen, and a clean projector lens. For a good presentation, you will also need some control over the lights near the projector, safe placement of cords and cables, and comfortable chairs for your audience. Sounds simple, doesn't it. But these specifications are rarely met in any nonprofessional projection situation, so we will improvise.

To solve the room problem at home, we show many of our films in the basement. It can usually be made dark enough by blocking off the small windows and there is usually enough open space to set up the projector and screen at a reasonable distance. If you must use an upstairs room, pick one that is longer than it is wide, and make sure that it can be made sufficiently dark. Regardless of which room you choose, place the screen in the darkest spot, preferably with its back toward the windows. Place it perpendicular to the path of projection and high enough so that it can be seen by everyone in the room (Fig. 11-3).

Set up the projector opposite the screen and perpendicular to it. Run the power cord off the back of the projection table to the nearest outlet. If the cord might trip someone as people are entering or leaving the room, leave it unplugged or tape it to the floor.

Place the extension speaker up front, under the screen but off the floor, and carefully run its cable back to the projector. Locating the speaker near the screen enhances the illusion that the sound is coming from the images on the screen. And keeping the speaker off the floor helps to improve the reproduction of the treble range of sound.

If everything in your projection room was perfectly placed, the light switch would be right next to the projection table. But since this is hardly ever the case, we usually put a small table or floor lamp near the projection table within easy reach of the projectionist. This is the last light turned off before showing the film and the first one turned on after the show is over.

Now that you are all set up, clean the projector lens and film path. Treat the lens like any other optical glass. Blow it clean, wipe it with moistened tissue, and dry it carefully. Blow out the film path and wipe the gate and sprockets of the projector with a brush or soft cloth.

SHOWING THE FILM

Thread the projector and focus before beginning to show the film. Then, back up to the first frame of the picture (or the title). That way, the first image seen by the audience will be the film, not the leader or a blinding white screen. And, they will not be annoyed by the time that it takes to thread the machine.

With sound films, check the volume level before projection. This should be part of your speaker setup and is just to make sure that the extension cables are connected and working. When projecting in a large room, remember that a room full of people requires more

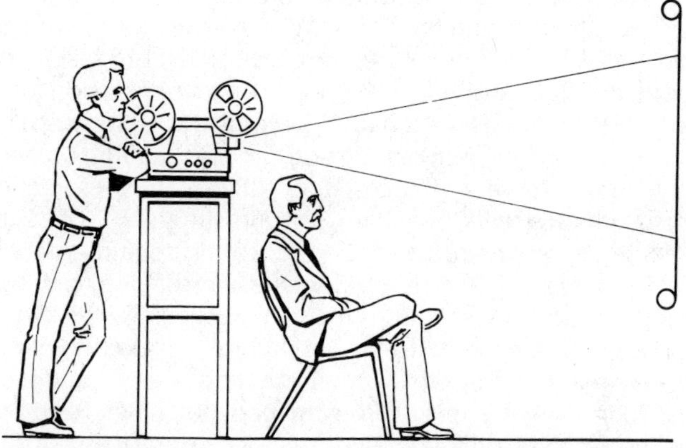

(A) The projector should be above the heads of the audience.

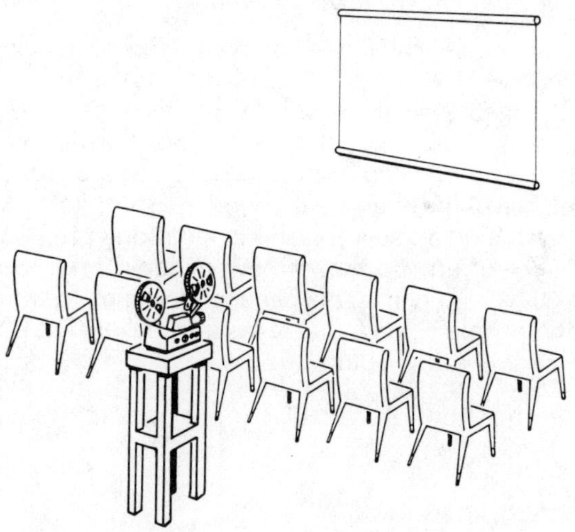

(B) But, level with and perpendicular to the screen.

Fig. 11-3. Setting up the projector.

volume than the same room empty, so set your volume a little higher than is necessary for the empty room.

Keep repair and cleaning materials around during film showings. By using tape splices, most breaks can be repaired immediately in order to finish showing the film. The cleaning brush, blower, and lens tissue might be necessary to remove that stray hair from the film gate, or to wipe the smudge off the lens.

Now that you are about to show the film, consider two more things—reel changes and rewinding. We usually mount our films on 600-foot reels (which will hold 40 minutes of film at 18 fps) so that we can avoid reel changes. If we are showing a number of short films, we often use 400-foot reels (which run 26 minutes at 18 fps), and have a short intermission between reels. If you can put your film on one reel, however, do it, as reel changes slow down your presentation.

If you do change reels, do not rewind until the show is over. In fact, we prefer not to rewind on the projector at all. If contemporary Super 8 projectors have a serious flaw, it is in the way that they rewind film. Most of them do it loosely and unevenly, especially with 400-foot reels or larger. Film should be wound tightly and evenly, of course. So, we take our reels back to the rewind bench and do them by hand. Oh yes, do not forget to let the projector cool down before you pack it away. The lamp is very sensitive to shock when it is hot.

THE JOY OF FILM MAKING

Now you are done. You have shown your film to an appreciative audience, received their compliments, answered all their questions, and made arrangements for the party later. This is the time to sit back and reflect on what you have accomplished. All that time and energy and thought has culminated in a finished motion picture. What you have created here is the equivalent of writing a short story, directing a play, and producing a television show, all in one piece. You have created a work of art, no matter how minor it may seem at the moment. You have joined that rather exclusive club to which only a few thousand people belong, that of the film maker. The satisfaction you feel now is the joy of film making.

Index